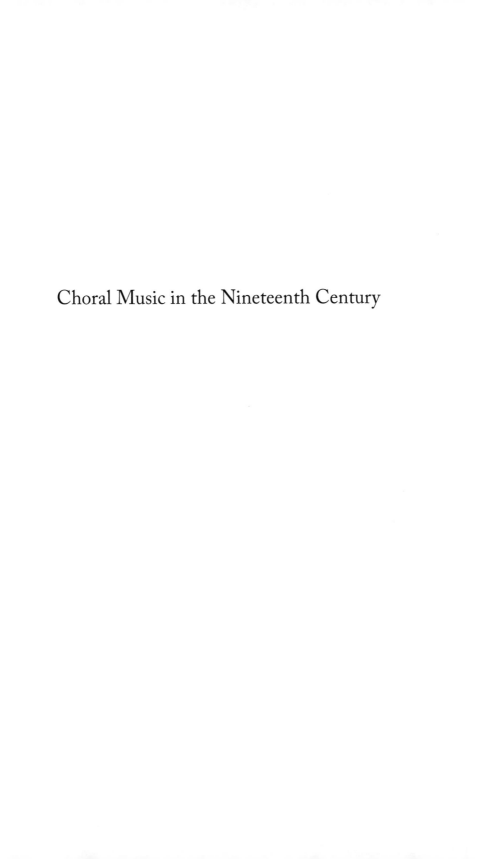

Choral Music in the Nineteenth Century

Choral Music
in the Nineteenth Century

Nick Strimple

AMADEUS
PRESS

AMADEUS PRESS

AN IMPRINT OF HAL LEONARD CORPORATION

NEW YORK

Published in 2008 by Amadeus Press
An Imprint of Hal Leonard Corporation
7777 West Bluemound Road
Milwaukee, WI 53213

Trade Book Division Editorial Offices
19 West 21 Street, New York, NY 10010

Printed in the United States of America

Book design by Mark Lerner

Library of Congress Cataloging-in-Publication Data is available upon request.

ISBN: 978-1-57467-154-4

www.amadeuspress.com

For my teachers

Robert H. Young

and

James H. Vail

Contents

Acknowledgments   ix

1 A Brief Overview   1

2 Austria and Germany   11

3 France, Switzerland, and the Low Countries   81

4 The British Isles   103

5 The Czech Lands, Slovakia, Hungary, and Poland   121

6 Russia, Scandinavia, and the Baltics   147

7 The Iberian Peninsula and Italy   171

8 The Americas   195

9 Epilogue   225

Works Lists   231

   Compositions for Mixed Chorus   231

   Compositions for Boys' or Children's Chorus   247

   Compositions for Female or Treble Chorus   248

   Compositions for Male Chorus   250

Bibliography   255

Index   271

Acknowledgments

The author extends his heartfelt thanks to the following, without whom this book would never have been completed:

Fisk University Franklin Library's Special Collection for the photograph of the Jubilee Singers and their accompanist

The Roy E. Atherton Collection for the original Brahms letter

Monir Tayeb and Michel Austin (www.hberlioz.com) for the cartoon image by Gustave Doré of Berlioz conducting a choir

The Denver Public Library's Western History Collection for the photo of the Greeley Methodist Choir

The National Archives and Records Administration—Pacific Alaska Region (Anchorage) for the photo of the Metlakahtla Indian Church Choir

The Adelaider Liedertafel 1858 for the photo of the Adelaider Liedertafel Choir

The *Illustrated London News*/May Evans Picture Library for the image of the Great Handel Festival at the Crystal Palace

Leonardo Ciampa for the Perosi letter

The Oratorio Society of New York for the image of the Society's 1881 Festival

Phil Hatton for reproductive photography

Gregory Cherninsky for preparation of the examples

Thanks also to my graduate assistants at the USC Thornton School of Music—Lesley Leighton, Karen Cooksey, Dominic Gregorio, and Nové Deypalan—who assisted with research and prepared the index and appendices, and to Professors Michael Lancaster

(Southern Baptist Seminary, Louisville, Kentucky) and Magen Solomon (University of Southern California), who read the manuscript and made many valuable suggestions.

Many, many thanks to my friends at Vendely Communications—Anne Pearson, Maggie Nye, and Elizabeth Vendely—who helped in myriad ways, not the least of which was researching photos and permissions.

Lastly, my deepest thanks to John Cerullo, Carol Flannery, and Gail Siragusa at Amadeus Press; to my wonderful editor Barbara Norton; and especially to my family, for demonstrating patience beyond all human expectations.

Nick Strimple
Los Angeles

1

A Brief Overview

Nineteenth-century choral music properly begins in 1796 with the composition and performance of the first two of the last great Masses of Franz Joseph Haydn, works that would have profound impact on virtually all later music. These Masses not only established a more or less standard duration for such works, but also introduced symphonic formal structures and an innovative approach to tonality, both of which helped to transplant the Mass and other liturgical forms directly into the realm of concert music.

Several performance trends that would become commonplace in the nineteenth century also began during the eighteenth. First, women were allowed to sing in worship as soloists in isolated areas of Italy and Austria (Eisenstadt, for example), and by 1850 women were singing in Protestant and Catholic choirs throughout Europe. The inclusion of women had begun somewhat earlier in England, where small singing societies had been formed by churches in Lancashire early in the eighteenth century to teach young men and women to sing psalms. Shortly thereafter, in rural communities in England where parish churches had neither organ nor formally organized choirs, singers and instrumentalists (including women) from the congregation formed ensembles to lead the worship service, improvising anthems from hymns already known to them. This became known as the West Gallery Tradition and would continue well into the nineteenth century. Second, the bringing together of large numbers of singers for commemorative concerts or festivals began in the early 1700s. The oldest English festival for instance, Three Choirs, began as early as 1715 using a conglomerate of singers from cathedrals in Gloucester, Worcester, and Hereford. The first mixed community choir independent of any connection to religion seems to have been the Stoughton Musical Society, formed in Stoughton, Massachusetts, on 7 November 1786. A few years later, in 1791, the Berlin Singakademie was formed. Similar organizations in Germany, Austria, England, and the United States followed in short order (Krehbiel 2007, 109).

A very important aspect of nineteenth-century life that would impact choral music was the political unrest that first erupted after the Napoleonic Wars, engulfing Europe and America during the middle of the century. In Venezuela, for instance, composers were killed or imprisoned; in Europe some composers, such as Smetana, entered exile, while others, such as Berlioz, Verdi, and Brahms, actively supported nationalistic political struggle. In the Baltic and Balkan regions political repression stymied the development of organized choral singing until very late in the century (the national singing festivals that would distinguish Baltic choral music in the twentieth century did not begin until 1873; Croatia's first secular choir was not organized until 1899).

In the first decade of the nineteenth century independent men's choruses began to be formed that had no connection to the old college singing clubs. Not only were these new TTBB ensembles the impetus for composers to write an enormous amount of music for a new genre, but in many cases they also became actively involved in the numerous revolutionary movements that spread through Europe around 1848. Especially among German-speaking people, men's choirs became culturally important, with German immigrants organizing *Männergesang* and attendant annual singing festivals in the United States and Australia, greatly enhancing the development of choral music there.

Many Germanic composers, beginning with Beethoven and Schubert, followed Haydn's lead and developed a tonal language that relied heavily on movement to the submediant or mediant. Schubert and others also explored the expressive possibilities of the part-song and led the way in compositions for TTBB male chorus.

The Enlightenment, of which the works of Haydn, Beethoven, and Schubert were representative, resulted in drastic reforms in Christian and Jewish sacred music. By the middle of the century conservatives in the Roman Catholic Church, exasperated with the operatic accretions to the liturgy in which most late eighteenth- and early nineteenth-century composers had indulged, stepped in to purify liturgical music. Following the example of church musicians in Italy and France who were exploring Renaissance music (see below), Karl Proske (1794–1861) began the reform efforts in Germany. Continuing his work, the Caecilian Society (Allgemeiner Deutscher Caecilienverein), organized in 1868 by Franz Xaver Witt (1834–1888), became a kind of moral watchdog over Roman Catholic music. For the duration of the century it endeavored to rid the church of the most recent musical epochs' operatic influences and return it to the purity of Gregorian chant and of the post-Tridentine unaccompanied polyphony of Palestrina. Although the Caecilian Society hounded important composers throughout the Catholic sphere of influence—such as Liszt and Bruckner—it could not keep them in the fold and ultimately converted only mediocre composers to its mission. Still, it exerted enormous influence through its publications and the relentless pressure Witt brought to bear against all who opposed his ideas.

The evangelical church in Germany was also in a reforming mood, freely allowing women singers and emphasizing a simplified, congregationally friendly music that contrasted with the rigid polyphonic complexities of J. S. Bach. The Caecilian movement also impacted the evangelical church as well as the newly organized secular choruses, so that a much greater awareness of Renaissance Italian and early seventeenth-century German composers developed. Church choirs flourished, or not, depending on the size of the congregation, the musical taste of the pastor, and the ability of the Kapellmeister (see Blume 1975, 317–404). In 1852 the American traveler Lowell Mason observed the variety found in German churches at the time: although some choirs had only a few singers—for instance, St. Peter's in Leipzig had only a male quintet (three boys and two men)—others boasted of flourishing choral organizations, such as the Thomas Church, also in Leipzig, which boasted a fifty-voice choir of men and boys (this choir's un- accompanied singing of part-songs by Mendelssohn and motets by J. S. Bach was apparently astounding; see Mason 1854, 80–82 and 88–91).

An important ancillary to the Enlightenment occurred in the Jewish community, a leader of which was the philosopher Moses Mendelssohn (grandfather of the composer Felix Mendelssohn). Essentially Moses Mendelssohn believed it important for Jews to be perceived as German. His ideas were put into practice by the Viennese singer-composer Salomon Sulzer, who composed— and commissioned—many works for the Jewish liturgy. His torch would be taken up later in the century by the outstanding Polish German composer Louis Lewandowski.

During the first three decades of the century French composers still produced secular or pantheistic compositions in the bloated syntax of the Revolution. The dimensions of these works, at least, gained some credibility in the hands of Hector Berlioz, who helped reintroduce liturgical texts and brought gigantic concepts to vivid life. In a climate of renewed interest in religion, Alexandre-Etienne Choron (1772–1834) founded the Institution Royale de Musique Classique et Religieuse in 1817; in 1833 Dom Prosper Guéranger founded the Benedictine Congregation of France (known ever since as the Solesmes Benedictines) which revolutionized the study and performance of Gregorian Chant; concerts of sacred music were begun in Paris, and often in provincial cities as well, creating a market for concert works on sacred subjects. Following the example of Sulzer in Austria, Samuel Naumbourg added to the growing repertoire of Jewish liturgical music for cantor and chorus. The oratorios of Gounod became famous throughout Eu- rope (and quite influential in England), and exquisite composi- tions by Fauré and, to a lesser extent, Saint-Saëns, took their place in the repertoire.

In the United Kingdom the great regional music festivals revived after the Napoleonic Wars, creating a demand for a steady stream of new cantatas and oratorios; new choral societies were established to meet this need as well. Unfortunately, at this time the British had few composers with strong artistic personalities. After 1846 Mendelssohn and, later in the century, Gounod became models for English creativity, a situation that did not guarantee an increase in the quality of works produced there. Success at the English festivals also provided a springboard to international fame for Antonín Dvořák, who composed several important large choral works for the English public. Throughout the century composers produced liturgical works for Anglican and Roman Catholic churches, often influenced in the latter half of the century by the high-minded and conservative Oxford Movement, whose views concerning music were similar to those of the Caecilians in Germany. Composers also churned out part-songs, madrigals, and glees for college and community singing. The advent of Edward Elgar, Hubert Parry, Charles Villiers Stanford, and Arthur Sullivan during the last two decades of the century signaled a renewal of fortune for British music, not only in regard to church music and small unaccompanied secular pieces, but in the realm of cantata and oratorio as well.

The immigration of Czech musicians to Western Europe that had begun in the eighteenth century continued early in the next. Among these were Antonín Rejcha, who became a friend of Beethoven and an exceptionally important teacher in Paris, and his compatriot Jan Hugo Voříšek, who greatly impressed Schubert. The rise of nationalism provided artistic direction for Bedřich Smetana and Antonín Dvořák, resulting in compositions—some of them masterpieces—that came to be internationally acclaimed. The Caecilian Society was also strong in the Czech lands, influencing the quantity and quality of church music, while the rising popularity of male choirs was aided and abetted by Pavel Křižkovský, Bedřich Smetana, and the young Leoš Janáček.

Although nationalism was promoted by many composers in Hungary, its development was slowed somewhat by an infatuation with Gypsy music, as well as by the predominantly German outlook of its leading composer, Franz (Ferenc) Liszt.

In Poland, Lithuania, and other locales with large Jewish communities, singing societies were very popular. These were often affiliated with Der Arbeiter Ring (The Workman's Circle), a secular organization that supported liberal causes and provided highly organized choral activities for children and adults. Although they performed standard European repertoire, these organizations also created a distinct repertoire of Yiddish choral song, popular throughout Eastern Europe until World War II.

Russian choral music was dominated early in the century by the director of the Imperial Court Chapel, Dmitri Bortniansky, who continued the Italianate classical style inherited from his teacher, Baldassare Galuppi. This common European style would permeate Russian music until nationalism, fomented by the operas of Mikhail Glinka, crystallized Balakirev and others to base liturgical works on traditional Russian models, thus creating the Moscow school of church composition. Although Tchaikovsky and Tanaiev produced impressive works colored by their cosmopolitan views, the group known as "the Five" (Balakirev, Borodin, Cui, Mussorgsky, and Rimsky-Korsakov) explored the possibilities inherent in Russian nationalism.

In Scandinavian countries the spirit of nationalism began early, in Sweden around 1809, when Russia made it a duchy, and in Norway around 1814, when it separated from Denmark. Composers, most of them influenced by German romanticism, focused on the development of national opera and the utilization of folk genres in symphonic and choral works.

In Portugal and Spain the Roman Catholic church controlled choral music. In Italy, too, the church was very strong, with many parishes throughout the country boasting of hardworking music directors who routinely churned out choral pieces for worship. Interest in early music was sparked by Giuseppe Baini's 1828 monograph on Palestrina, and important opera composers such as Rossini and Verdi produced sacred works more important for their inherent drama than for any projection of religious sentiment. Oratorio, though important in other regions such as England, faded in importance, and late in the century church reformers, encouraged by the Caecilian Society, finally succeeded in getting the pope's attention. In 1903 Pope Pius X issued a *motu proprio*—essentially a restatement of the principles of the sixteenth century's Council of Trent—establishing the following guidelines for Roman Catholic liturgical music: (1) Gregorian chant was the ideal vocal medium, (2) polyphony, if used at all, should be in the style of Palestrina, (3) new music was to be devoid of theatrical influences, (4) clear projection of the text was paramount in vocal music, and (5) instrumental accompaniments were severely restricted.

At the beginning of the century American choral music was largely defined by that relic from colonial days the itinerant singing master, whose self-published books were often the only source of repertoire and musical instruction for churches in rural America. Some large urban churches—including the newly organized independent African American congregations in New York City and Philadelphia—could provide more sophisticated fare, but, in general it was not until the second third of the century, and mostly through the efforts of Lowell Mason, that music began to be taught in the urban public schools, thus enabling large singing societies such as the newly organized Boston Handel and Haydn Society to flourish.

Simultaneously existing outside this mainstream were the German Moravian communities of Winston-Salem, North Carolina, and Bethlehem, Pennsylvania, which had flourished since the early eighteenth century. Moravian artistic sensibilities, at least regarding music in worship, developed along Lutheran lines. When they immigrated to America, they brought music and composers highly skilled in German baroque and *style galant* practices. Unfortunately, by the early nineteenth century the major Moravian composers had died, so this unique repertoire stream dried up. Later in the century, though, J. Fred Wolle organized the Bethlehem Bach Choir, which gave the first American performances of J. S. Bach's *St. John Passion* (1888), B Minor Mass (1900), and *Christmas Oratorio* (1901).

During the middle third of the century young composers began traveling to Germany for training, a development that would color the outlook of American music until the end of World War I. At the same time the nation was gripped by the political realities that resulted in the Civil War. In the foreword to *Lincoln and the Music of the Civil War*, Kenneth Barnard observed that "during the first year alone, an estimated two thousand compositions were produced, and by the end of the war more music had been created, played, and sung than during all our other wars combined. More of the music of the era has endured than from any other period in our history" (Bernard 1966, xvii).

At century's midpoint there was also a desire among many large urban churches to separate themselves from small congregations who relied heavily on congregational singing. But instead of building up large choirs, these urban institutions hired professional quartets who sang, usually, from side galleries. In 1856 the *San Francisco Bulletin* reported that "the First Presbyterian Church has a choir of ten instead of the fashionable quartet so much in vogue in other churches" (Stevenson 1966, 112–13). So the numerous anthems written by Dudley Buck and others were actually composed with solo voices in mind.

In Canada choral music was confined to churches, with large establishments in the eastern cities utilizing European and English cathedral repertoire. On the frontier, choral activity, even in churches, was largely a hit-and-miss proposition.

South of the United States, choral music had flourished in churches since the time of the Spanish and Portuguese conquests. Now this development stagnated in Mexico while continuing with nationalistic fervor in several South American countries, spurred on by composers returning from study in Europe and by newly acquired revolutionary zeal and the resultant interest in indigenous music.

In the Pacific Rim, choral music had not developed at all except in the Philippines, where the repertoire was confined to works brought by the early Spanish missionaries, and Australia and New Zealand, where English settlers established church choirs and German immigrants established festivals for *Männergesang*. As in the Philippines, repertoire essentially consisted of European imports.

Everywhere, opera flourished and arguments concerning the proper nature of sacred music abounded. Composers became simultaneously fluent in academic counterpoint and folk-inspired styles. And although the last third of the century witnessed animated discussion—emanating primarily from Austria and Germany—on the direction of new music, no one anticipated the musical revolutions that would shake the next century.

2

Austria and Germany

When Prince Nicolaus II of Esterházy was reestablishing the Esterházy court orchestra in 1795, he requested his absent *Kapellmeister*, Franz Joseph Haydn (1732–1809), to return from London. In addition to normal administrative duties, Haydn would be required only to compose a new Mass each year in celebration of the name day of Prince Nicolaus's wife, the Princess Josepha Maria of Esterházy. Her name day was 12 September, and, as a rule, a new Mass would be performed each year on the Sunday morning closest to that date in the Bergkirche at the Esterházy estate in Eisenstadt.

Haydn dutifully returned and from 1796 to 1802 produced six masterpieces that, collectively, were to have a profound impact on later music. The late Masses, and their keys, are:

Missa Sancti Bernardi von Offida ("Heiligmesse"), in B-flat major (1796)
Missa in tempore belli ("Paukenmesse") in C major (1796)
Missa in angustiis ("Nelsonmesse") in D minor (1798)
Mass in B-flat ("Theresienmesse") (1799)
Mass in B-flat ("Schöpfungsmesse") (1801)
Mass in B-flat ("Harmoniemesse") (1802)

There is no clear chronology concerning the first two Masses since both the *Missa Sancti Bernardi von Offida* (Mass in Honor of Saint Bernard of Offida) and the *Missa in tempore belli* (Mass in Time of War) are dated 1796. The situation was clarified some-what in 1968 with the publication of the diaries of Joseph Carl Rosenbaum, an employee of the Esterházy family and the par-amour (later the husband) of the soprano Therese Gassmann. Rosenbaum's entry for 28 September 1797 reads: "two choral sing-ers arrived from Pressburg: Anna Rhumfeld, a soprano, and Frl. Hammer, an alto; the former is already in service, the latter will also be engaged" (Radant 1968, 2e). The next day, 29 September, he wrote that "a new mass in C by Haydn was performed; both women sang and both were very successful." (While it may appear unusual that the celebration would take place on a Wednesday, over two weeks removed from the princess's name day, the delay can surely be explained by any number of logistic, technical, or domestic reasons; nor is it the only one of the late Masses to have been so delayed.)

This little piece of information—almost an afterthought to the diarist's interest in the new singers—is surprising because the C major Mass, *Missa in tempore belli*, appeared to be older. Character-istics that separate it from the other late Masses are so acute that one biographer, J. Cuthbert Hadden (writing in 1902), thought it was written in 1790, before the first London visit (Hadden 1934, 184). For one thing, it utilized telescoped text (that is, simultane-ous declamation of different texts) in the Gloria and the Credo, a technique common in Haydn's earlier Masses (and Masses by other composers as well, including Mozart) but absent from the other late Masses. Also, a version of the Mass with much more opulent orchestration than that available in Eisenstadt was known to have been performed in Vienna's Piaristenkirche on St. Stephen's Day (26 December) in 1796. The conventional thinking was that Haydn, after the supposed Eisenstadt premiere in September of that year, simply expanded the orchestration for the Vienna performance.

It was also thought that because St. Bernard's name day was one day before the princess's and, further, that these fell on Sat-urday and Sunday in 1797, Haydn decided to honor both the new saint (canonized in 1795) and the princess with that year's new Mass. But Rosenbaum is difficult to dispute because the new Mass performed in 1797 obviously made an impression on him: of the several diary entries confirming performances of Haydn's Masses, this is the only one to specify a key. And because he was himself a good amateur musician, married to an excellent professional one, it is unlikely that he would have gotten the key wrong.

So it now seems that *Missa Sancti Bernardi von Offida* was the first new work by Haydn after his return from England and was performed for the Princess Esterházy on 11 September 1796 (still serving double duty in honoring St. Bernard). The "Paukenmesse" was composed shortly after for a festive St. Stephen's Day Mass in Vienna later that year, Haydn's backward glances in terms of form, style, and text setting being largely the result of haste in preparing a large new work for rehearsals and performance in such a short span of time. Consequently, it was performed again for the (delayed) name-day celebration on 29 September 1797 in Eisenstadt, in an abridged instrumentation to accommodate the limitations of the Esterházy orchestra.

Both Masses are still very popular, but the "Heiligmesse" is more impressive. In it Haydn established a number of new parameters that would not only become the norm in his later Mass settings, but would also influence most nineteenth-century Masses: a duration of approximately forty minutes; a reliance on sonata form for the opening movement; and the abandonment of simultaneous setting of different texts. Even more important were the quietly revolutionary modulations to keys a third apart and the extensive use of flat keys, which, in combination with the tonal third relations, provided a fertile source of inspiration and experimentation for virtually all nineteenth-century composers.

Frequently encountered modulations in the late Masses are between the home key and a key a third away. But in the fantastic "Cruxificus" section of the Credo of the "Heiligmesse," Haydn finds himself in the extremely remote key of E-flat minor, which moves to G-flat major and thence to E-flat major. The ensuing "Et resurrexit" is in C minor, the first of three minor-key settings of this text (the others being the "Nelsonmesse" and the "Theresienmesse"). It should be pointed out here that flat keys, while easy for wind instruments, are difficult for strings because when five or more flats are involved, the players cannot use an open string to help with intonation. In Haydn's day E-flat minor probably lifted the powdered wigs right off the string players' heads.

The work's nickname is derived from the inclusion of a vernacular church tune in the inner voices of the Sanctus ("Heilig"

Above and opposite: The "Crucifixus" section of the Credo from Franz Joseph Haydn's "Heiligmesse."

in German; Haydn may have been giving a nod of recognition to a rather new Austrian tradition of Mass settings in German, a tradition to which his younger brother Michael contributed, as would Franz Schubert). At "Et incarnatus est" the solo ensemble is expanded to two pairs of three voices (SSATBB); here Haydn also borrows a preexisting tune, one he had created earlier as a three-voice canon to the words "God in your heart, a good wife in your arms." This minor indiscretion aside, the "Heiligmesse" projects an air of festive solemnity, enhanced by the richness of its B-flat major tonality. Scored for winds in pairs (oboes, clarinets, bassoons, trumpets), timpani, strings, and organ, the composer later expanded the clarinet parts and added French horns to double the trumpets in the tuttis.

The flamboyance of the *Missa in tempore belli* is intensified by the martial character of the trumpets and drums in the Agnus Dei (hence the nickname "Paukenmesse," [Timpani Mass]). The warlike feeling is further accentuated by the key of C major, often associated with military music. Another notable feature of this Mass is the central section of the Gloria, in which Haydn achieves exceptional contrast with the agitated, declamatory outer sections by means of a serene duet in A major for bass soloist and cello, which alternates with intense interludes for the chorus. Although Haydn does not set the conclusion of the Gloria as a fugue, he begins the Credo with a fugal exposition of some length and ends that movement in traditional fashion by setting "Et vitam venturi" as a fugue. As mentioned earlier, the telescoping of text in this work may have resulted from lack of time. But no matter what the reason, this antiquated technique at the beginning of Credo vividly portrays a sense of doubt and confusion that all must have felt at this critical time in the Napoleonic Wars, when French troops were already camped on Austrian soil.

From its Latin title, to the severity of its orchestration, to the profundity of its musical thought, the *Missa in angustiis* is a singular masterpiece. The meaning of *angustiis* in this case is enigmatic, because the literal meaning of the word is "tightness" or "constriction." So the Mass's title is usually translated as "Mass in Time of Anxiety," or "Mass in Time of Danger." The anonymous author of *Über Musik und Schauspielkunst in Wien* (Notes on Music and Dramatic Art in Vienna), published in 1800, created the legend of the Mass's nickname—"Nelsonmesse"—by asserting that Haydn told him that the news of Lord Nelson's victory over the French fleet at the Battle of Aboukir (also known as the Battle of the Nile) reached Eisenstadt just as he was beginning the composition of the remarkable Benedictus. The time line alone refutes this claim: Haydn composed this Mass between 10 July and 31 August

1798; news of the battle, which occurred over the first three days of August, did not reach Austria until mid-September, about the time of the Mass's premiere (as in the case of the "Heiligmesse," the premiere was delayed: this year it occurred on 23 September). But the nickname stuck anyway, perhaps because listeners equated the dramatic and powerful trumpet calls in the Benedictus—quite unlike the usual lyrical settings in most Austrian Masses—with the advent of a savior more immediate than Jesus Christ: the victorious Lord Nelson. The "Nelsonmesse" is scored for SATB soloists, mixed chorus, and orchestra of three trumpets, timpani, organ, and strings. An additional soprano soloist is required for four measures at the "Christe eleison" in the opening movement. The organ, in the absence of woodwinds, is treated as an obbligato instrument; and the third trumpet is only used when all trumpets play in unison. Otherwise the economy of orchestration is matched by an economy of gesture and emotion: it maintains a remarkable intensity from beginning to end. Contrapuntal forms are prominent but are not necessarily used in traditional ways. For instance, the fugue that concludes the Gloria is delayed until the words "in Gloria Dei Patris, amen"; although there is no fugal ending for the Credo, that movement begins with an accompanied canon at the fifth, in octaves; the final section of the work, the "Dona nobis pacem," is a fugue, accompanied by a running figure in the violins that has no pattern or shape—perhaps an indication of unbridled ecstasy at the thought of peace. Overall, the "Nelsonmesse" is more closely aligned with the political realities of the day than the earlier "Paukenmesse." This is also borne out by the orchestration, which may not reflect Haydn's conception, but rather was necessitated by a sudden reduction in the Eisenstadt orchestra's size. It is known that the orchestra was again increased by eight players in 1800, and additional wind parts (flute, two oboes, two clarinets, and two horns) exist in the Eisenstadt archive. These parts were included in the first published edition (1803) but may not be by Haydn.

The 1799 Mass in B-flat ("Theresienmesse") may derive its nickname from a private royal performance in Vienna in which the soprano solos were apparently sung by Empress Maria Theresa. It is certainly the most introspective of the late Masses and gives more prominence to the solo voices. The orchestration, for pairs of clarinets and trumpets (both in B-flat), timpani, organ, and strings, is also a bit unusual for Haydn. Edward Olleson referred to the clarinet as "the Cinderella of Haydn's orchestra" because Haydn used it so infrequently (Wellesz and Sternfield, 323). Here they add undisguised warmth to the proceedings. Unlike in the "Heiligmesse," for instance, the profound "Et incarnatus est" section is maintained in the key of B-flat minor without modulation until the rather restrained "Et resurrexit" in G minor. The Credo ends with a lengthy fugue in 6/8, while the traditional fugal ending of the Gloria is reduced to a brief fugal exposition on the word "Amen."

There was no new Mass in 1800 because Lord Nelson's mistress, Lady Hamilton, was visiting Eisenstadt at the time. Instead, the *Missa in angustiis*, already associated with the great admiral and very popular, was performed in her honor.

However, the popularity of the next Mass—composed quickly in 1801—was hampered from the outset by the negative reaction of Empress Maria Theresa, who took exception to Haydn's borrowing of the theme in the middle section of Adam and Eve's love duet in *Die Schöpfung* for use with the text "qui tollis peccata mundi" (that takes away the sin of the world). At her insistence Haydn excised the offending passage from her copy of the new Mass. And in fact, her sensibilities may have been correct, for the quote is a curious intruder. Used as an introduction to the section in question in the Gloria, it has nothing to do with the surrounding music and functions only as a peg on which to hang the nickname, "Schöpfungsmesse." Even without the composer's little joke, this work is the most consistently sunny and lightweight of the late Masses. The two fugues—at "In gloria Dei Patri" and "Dona nobis pacem"—are each constructed from chromatic subjects. Especially endearing is the Benedictus, whose gentle, songlike quality conforms to the traditional Austrian preference for such movements more than any other late Mass. The orchestration is fuller than in the previous Masses, too: pairs of oboes, clarinets, bassoons, horns, trumpets, and timpani, with obbligato organ and strings.

The last Mass gets its nickname, "Harmoniemesse," from the German terminology for a kind of wind ensemble, *Harmonie*. (Knowledge of this terminology also provides the uninitiated with a guide to the differences between European *symphony* orchestra, with flutes, oboes, clarinets, bassoons, horns, and trumpets in pairs, three trombones (perhaps), timpani and strings; and a *philharmonic* orchestra, the concert persona of an opera-house orchestra, with additional winds such as piccolo, English horn, bass clarinet, tuba, additional percussion, etc.) The orchestration is the same as for the preceding Mass, with the addition of a flute part, making this the fullest orchestration of any Haydn Mass. According to the composer's correspondence with his employer, this Mass did not come easily for him. And it is no wonder, for there were many new things to be worked out: the spacious opening Kyrie never breaks free of its adagio tempo, the initial choral entrance is on a loud diminished chord, and the traditional closing fugues in the Gloria and the Credo are on unusual chromatic subjects. Further, the "Qui tollis peccata mundi" is the most dramatic and serious in any Haydn Mass, perhaps an appreciative gesture in the empress's direction. Also, Haydn here seems to approach a systemization of mediant tonal movement: the recapitulation of the Kyrie and the concluding "Dona nobis pacem," both in B-flat, are approached from G minor via a D major chord.

His two late oratorios, *Die Schöpfung* (The Creation, 1798, on text by Lidley, revised and translated by Gottfried van Swieten), for STB soloists, mixed chorus, and orchestra; and *Die Jahreszeiten* (The Seasons, 1801, on text by James Thomson, adapted by van Swieten), for STB soloists, mixed chorus, and orchestra, are lesser masterpieces than the late Masses but are significant nonetheless. *Die Jahreszeiten*, in spite of its relentless good nature and many fine individual passages, is rarely performed now, owing mostly to its inordinate length. Also, unlike *Die Schöpfung*, it lacks the spark of innovation that resides in the Masses.

However, *Die Schöpfung* abounds in new things: the exceptionally modern depiction of chaos, the single C major chord on the word "light" ("and there was light," which seems, initially, to establish the oratorio's tonality), the accompanied recitative in which the musical expression of natural events is followed by the verbal explanation ("And God made the firmament"), movement to mediant tonalities, and the final choruses of parts 2 and 3 in a brand-new key (B-flat major). And yet, structurally, *Die Schöpfung* stumbles a little: the third part, where we meet Adam and Eve in the Garden of Eden, bears little or no relation to the preceding sections. *Die Schöpfung* has always been very popular, and individual movements, such as the beautiful soprano aria "With verdure clad" and the magnificent chorus with solo trio "The Heavens are telling," show no signs of falling out of the repertoire. But it has always had detractors, too. Beethoven thought the imitation of birds and beasts amusingly childish; Schiller dismissed it as a meaningless hodgepodge (Thrall 1908, 121). Ultimately, the importance of *Die Schöpfung* lies in the opportunities it provided Haydn, away from the liturgy, to expand his experiments in tonal movement. And this is obvious throughout the work, from the opening chaos to the lowered final key.

Ludwig van Beethoven

Ludwig van Beethoven (1770–1827) is not usually thought of as a composer of choral music, except in relation to his monumental *Missa solemnis*, Op. 123 (1818–23), and the equally monumental Ninth Symphony, Op. 125 (1825). Throughout his career, however, Beethoven composed choral music, and most of it is of very high quality.

Beethoven's earliest choral works, the *Cantata on the Death of Emperor Joseph* (1790), and the *Cantata on the Ascension of Emperor Leopold* (1790), both for SATB soloists, mixed chorus, and orchestra, are sturdy, workmanlike pieces. Beethoven must have been pleased with the first of these, at least, because he showed it to Haydn in 1792, when Haydn passed through Bonn on the way home after his first London visit. Haydn was apparently impressed. It is unclear, however, whether Haydn encouraged the young composer to move to Vienna or suggested that Beethoven study with him. In any case, Beethoven moved to Vienna in November of that year and at some point soon thereafter began studying with Haydn. However, Haydn was apparently an uninterested teacher, and Beethoven ceased studying with him at least a year before Haydn left for his second London sojourn in 1794. Even so, Beethoven held Haydn and his work in high esteem, and the two men remained on friendly terms.

Beethoven subsequently studied with the theorist Johann Schenk; with Johann Georg Albrechtsberger, who taught him counterpoint; with Antonio Salieri, from whom he learned finer points of text setting; and finally with Aloys Förster, from whom he learned to write for string quartet.

Haydn may not have been a diligent teacher, but Beethoven still learned much through familiarity with the older master's work. The example of Haydn's Masses is particularly strong in Beethoven's Mass in C Major, Op. 86 (1807), for SATB soloists, mixed chorus, and orchestra, which was commissioned by Prince Esterházy as a continuation of the annual celebrations surrounding his wife's name day. As in Haydn, Beethoven's score allows for the inclusion of organ by retaining the old fashioned figured bass; it also incorporates the popular Austrian custom (encountered in Haydn's early Masses) of bringing back the Kyrie theme for the "Dona nobis pacem," as well as the more universal tradition of closing the Gloria and Credo movements with fugues (a practice that Haydn's late Masses continues with considerable freedom). But Haydn's presence is mostly felt in the use of third relations, not only between sections, as in the unprepared movement from A major to F major at the Benedictus and the opposite motion—A major to C minor—at the Agnus Dei (itself a lengthy modulation that eventually achieves the home tonic at "Dona nobis pacem"), but also by the extended progression of chords a third apart which sets up the approach into the final climax of the Gloria.

While Haydn's influence is apparent, this Mass is also stamped by the forcefulness of Beethoven's singular personality. For instance,

A section of the Gloria in Ludwig van Beethoven's C Major Mass showing chord progression by thirds.

the previously mentioned Benedictus begins with unaccompanied singing by the solo quartet, a stark—and startling—affect that looks forward to *Missa solemnis*. The quiet, almost devotional opening of the Sanctus is noteworthy, as is the "qui tollis peccata mundi," which, with its seemingly static string accompaniment and great tutti unison outburst, could only have been conceived by Beethoven.

The Mass in C Major was thoroughly unappreciated by Prince Esterházy, who exclaimed with undisguised disappointment, "Beethoven, what have you done?" Public opinion sided with the prince.

Still, Beethoven was fond of his Mass and saw an opportunity to get more mileage out of it by substituting text more suitable to concert presentation and, not incidentally, acceptable to Protestants as well. The resulting *contrafactum*, known as *Three Hymns*, Op. 86a, is textually divided into three large sections, the first encompassing the Kyrie and Gloria, the second the Credo, and the third the remaining movements. It is remembered today mostly because of the composer's freewheeling business ethics. Beethoven had sounded out a friend, Joseph Röckel, about the possibility of fitting German words to the music shortly after the premiere on 13 September 1807. Whether or not anything came of this is unknown. However, in 1810 Beethoven asked his publisher, Breitkopf & Härtel, the same question. That firm subsequently hired a Lutheran theologian, Dr. Christian Schreiber, to prepare a German text. After some negotiation the composer approved Schreiber's text, and it was printed along with the Latin in Breitkopf's first published edition of the Mass. In 1825, though, Beethoven offered the Mass to the Mainz publisher Schott, with a new text by one Benedikt Scholz. Schott declined the opportunity.

Beethoven's C Major Mass was generally viewed as clumsy and uninspired until 1970, when Carlo Maria Giulini conducted a revelatory performance (and subsequent recording) in London with the New Philharmonia Orchestra and Chorus. Since then it has steadily gained in favor with conductors, singers, and audiences, and no longer lives in the shadow of *Missa solemnis*.

Beethoven was accustomed to producing concerts, or *Academies*, of his own music. In December 1808 he produced one that included the Gloria, Sanctus, and Benedictus of his Mass, the concert aria "Ah! perfido," and the premieres of the Fifth and Sixth Symphonies as well as the G Major Piano Concerto. Beethoven decided that this four-hour extravaganza needed a big finish and in less than a month completed the Fantasie, Op. 80 (1808), for solo piano, mixed chorus, and orchestra. The Fantasie is a miniature piano concerto with chorus, best known because in some aspects it seems to be a warm-up for the Ninth Symphony: its thematic material is similar to the main theme of the Ninth's finale, and a specific climactic chord change (from a major chord to another major chord a third below) occurs in much the same way in both pieces. However, this chord progression, in different guise, had already made its presence known in the C Major Mass (see above). And, even though the shock value is the same in the Fantasie and Ninth Symphony, the succeeding material in both works is quite different.

Beethoven's only oratorio, *Christus am Ölberg*, Op. 85 (Christ on the Mount of Olives), for STB soloists, mixed chorus, and orchestra is not often performed, although the final scene is a very effective ensemble piece for the soloists, and there is a significant amount of fine music for male chorus earlier in the work (not unlike the men's choir writing in his opera, *Fidelio*, Op. 72, which, by the way, is occasionally done in concert). The concluding chorus has long been popular with English and American choirs, who know it as "Beethoven's Hallelujah," although the English text has little to do with the original German.

Another neglected large work is the cantata *Der glorreiche Augenblick*, Op. 136 (The Glorious Moment, 1814, on text by Aloys Weissenbach), for soloists, mixed chorus, and orchestra. Commissioned for the closing ceremonies of the Congress of Vienna, which brought an end to the Napoleonic Wars, Beethoven was saddled with the worst kind of occasional text: one that deals with a specific political event. This is why it is performed now only rarely. It also has the undeserved reputation of being "throwaway" music. But this is surely not the case: although Beethoven may not storm heaven and earth in this cantata, it contains lovely and entertaining music, not the least of which are the beautifully lyrical soprano aria with chorus, "Dem die erste Zähre" (Pray to him above), and the exciting final chorus, "Es treten vor die Scharen" (The crowds press forward), which briefly includes a children's choir. Beethoven, obviously not wanting to waste a good thing, allowed it also to be published under the title *Preis der Tonkunst*, with an appropriate text (by F. Rochlitz) extolling the glories of music.

Other works include the popular small cantata *Meeresstille und glückliche Fahrt*, Op. 112 (Calm Sea and Prosperous Voyage, 1815, on text by Goethe), for mixed chorus and orchestra; *Elegischer Gesang*, Op. 118 (Elegiac Song, 1814), for vocal quartet and string orchestra without double basses (often performed by mixed chorus with accompaniment of either piano or string quartet); two versions of *Opferlied*, Op. 121 (1823 and 1824), the earlier for SAT soloists, clarinets, horn, and low strings, and the later for soprano solo, mixed chorus, clarinets, bassoons, horns, and strings; the charming *Bundeslied*, Op. 122 (1822–23), for soprano and alto soloists, three-part chorus, and pairs of clarinets, bassoons, and horns; several choruses (some with incidental solos) with orchestra contained in incidental music for the plays *Die Ruinen von Athen*, Op. 113 (1811, on text by Kotzebue), *König Stephan*, Op. 17 (King Stephan, on text by Kotzebue) and *Die Weihe des Hauses*, Op. 124 (The Consecration of the House, on text by Carl Meisl); as well as numerous riddle canons and canons for three to six voices.

Missa solemnis and the Ninth Symphony

Missa solemnis, Op. 123 (1818–23), and the Ninth Symphony, Op. 125 (1825, on text by Schiller), both for SATB soloists, mixed chorus, and orchestra, are watershed works in the history of music. The symphony is the more frequently performed, but *Missa solemnis*, as the leading edge of this double-edged sword, is more important. Though a couple of years (and *Die Weihe des Hauses*, a relatively insignificant work) separate their completion, they are part of the same creative impulse, representing, respectively, the sacred/personal and the secular/communal aspects of life. Taken together, their attempt to reconcile humankind with God and with itself form the highest artistic achievement of the Enlightenment. We know from Beethoven's sketchbooks that he worked on them at the same time, seeking to come up with the "pacem" theme of the Mass and the symphony's "joy" theme almost simultaneously (Fiske 1979, 83).

Missa solemnis represents a paradigm shift in musical composition similar to that exemplified first by the introduction of parallel organum, later by Monteverdi's Vespers of 1610, and, more recently, by Penderecki's *St. Luke Passion*. In each case new elements were synthesized with old in such a way as to make the continuance of tradition possible within the framework of innovation. Each of these therefore exemplifies what the American theologian Robert Webber called ancient/future rhetoric. This does not mean that Monteverdi, Beethoven, and Penderecki were the originators of every innovation found in these works; rather, it means that in these respective compositions the path of the future was first fully realized.

Missa solemnis's reliance on tradition is apparent in the occasional use of old church modes, the frequent use of trombones to double lower voice parts (according to traditional Austrian usage), the liturgical text itself, the presence of standard early nineteenth-century performing forces, the fugal endings of the Gloria and the Credo (the Credo actually ending with two fugues), and the incorporation of fairly recent but already universally accepted practices, such as tonal movement to the mediant (conspicuous in the B-flat major Credo, other movements being in D major).

New elements include the expansive duration (although Cherubini's *Missa solemnis* in D is 634 measures longer), the extended high choral tessitura, the introduction of extraliturgical text for dramatic and emotional purposes ("O" before "miserere nobis" in the Gloria, rendering the work officially unusable in Roman Catholic worship), a violin solo so extensive in the Benedictus as to turn it into a concerto movement, and in the Agnus Dei a kind of reverse text painting so violently descriptive as to force the "Dona nobis pacem" text to take the offensive against the aggressive onslaught of the orchestra. Also new is the absolute refusal to attempt text painting at "Et resurrexit." And the simple, unaccompanied, forceful declamation of this text makes it one of the most effective in the repertoire.

The most profound innovation, however, occurs at the Sanctus. This text is based on Isaiah 6, which shows God sitting on a throne with worshiping angels saying "Holy, Holy, Holy, Lord God almighty. Heaven and earth are full of your glory! Hosanna in the highest!" Robert Shaw recognized the significance of Beethoven's setting and attempted to explain it in essentially musical terms:

> B minor is said to be a very rare and dark tonality for Beethoven. Though he is clearly in D major by m. 9, the exclusive use of low instruments, the solemn presence of trombones, the use of the solo Quartet's lowest registers and the *messe voce* admonition to soloists yield a texture of obscurity and mystery. Contrast this with the splendour and swinging rhythms of Bach's *Sanctus* (*B Minor Mass*)—and nearly every other setting you can recall. (Mozart's in the *Requiem* and *C Minor Mass* begin with brilliance—though the latter falls back shortly into a ghostly shudder. The late Haydn *Sancti* most frequently begin *piano*, but principally to dramatize a *crescendo* to *forte* before *Pleni sunt coeli*.) Already Beethoven in his early *C Major Mass* had written a *Sanctus* which was entirely *piano*.—But this later one, in his rarest of tonalities, is a mastery of mystery. (Blocker 2004, 178; italics in original).

In every previous setting of Sanctus God was perceived as king, and people bowed accordingly. Beethoven's achievement in *Missa solemnis* was in understanding that God is something much greater than a temporal ruler. Therefore he approached God not as did the Pharisee who pointed out in his prayer that he gave the synagogue 10 percent of his income, but rather as the publican—off in the shadowed corner, prayer shawl over his head—beating his breast and pleading, "God, be merciful to me, a sinner."

The Ninth Symphony expresses the same desire for community and peace in secular humanistic terms. Its connections to tradition, or to recently accepted currency, are obvious in the four-movement scheme, the progression from minor to tonic major (as in the Fifth Symphony), and the standard nineteenth-century performing forces. New elements include the reordering of symphonic

movements (here the Scherzo comes second) and the inclusion of
chorus and vocal soloists. Schiller's "Ode to Joy" (with amplifying
additions by Beethoven) expands on sentiments expressed in the
last pages of the *Missa solemnis*.

Whereas commentary on the *Missa solemnis* has been frequently concerned with the difficulty of its choral writing—notably the
extended high tessitura—and the meaning of the violin solo, criti-

Above and opposite: The opening measures of the Sanctus from Ludwig van
Beethoven's *Missa solemnis*.

cism of the Ninth Symphony has focused on perceived extramusical meanings in the first three movements (for instance, is the opening a depiction of chaos and creation?) and frustration over the definition of the last movement's structure (is it some variant of a rondo, as Vaughan Williams suggested, or a self-contained four-section symphony?).

Further, in both works listeners were forced as never before to come to grips with other unsettling aspects of Beethoven's art. Leonard Bernstein, in a Young Person's Concert, made the point that everything seems inevitable in Beethoven's music. But there is a troubling, sometimes confounding dichotomy, too, a dichotomy quite beyond the notion of ancient/future rhetoric. And nowhere is this dichotomy more apparent than in the *Missa solemnis* and the Ninth Symphony. After hearing her brother, Felix, conduct the Ninth Symphony in 1836, Fanny Mendelssohn—who knew nothing of ancient/future rhetoric—wrote: "This gigantic Ninth Symphony, which is so grand and in parts so abominable, as only the work of the greatest composer could be … A gigantic tragedy with a conclusion meant to be dithyrambic, but falling from its height into the opposite extreme—into burlesque" (Grove 1898/1962, 392). This dichotomy was viewed somewhat differently, and from a greater distance, by Donald Francis Tovey, who remarked: "it is a fundamental principle with Beethoven that not only tragedy and comedy, but beatific visions and common daylight, are inextricably mingled" (Tovey 1944, 133).

The dichotomy is not only artistic, it is moral: consider, for instance, the unfortunate juxtaposition of Beethoven's lofty artistic morals with his frequently shoddy business practices. The American critic Henry E. Krehbiel took Beethoven to task over this, particularly in regard to *Missa solemnis*:

> At no time have these blemishes been so numerous or so patent as they are in the negotiations for the publication of the *Missa Solemnis*— a circumstance which is thrown into particularly strong light by the frequency and vehemence of his protestations of moral rectitude in the letters which have risen like ghosts to accuse him, and by the strange paradox that the period is one in which his artistic thoughts and imagination dwelt in the highest regions to which they ever soared. (quoted in Sullivan 1960, 127)

J. W. N. Sullivan jumped to Beethoven's defense, however:

> [Beethoven's] morality, as is the case with most artists, was not identical with that professed by business men. His morality may perhaps be summed up as consisting of unfaltering courage in be-

ing true to his own experience . . . That a man should write the *Missa Solemnis* and at the same time fail to fulfill certain commercial contracts may or may not be an interesting psychological fact. It only becomes a moral problem and the *Missa Solemnis* a paradox if it be assumed that the creation of the *Missa Solemnis* implies reverence for contracts. . . . Only a very great spirit could have written the *Missa Solemnis*. And it is highly probable that a man guilty of certain moral "lapses" could not attain such heights. But that a certain unscrupulousness in relation to publishers is not incompatible with such heights is proved by the existence of the *Missa Solemnis*. (Sullivan 1960, 127–28)

Frankly, *Missa solemnis* and the Ninth Symphony would be much bigger surprises had Beethoven been some kind of saint: a monk or priest unblemished by any scandal, for instance, or a happily married gentleman with perfect kids and a country cottage resembling something from a hideous Thomas Kinkade painting. We recognize the styles—the artistic personalities— of great composers prior to Beethoven, whose art is capable of engendering a profound and satisfying response. But even in the masterworks of the greatest of these—Josquin, Monteverdi, Bach, or Mozart, for instance—the essence of their human personalities is hidden from us. Beethoven is the first composer to reveal himself, warts and all, in his music. Ralph Waldo Emerson wrote that "a foolish consistency is the hobgoblin of little minds," and Beethoven, in his greatest works, shares with us his entire life's experience, including the inconsistencies. We are somehow included as he doubts, confronts, struggles, and, ultimately, triumphs. To paraphrase Schiller's poem, we are all his brothers. This is why he is the most universally popular of all composers: not because of his artistic mastery, nor because we admire his struggle with the singular adversity of deafness, but rather because we all identify with his daily battles. When he wrote "From the heart—may it go to the heart" on the first page of the *Missa solemnis*, we know that he meant it; and we know that he meant it for us.

Schubert, Schumann, and Mendelssohn

After Beethoven, the most important Germanic composers in the
first half of the century were Franz Peter Schubert (1797–1828),
Robert Schumann (1810–1856), and Felix Mendelssohn (1809–1847).
These men composed in all genres and made especially significant
contributions to the choral repertoire.

Franz Schubert was particularly adept in small forms, and his
many part-songs provide ample evidence of his gifts. During
the middle of the twentieth century his songs for men's choir so
dominated the repertoire that some collegiate glee clubs—at the
University of California, Santa Barbara, for instance—were called
the Schubertians. He also composed exquisite songs for treble
and mixed choirs. Outstanding examples include "Lebenslust"
(1818), for mixed chorus and piano; "Gott in Natur" (1822, on text
by Ewald von Kleist), for treble chorus and piano; four settings
of "Trinklied" (all 1815, on different texts), for male chorus and
piano; "An die Frühling" (c. 1816, on text by Schiller), "Die Nacht"
(c.1822, on text by Friedrich Krumacher), and "Ewige Liebe" (c.
1825, on text by Ernst Schulze), for unaccompanied male chorus;
and "Christ ist erstanden" (1816, on text from Goethe's *Faust*), for
unaccompanied mixed chorus.

Perhaps more important are the slightly larger works with piano, for example the second version of *Ständchen* (1827, on text by
Grillparzer), for contralto solo and women's chorus; and *Nachtelle*
(1826, on text by Seidl), for tenor solo and male chorus, which
achieve near perfection in the partnership of performers.

A most impressive large work (about twenty minutes) for soprano solo, mixed chorus, and piano is *Mirjams Siegesgesang* (Miriam's
Song of Triumph, 1828). Here Schubert's humanism rejoices with
the Israelites and most effectively mourns with the Egyptians.
The piano colorfully sets the dramatic scenes, the soprano solos
are brilliant and idiomatic, and the choral writing is appropriately
powerful or reflective as necessary. It is a virtually flawless setting
of the biblical text.

Schubert was a freethinker, and this attitude is obvious in his liturgical works. For example, he freely omitted large chunks of text in all his Masses, a particularly notable example occurring in the Credo of the exquisite early Mass No. 2 in G Major (1815), for SATB soloists, mixed chorus, and string orchestra. Still, this Mass is set apart from the others of his youth by virtue of an exceedingly warm harmonic vocabulary and an innate lyricism apparent even when declamation of text is reduced to its most basic form. However, in the other early Masses—No. 1 in F Major (1814, revised 1815), No. 3 in B-flat Major (1815), and No. 4 in C Major (1816), all for SATB soloists, mixed chorus, and chamber orchestra—the writing is almost exclusively dry and academic. The most interesting aspect of these is the exceptionally virtuosic Benedictus for soprano solo in the C Major Mass. Here the writing proved so difficult that Schubert, late in life, provided an alternate version for chorus alone. He was better able to camouflage religious indifference in the Masses No. 5 in A-flat and No. 6 in E-flat, which are the products of artistic maturity. While not exactly profound, they contain much excellent music. The orchestrations here have expanded to the normal nineteenth-century standard, and Schubert makes full use of the newly available woodwind colors. Also, the solo writing possesses the easygoing naturalness of his lieder. Especially interesting is the "Et incarnatus est" trio for soprano and two tenors in the E-flat Mass, the only instance where Schubert varies the SATB solo configuration.

Schubert was more at home setting religious texts reflecting his humanism (in this regard, the most heartfelt music in his Masses usually occurs at "Et incarnatus est"). Good examples are the *Deutsche Messe* (1826 or 1827, on text by Johann Philipp Neumann), for mixed chorus and wind band, and the late motet *Intende voci* (1828), for tenor, mixed chorus, and chamber orchestra. The text of the *Deutsche Messe* is far beyond a paraphrase of the Latin. Rather, it neutralizes Roman Catholic dogma into a kind of pantheism appropriate to any religion, at any time, in any situation. It can also be performed with organ, each movement being easily extracted as an independent piece. And because the instrumental parts largely double the voices, some movements—the popular and profoundly simple "Heilig," for instance—can be effectively performed without accompaniment. The position of the *Intende voci* in Schubert's catalog is similar to that of the *Ave verum corpus* in relation to Mozart's work. And like Mozart's late motet, *Intende voci* is remarkable for its clarity of thought and richness of harmony.

Another piece with religious text that deserves mention is the *Magnificat* (1816), for SATB soloists, mixed chorus, and chamber orchestra of two oboes, two trumpets, timpani, and strings. Like the G Major Mass, it is slightly marred by an uncharacteristically high tenor tessitura. Otherwise it sits comfortably astride two worlds: divided into three sections, the joyfully academic choruses surround a central solo ensemble movement of ravishing beauty.

Schubert's brother Ferdinand (also a composer and choral conductor) attempted to increase the marketability of Schubert's music after his death by orchestrating *Mirjams Siegesgesang* and adding winds and timpani to the G Major Mass. Also, a *Deutsche Trauermesse* (German Requiem, 1818) for unaccompanied mixed chorus, long thought to be Ferdinand's, was actually ghostwritten by Franz in an effort to promote his brother as a composer.

Other works include several Latin motets, the charming *Gesang der Geister über den Wassern* (Song of the Spirits over the Water, 1820, revised 1821, on text by Goethe), for men's chorus and low strings; the cantata *Lazarus* (1820, on text by August Niemeyer), for soloists, chorus, and orchestra; and several occasional cantatas.

Robert Schumann was, like Schubert, a master of the miniature. He composed a large number of part-songs, most of which are homophonic. They are more objective than his lieder and less interesting rhythmically than his other music. Still, many exude undeniable charm and are otherwise noteworthy for the literary astuteness Schumann demonstrated in selecting his texts. Poets represented include Eichendorff, Mörike, Rückert, Heine, Goethe, and Klopstock. There are two volumes of *Romanzen* for women's choir with optional piano accompaniment (Opp. 69 and 91, 1849), with six songs in each volume. There are six sets of part-songs for men (a total of twenty-one songs) and seven sets for mixed chorus (thirty-three songs). Of these, several deserve mention, including the five *Jagdlieder*, Op. 137 (Hunting Songs, 1849), for men's choir and four horns ad libitum; "Die Lotusblume," Op. 33, No. 1 (1840), for men's choir; "Gute Nacht," Op. 59, No. 4 (1846), for mixed chorus; and "Das Schifflein," Op. 146, No. 5 (1849), for mixed chorus, flute, and horn. Some of his vocal quartets with piano have also been occasionally performed by choirs, especially the delightful "Zigeunerleben," Op. 29, No 3 (1840), with optional triangle and tambourine.

Schumann's largest choral works are *Das Paradis und die Peri*, Op. 50 (1841–43, on text by Thomas Moore, translated by Emil Flechsig with adaptations and additions by the composer) and the oratorio-like *Szenen aus Goethe's "Faust"* (1844–53), both for soloists, mixed chorus, and orchestra. In the former Schumann achieved what he thought to be a new form of secular romantic oratorio and considered it to be his most important work up to that time. Both pieces clearly reveal Schumann's inability to write dramatic music and are saved only by sections in which his innate lyricism comes to the fore. George Upton, commenting on *Das Paradis und die Peri* in 1886, wrote: "Had the narrative passages been omitted, it would unquestionably have enhanced the interest and perhaps relieved the monotony and weariness of some parts of the work" (Upton 1886, 275). Still, it remained popular for many years and counted Felix Mendelssohn among its admirers. Concerning *Faust*, Josephine Thrall, writing around 1908, claimed the final part—in which Faust's soul is taken to heaven—was Schumann's masterpiece (Thrall 1908, 173). But during the twentieth century *Faust* simply gathered dust until revived by Benjamin Britten and Peter Pears in 1973. Since then it has been performed occasionally, with some success.

Schumann's best choral works are the exquisite *Requiem für Mignon*, Op. 98b (1849, on text from Goethe's *Wilhelm Meister*), for soloists, mixed chorus, and orchestra; and the unique song cycle *Der Rose Pilgerfahrt*, Op. 112 (The Pilgrimage of the Rose, 1851, on text by Moritz Horn), for soloists, mixed chorus, and piano (later orchestrated). *Requiem für Mignon* does not fit neatly into any formal category. It is simply a text, of moderate length, set to music for voices and orchestra. Whereas Schumann's commonplace orchestration mars all of his other compositions for chorus and orchestra, here everything works. The text is brief enough for his natural inclination toward compact expression to be effective, and intimate enough for his lyricism to carry the day. *Der Rose Pilgerfahrt*, composed for a musicale in Schumann's home involving only a few performers, is through-composed: each song, while a distinct entity, flows without pause into the next. There is admirable variety and good balance between the solo and choral movements, and particularly lovely writing in the sections for treble choir. The original version for piano is much preferable to the later one, where the orchestration destroys the work's intimacy.

In 1852 Schumann became fleetingly interested in Roman Catholic liturgical music, composing a Mass, Op. 147, and a Requiem, Op. 148, both for mixed chorus and orchestra. Neither is among his best works, although each is occasionally performed. The same year he also orchestrated his German motet, *Verzweifle nicht im Schmerzenstal*, Op. 93 (1984), which was originally for double men's chorus with ad libitum organ.

Other works include the once popular *Adventlied*, Op. 71 (1848), for soprano soloist, mixed chorus, and orchestra; several "choral ballades," including *Der Königssohn*, Op. 116 (1851), *Des Sängers Fluch*, Op. 139 (1852), *Vom Pagen und der Königstochter*, Op. 140 (1852), and *Das Glück von Edenhall*, Op. 143 (1853), all for soloists, mixed chorus, and orchestra; and occasional pieces such as *Beim Abschied zu singen*, Op. 84 (1848), for chorus and wind instruments; and *Festival Overture on the "Rheinweinlied,"* Op. 123 (1853), for chorus and orchestra.

Felix Mendelssohn was a grandson of the great Enlightenment philosopher Moses Mendelssohn (1729–1786), who was, in turn, a disciple of the important philosopher and playwright Gotthold Ephraim Lessing. Moses Mendelssohn thought it important that the primary allegiance of German Jews be to Germany. Not only did this place him in the forefront of reforming forces within Judaism, it also resulted in his children's converting to Christianity (two daughters became Roman Catholics, and two sons became Protestants, including Felix's father, Abraham, a successful banker). Felix's father added "Bartholdy" (the name of their estate on the Spree River) in an effort to Christianize the family name.

Since childhood Mendelssohn had been attracted to the music of J. S. Bach. Late in 1827 he formed a group of sixteen friends who began rehearsing the *St. Matthew Passion* in his home. One of these—the actor Eduard Devrient—recognizing that *St. Matthew* had not been performed outside Leipzig since Bach's death, convinced Felix to approach his old teacher Carl Friedrich Zelter about producing *St. Matthew* with the Berlin Singakademie. Zelter loved the idea. He put the full resources of the Singakademie behind it and turned the conducting duties over to Mendelssohn, since he was already recognized as a consummate choral conductor. This performance, on 11 March 1829, began the resurrection of Bach's music. Over the next several years Mendelssohn conducted other notable performances of Bach, including the cantata *Gottes Zeit ist die allerbeste Zeit* and portions of the B Minor Mass in Frankfurt in 1835, and the *St. Matthew Passion* in Leipzig in 1841. Referring to the famous 1829 performance of the *St. Matthew Passion*, Mendelssohn later commented that "it was an actor and a Jew who restored this great Christian work to the people."

When Felix Mendelssohn's own choral music is considered today, one immediately thinks of the oratorio *Elijah*, Op. 70 (1846), for soloists, mixed chorus, and orchestra. It was premiered at the Birmingham Festival the same year and caused a sensation in Britain. For well over two hours listeners were spellbound by Mendelssohn's colorful retelling of the story of the prophet: dueling with the priests of Baal, bringing fire down from heaven, raising a widow's lifeless son, successfully praying for rain to end a devastating drought, being consumed with disappointment and fear, and eventually being taken off to heaven in a fiery chariot. *Elijah* is a great work, but it is not perfect by any means. For one thing, it is too long; for another, most of the compelling drama occurs in Part I, leaving Part II to pick up the pieces. Still, there is much to recommend it: exceptionally powerful choruses, effective projection of dramatic urgency (especially in Part I), beautiful solo and small ensemble writing and, in the character of Elijah, one of the great baritone roles of all time. With the right Elijah the work is stunning. Its popularity was in decline around the middle of the twentieth century, but in 1970 a rejuvenating new recording with Dietrich Fischer-Dieskau confirmed its lasting place in the repertoire.

Still, lovers of choral music should know that *Elijah* is not Felix Mendelssohn's only choral work, nor is it his best. That honor may fall to *Die erste Walpurgisnacht*, Op. 60 (first version, 1832; second version, 1843, on text by Goethe), for soloists, mixed chorus, and orchestra. Goethe's text about the continuance of pagan religious practices in the German countryside and, on at least one occasion, the defeat and routing of local Christians by adherents of the old religion is a paean to German art and culture. And the music reflects this totally: it doesn't sound Christian (or anti-Christian), or Jewish, or pagan. It sounds German. *Die erste Walpurgisnacht* contains all the attractive and effective elements found in *Elijah*, but is of more manageable length and contains not one ounce of sentimentality.

Mendelssohn composed two other oratorios, *Christus*, Op. 97, which remained unfinished at the composer's death, and *St. Paul*, Op. 36 (Paulus 1836). *St. Paul* was quite popular for a time, but audiences eventually tired of its length and, compared to *Elijah*, relatively anemic dramatic punch. A large portion was resuscitated for a while by Charles C. Hirt's separate edition of Part I, published as *The Conversion of St. Paul* (1970), and individual movements—Part II's beautifully flowing "How Lovely Are the Messengers," for instance—have remained staples of the church anthem repertoire.

Christus is not usually performed as a whole because of its fragmentary nature: the surviving music jumps from Epiphany to Good Friday. However, the opening male trio, one of the best representations of the Three Kings in the repertoire, and superlative chorus "There Shall a Star Come out of Jacob" are well-known to folks who enjoy church Christmas concerts.

Mendelssohn's Symphony No. 2, "Lobgesang," Op. 52 (Hymn of Praise, 1840) is often referred to as a "symphony-cantata." The first three sections, played without pause, equate to the standard movements of a symphony. The finale, however, is a multimovement cantata on religious texts and begins with thematic material taken from the opening section. The earliest German progeny of Beethoven's Ninth, the cantata portion—peppered with Lutheran chorales and delightfully contrapuntal choruses—is even more closely modeled on the cantatas of J. S. Bach. Like *Elijah*, *St. Paul*, and *Christus*, it has some individual movements that have become standard repertoire in schools and churches.

The impact of *Die erste Walpurgisnacht*, the independent success of the finale of "Lobgesang," and continued popularity of the Violin Concerto, the Third, Fourth, and Fifth Symphonies, and various chamber works bear witness to Mendelssohn's considerable abilities in writing music that grips the listener for thirty or forty minutes. Within this category are several works for mixed chorus and orchestra which are finely wrought and beautiful examples of Mendelssohn's craft. Among them are the Latin cantata *Lauda Sion*, Op. 73 (1846); the settings of Psalm 42, Op. 42 (1833), and Psalm 95, Op. 46 (1839, with tenor solo); and the typically lovely *Hear My Prayer* (*Hör mein Bitten*; organ version 1844, orchestrated in 1847), with soprano solo.

Like most German composers of his generation, Mendelssohn composed a large number of part-songs: five sets for unaccompanied mixed chorus (twenty-eight songs), and four sets for unaccompanied male chorus (eighteen songs). The first set for mixed chorus, *Six Part-songs*, Op. 41 (c. 1834) is intriguing because three are arrangements of German folk tunes, with texts by Heinrich Heine. The most frequently performed of the part-songs may be the beautiful *Die Nachtigall*, Op. 59, No. 4, which is notable for its canonic writing.

Of more interest are the settings of sacred texts for unaccompanied mixed choir, among them the *Six Anthems*, Op. 79 (1843;

one each for Christmas, New Year's Day, Ascension Day, Passion Week, Advent, and Good Friday), for eight-part chorus; the great double-chorus motets *Ehre sei Gott* and *Heilig*; and the exquisite setting of Psalm 100.

Also of interest are the cantata-like works for male chorus in which Mendelssohn endeavored to raise men's ensemble singing to a high level: *Der Jäger Abschied*, Op. 50 (1840, on text by Eichendorff), with four horns and bass trombone; *An die Künstler: Festgesang*, Op. 68 (1846, on text by Schiller), with brass; and *Festgesang*, written for the anniversary of the publication of the Gutenburg Bible (1840), with orchestra.

Other works of Mendelssohn's that deserve mention include the *Three Latin Motets*, Op. 39 (1830), for treble chorus and organ; the choruses that form part of his incidental score to Racine's *Athalie*, Op. 74 (1843, overture completed 1845), with orchestra; and the several pieces composed for the Anglican church.

Other Composers Active in the First Half of the Century

After composing several cantatas and a Mass (all for mixed chorus and orchestra), David August von Apell (1754–1832) composed his *Missa pontificale*, for soloists, mixed chorus, organ, and strings (1800), for Pope Pius VII. This work, consisting only of the Kyrie, Laudamus, Crucifixus, and Benedictus, was so well received that the composer received the Papal Order of the Golden Spur; further, the Crucifixus and Benedictus were published separately. Thereafter he composed several other sacred works, culminating in a Te Deum (1815), another Mass (1817), and a *Magnificat* (1818), all for mixed chorus and orchestra, but these works did not achieve the fame of *Missa pontificale*.

Carl Friedrich Zelter (1758–1832) was an important teacher and composer who was affiliated with the Berlin Singakademie from its inception, first as accompanist and then, after the death of Johann Friedrich Fasch, as director. He was a friend of Goethe and a teacher of Mendelssohn. Although he composed several large choral works, including a Requiem and a Te Deum, his lasting importance lies in his relationship to Mendelssohn, to whom he gave the score of Bach's *St. Matthew Passion* for study, resulting, eventually, in the performance and resurrection of that work.

Ludwig Abeille (1761–1838) was active as a musician in the court of the Duke of Württemberg. His *Aschermittwoch Lied* (Ash Wednesday Song, 1798, on text by Jacobi), for four voices and piano, was a popular work that may have influenced the vocal quartets of Schubert and Schumann.

Johannes Andreas Amon (1763–1825) was a German conductor and horn player who also composed several cantatas, a couple of Masses, and a Requiem that was performed at his own funeral.

Joseph Eybler (1765–1846) was a student of Johann Georg Albrechtsberger and an exceptionally successful choirmaster who succeeded Antonio Salieri as imperial Kapellmeister in 1824. His teacher thought his abilities second only to those of Mozart, and his works, in all genres, were frequently performed during his life. His sacred music, however, was the most durable, and his liturgical works were performed long after his death. Chief among them is the Requiem in C Minor, for soloists, mixed chorus, and orchestra. Other works include a couple of Te Deums, several Masses, and a significant number of smaller pieces.

Johann Anton Andre (1775–1842) continued the music publishing business founded by his father, Johann Andre (1741–1799). He is primarily remembered for his early, and reliable, editions of works by W. A. Mozart, and in particular helped establish the authenticity of Mozart's Requiem. As a composer he was, in the words of Wolfgang Plath, "perhaps among the most considerable of the many composers of his period who now stand in the shadow of Beethoven and Schubert" (Wolfgang Plath, "Johann Anton Andre," in Sadie 1980, 1:404). Among his choral works are the *Missa solemnis*, Op. 43, for soloists, chorus, and orchestra (1819); *Vater unser*, Op. 50, for two choirs and orchestra (1827); the Te Deum, Op. 60, for soloists, chorus, and orchestra (1829); several part-songs and vocal quartets with piano accompaniment; and three sets of pieces for male chorus: *Liederkranz*, Op. 57 (c. 1830), *Liederkranz*, Op. 61 (c. 1830), and *24 Maurergesänge* (n.d., without opus number).

Johann Kaspar Aiblinger (1779–1867) studied in Munich and Italy, where he collected old music on behalf of Ludwig I of Bavaria. Working at the Allerheiligen-Hofkirche in Munich, he strove tirelessly for the enrichment of church music and became an adept composer of it, writing over thirty Masses, some unaccompanied and some with orchestra, and many other sacred choral works of all types common to the Roman Catholic liturgy. His style is marked by a balanced, classical approach that leans heavily on Renaissance models while eschewing the more dramatic elements associated with his immediate Austrian and German predecessors. Lowell Mason attended a service at Aiblinger's church in May 1852. His account clearly shows that Catholics, at least in Munich, were catching up with their Protestant brethren in regard to chorus personnel:

> The choristers number about twenty-four, or six on a part, being composed of the best professional vocalists, or opera singers, in Munich. The organ was played very well, but never as an accompaniment, as the vocal music was without any accompaniment whatsoever. There was, in the performance of this choir all the full, clear, and certain delivery and union of vocal tones that the most fastidious critic could desire; though less of the *crescendo* and *diminuendo* than in the Dom choir at Berlin; but in one respect, the Munich choir had a great advantage,—*the Soprano and Alto parts were sustained by female voices.* (Mason 1854, 129; italics in original)

Louis Spohr (1784–1859), in addition to having an international career as a violinist, was a composer of some renown during his lifetime. An acquaintance of Beethoven, he was a great champion of the early string quartets but simply could not understand Beethoven's later music. He became one of Richard Wagner's earliest advocates even though his own music is conservative in the extreme. For a composer essentially committed to instrumental music, he composed a significant number of works for chorus, including *Six Part-songs*, Op. 44, and *Six Part-songs*, Op. 90, both for unaccompanied male chorus; *Six Part-songs*, Op. 151, for unaccompanied mixed chorus; *Psalm Eighty-four*, Op. 134 (after Milton), for soloists, mixed chorus, and orchestra; several oratorios commissioned by the English festivals; and a Mass, Op. 54, for solo voices and double mixed chorus.

Carl Maria von Weber (1786–1826), the founder of German romantic opera, was also a composer of rather interesting choral music. The early cantata *Der erste Ton*, Op. 14 (1818), for speaker, mixed chorus, and orchestra, was an unsuccessful precursor to the melodrama, a form that would become popular later in the century. Of his other secular works, mention should be made of *Jubal-Cantata*, Op. 58 (1818, on text by Friedrich Kind), for soloists, mixed chorus, and orchestra. One of the more successful occasional works of its kind, it was composed for the fiftieth anniversary of the accession of Frederick Augustus as King of Saxony. Weber's best choral music is found in his two Masses for soloists, mixed chorus, and orchestra. The first, in E-flat, Op. 75a (1818), projects an air of solemnity from start to finish. The second, in G major, Op. 76 (1818–19), has more buoyancy and also occasional fleeting references that remind the listener of Weber's operatic inclinations. Like other Mass settings from early in the century, they adapt well to concert presentation and should not be overlooked by enterprising conductors. Other works include offertories for each of the Masses; several sets of part-songs for male voices, including *Leyer und Schwert*, Op. 42 (1814, text on six poems of Theodor Körner); and several three- and four-part canons.

August Ferdinand Anacker (1790–1854) was primarily concerned with music education. In addition to his teaching posts in Freiburg, he also became Kantor at the cathedral and founded the Freiburg Singakademie in 1823. As a composer he focused mainly on choral music, both sacred and secular. Unlike many composers who are primarily choral-music educators, Anacker did not seek to compromise his natural proclivity toward modernity in exchange for easy-to-teach formulae. On the contrary, his music is noteworthy for emotional content that is exceptionally focused and taut. His oratorio *Bergmannsgruss* (1831–32) became one of the most popular choral works of the century.

Giacomo Meyerbeer (1791–1864) was the son of a wealthy Jewish banker. He demonstrated prodigious gifts as a pianist, including an apparent ability to read the most difficult orchestral scores as sight. His interest in composition led him to study with Zelter for a while, then with Bernard Anselm Weber, and finally with Abbé Vogler, in whose house he lived and where he met his lasting friend Weber. His earliest compositions, written at this time, included seven *Geistliche Oden von Klopstock* (c. 1810) for unaccompanied mixed chorus (his first publication); and the oratorio *Gott und die Natur* (1811), for soloists, mixed chorus, and orchestra, the performance of which received such favorable attention that he was appointed court composer. Meyerbeer's first visit to Paris in 1826 changed his life. The impression was so profound that he became virtually French in musical style. In 1842 the king of Prussia appointed him general music director, and in 1862 he was chosen to represent German music at the London International Exhibition. Although his fame rested on dramatic works, choral music remained important to him. There are great choruses in his operas, and in his official capacity in Berlin he composed several occasional cantatas for the Prussian royal family. In addition, he wrote a couple of pieces for the Berlin Cathedral choir: a setting of Psalm 51 for unaccompanied eight-part mixed chorus, and a *Pater Noster* for mixed chorus and organ. Works unpublished at his death include settings of twelve psalms, for unaccompanied double mixed chorus, as well as a *Stabat mater* and a Te Deum. His Jewish heritage later made his music, along with that of Mendelssohn and Mahler, the focus of relentless attacks by German musicologists during the Nazi era as part of the official effort to rid German music of *entartete Kunst* (degenerate art).

Salomon Sulzer (1804–1890) was an exceptionally influential innovator in choral music for the synagogue. A celebrated cantor, he served in his hometown of Hohenems before being called as *chazzan* (cantor) of Vienna's Seitenstettengasse synagogue in 1826.

The initial choral entrance of Psalm 21 from Salomon Sulzer's *Shir Zion*.

There he worked with the important Jewish rabbi and reformer Izaak Noah Mannheimer. Sulzer was one of the first to advocate the use of organ in Jewish worship and on at least one occasion also used string quartet. He was the first nineteenth-century Jewish composer to write liturgical music for four-part mixed choir. Further innovations appeared in his collection *Shir Zion* (1838), for cantor and mixed choir (many works with organ): not only did Sulzer eschew traditional Jewish melodies in favor of free composition in the style of secular Austrian music, but he also invited several non-Jewish composers to contribute, including Franz Schubert, who provided a setting of Psalm 92 for baritone solo and mixed chorus. A second volume of *Shir Zion*, published in 1865, reintroduced traditional Jewish materials. In 1860 he published *Duda'im*, a collection of liturgical songs for unison chorus and organ (or piano) intended for the purpose of training Jewish children.

Fanny Mendelssohn Hensel (1805–1847) lived and worked in the shadow of her famous brother Felix; some of her works were even published as his. Nevertheless, she was highly regarded during her lifetime as both a pianist and a composer, and the few works that appeared in published editions during the latter part of the twentieth century became deservedly popular. Her untimely death deprived Europe of an outstanding talent who could have become the first truly great female composer. Six of her part-songs for mixed chorus were published together, just before her death, under the title of *Gartenlieder*, Op. 3 (1846), and were reissued by Novello in 1878. Other choral works include the cantatas *Hiob* (Job, 1831), for SATB soloists, mixed choir and orchestra; and *Lobgesang* (1831), for soprano and alto soloists, mixed chorus, and orchestra (both published in 1992); *Oratorium nach den Bildern der Bibel* (1831), for SATB soloists, mixed chorus, and orchestra; and two works for mixed chorus and piano, *Zum Fest der heiligen Cäcilia* (1833) and *Einleitung zu lebenden Bilder* (1841, with speaker).

Others include Johann Simon Mayr (1763–1845), a distinguished pianist and opera composer whose career was spent mostly in Italy and who did not begin composing large choral works until 1791, thereafter turning out several *Stabat mater* settings and several impressive oratorios, including *La Passione* (1794), for soloists, mixed chorus, and orchestra; Leonhard von Call (1767–1815), whose numerous three- and four-part male choruses helped establish the popularity of the genre throughout Europe; August

Bergt (1771–1837), who was admired by Weber and literati such as E. T. A. Hoffman for his oratorios and cantatas, and whose smaller sacred pieces were popular in Germany during his lifetime; Gottlieb Benedikt Bierey (1772–1840), a very popular composer of singspiels, who also contributed part-songs, small sacred pieces, and some cantatas, including *Wie an dem stillen Abend* (1806), an Easter cantata for soloists, mixed chorus, and orchestra; Joseph Drechsler (178?–1852), who was appointed Kapellmeister at St. Stephen's Cathedral in 1844 and contributed a festive Psalm 150, for mixed chorus, to Salomon Sulzer's 1838 collection of new music for the Jewish liturgy; Antonio Diabelli (1797–1848), who composed the *Pastoralmesse* in F major, Op. 147, for mixed chorus and orchestra and several other popular Masses designed specifically for performance in small rural churches; Wilhelm Theodor Johannes Braun (1796–1867), an oboist and composer who contributed a Mass for mixed chorus and orchestra (c. 1830) and a couple of other choral works; and Robert Führer (1807–1861), a fine organist but an incredibly dishonest person, who lost several positions "because of his irregular life, embezzlements, etc." (Watson 1996, 145) and who wrote thirty-two Masses and fourteen Requiems as well as other sacred music, yet still found time to add trumpets and drums to a Schubert Mass and claim it as his own.

Bruckner, Brahms, and Mahler

The first names that come to mind when one thinks of late nineteenth-century Austro-German choral music—and symphonic music, too, for that matter—are the transplanted north German Johannes Brahms (1833–1897) and the native Austrians Anton Bruckner (1824–1896) and Gustav Mahler (1860–1911). Each man's work is marked by exceptional originality and depth of expression. And each, in one way or another, fell under the shadow of Richard Wagner (1813–1883).

As a composer of choral music Wagner is not important. But his ideas were revolutionary and remarkably influential: his music dramas were *Gesamtkunstwerke* (complete art works) in which every character, emotion, and important object was represented by its own musical idea, or leitmotif; in *Tristan und Isolde* (1857–59) he changed concepts of harmony forever; and to his everlasting shame he authored under a pseudonym an inflammatory anti-Semitic diatribe entitled "The Jew in Music," which later caught the eye and imagination of Adolf Hitler. Four of his seven choral works are for male voices, including *Das Liebesmahl der Apostel* (The Love Feast of the Apostles, 1843) for men's chorus and orchestra, which is still occasionally performed by very good choirs that can stay in tune for fifteen minutes or so before the orchestra enters. Others include the unaccompanied men's chorus *An Webers Grabe* (1844), which might be worth a revival, and the very early *Neujahrs-Kantate* (New Year's Cantata, 1834), for mixed chorus and orchestra.

Anton Bruckner (1824–1896) fell thoroughly under Wagner's spell. Most of his mature works reveal the direct influence of Wagnerian harmony, pacing, and orchestration (some of the symphonic works even require Wagner's new tubas). His dramatic sense, though, was formed by the Roman Catholic liturgy, not the stage, and his aesthetic was Austrian rather than Bavarian. Even within the spacious structures and monumental pronouncements of the great symphonic Masses—the so-called No. 1 in D Minor and No. 3 in F Minor—one hears Papa Haydn and the Austrian countryside. Bruckner's orchestrations are also defined by his prowess as an organist: solo lines are accompanied by instrumental groupings that change color as if stops were being pulled on and off.

Bruckner devoted his life to the church, much of it as organist and music director at the monastery of St. Florian, a short distance from Linz. His early compositions are generally uninspired, practical vehicles for the liturgy. The first in which his own formidable personality begins to emerge is the Requiem in D Minor (1848–49), still occasionally performed. Its duration of about thirty minutes and understated performing forces of SATB choir (with incidental solos), organ, horn, three trombones, and strings, reveal it to be a functional funeral Mass. Although Bruckner's mature violin writing is anticipated here, nothing else, either in the Requiem or in any of his other early Masses, motets, and miscellaneous church pieces, prepares us for the power of his later compositions.

The monumental qualities of duration and dynamic excess in Bruckner's symphonies are such that the great Masses of his maturity—D Minor (1864, revised 1876, 1881), E Minor (1866, revised 1869, 1876, 1882), and F Minor (1867–68, revised 1872, 1876, 1877, 1881, 1883, 1890–93)—as well as the remarkable Te Deum (1881, final version 1883–84), are often found guilty by association. This view is neither fair nor completely accurate. Even though the D Minor requires a soloist (or priest) to intone the Gregorian incipits for Gloria and Credo, both it and the F Minor Mass are essentially concert works written for a standard nineteenth-century orchestra, mixed chorus, and SATB soloists. Following Haydn's late example, they do not telescope text. Durations are mostly in line with those of other notable late eighteenth- and nineteenth-century Masses: the D Minor is the longest at just under an hour, and the E Minor and F Minor are about forty-two minutes each, which also keeps them in the ballpark with Haydn's late Masses. This kinship with Haydn caused the Caecilians to claim that Bruckner was simply writing symphonies with liturgical text.

The E Minor Mass may have been a reaction to that criticism. Designed to dwell in the parallel universes of concert hall and worship service, this severely gorgeous work is scored for eight-part mixed chorus and fifteen wind instruments. The Gloria and Credo begin with Gregorian incipits sung by a soloist (or priest); the instrumental accompaniment harkens back to the eighteenth-century Austrian tradition of the wind-band Mass, as perfected by Michael Haydn; counterpoint, following the lead of Palestrina, magically projects clear declamation of text; and austere modality mingles freely with Wagnerian chromaticism. Most strict Caecilians, on hearing it, must have been simultaneously enthralled and appalled. But, in fact, Franz Xaver Witt loved it, no doubt rationalizing the use of wind instruments as necessary under the circumstances of outdoor performance for which Bruckner wrote the piece.

These Masses contain particularly memorable passages, especially the ravishing "Et incarnatus est" of the E Minor Mass and the F Minor's "Et resurrexit," one of the most convincing in the repertoire.

The Te Deum, for SATB soloists, mixed chorus, and orchestra, is laid out in four sections, like a small symphony. Its sustained ultimate climax is exceptionally overpowering; but there is much quiet singing, too, and ample rest for the chorus between its outbursts while the soloists hold forth in virtuosic splendor. Even though the choral tessitura in the final section is unforgiving, the relatively brief duration of the whole (about twenty-five minutes) negates that problem if the chorus is large enough. And therein is the real difficulty of the Te Deum: not bombast or unrealistic vocal demands, but rather that most of the choral writing seems to have been conceived for a professional chamber choir. The vast number of large amateur choral societies simply cannot negotiate the contrapuntal intricacies that permeate the piece.

The motets are perhaps most familiar to choral enthusiasts. The *Ave Maria* (1861), for unaccompanied seven-part mixed chorus, is generally considered Bruckner's first masterpiece. Though obviously indebted to the eight-part polychoral works of Giovanni Gabrieli and other masters of the colossal baroque, Bruckner's chromaticism is also an obvious homage to Wagner, especially in the way it is used to create dramatic effects. Still, the quickly rising crescendos and massive climaxes, followed by expressive silences—which have an overpowering effect, especially in the St. Florian acoustic—are not the work of a student or disciple, but rather that of a superlative artist in full command of his material and surroundings. Incidentally, the dramatic pause is a common feature of Bruckner's style that, like much else in his writing, elicited criticism. The composer's response was: "Whenever I have something new and important to say, I must stop and take a breath first" (Watson 1996, 67).

Bruckner was very sensitive to criticism throughout his life and, even though he would eventually abandon the Caecilians, their attacks cut particularly deep. In addition to the E Minor Mass,

he answered them with the motet *Os justi* (1879), for unaccompanied mixed choir. It is a brilliantly conceived supposition of what
Palestrina might have done with the Lydian mode had he lived in
the nineteenth century. The counterpoint is flawless, the climaxes
perfectly timed, and the quiet, quasi-chant unison ending a stroke
of genius. In presenting this piece to Ignaz Traumihler, the music
director at St. Florian, to whom it is dedicated, Bruckner wrote:
"I should be very pleased if you found pleasure in the piece. It is
written without sharps or flats, without the chord of the seventh,
without six-four chord and without chordal combinations of four
and five simultaneous notes" (Watson 1996, 92).

Bruckner further nodded in the Caecilians' direction with an
unaccompanied setting of *Pange lingua et Tantum ergo* (1868) in the
Phrygian mode. Witt eventually published it but "greatly annoyed
Bruckner by 'correcting' some of the most poignant dissonances"
(Watson 1996, 92).

Other motets for unaccompanied mixed chorus that have retained places of honor in the repertoire include *Locus iste* (1869),
a simple, largely homophonic affair, and its contrapuntal and
harmonically complex sister *Virga Jesse floruit* (1885). *Virga Jesse*,
in particular, casts off Caecilian restraints in favor of Wagnerian
harmonic complexities.

Other sacred works of some interest include the popular Psalm
150 (1892), for soprano solo, mixed chorus, and orchestra; the early
Missa solemnis in B-flat minor (1854), for soloists, mixed chorus,
and orchestra; *Tantum ergo* in B-flat major (c. 1854), for mixed
chorus, two trumpets, strings and organ; and *Ecce sacerdos magnus*
(1885), for mixed chorus, three trombones, and organ.

Bruckner's Masses and best motets carry such weight that his
output of secular choral music goes unnoticed. But beginning with
the very early cantata *Vergissmeinnicht* (1845, on text by Marinelli),
for solo quartet, mixed chorus, and piano, he composed a significant number of secular works, most of them for male choir. These
include the cantatas *Auf, Brüder! Auf zur frohen Feier* (1852, on
text by Marinelli), for male quartet, mixed chorus, and brass; *Auf
Brüder, auf, und die Saiten zur Hand* (n.d., on text by Marinelli), for

male quartet, male chorus, mixed chorus, woodwinds, and brass; *Abendzauber* (1878, on text by Mattig) for baritone solo, three yodelers, male choir, and four horns; *Träumen und Wachen* (1890, on text by Grillparzer), for tenor solo and male chorus; and *Das deutsche Lied* (1892, on text by E. Fels), for male chorus and brass.

Johannes Brahms is regarded today, as in his own lifetime, as a consummate master of antique musical forms. Even Richard Wagner, before he had become permanently enraged with anyone who deviated from his views, wrote of Brahms: "One sees what can still be done with the old forms in the hands of one who knows how to deal with them" (Geiringer 1961, 76). Others of influence also appreciated Brahms's classical inclinations: early in his career he had been dubbed a musical messiah in Robert Schumann's last editorial for the *Neue Zeitschrift für Musik*.

But, as if Schumann's unabashed shout-out did not place enough pressure on the young composer, a bitter and ongoing dispute emerged between Wagner's circle and Brahms's friend Eduard Hanslick, the influential music critic, who not only questioned the musical principles of Liszt and Wagner, but also was unappreciative of the Wagnerites' self-righteous attitude. Brahms, caught in the middle, became a target for the Wagnerites, who considered his music to be more than old-fashioned. Hugo Wolf, for instance, wrote that Brahms's music was "disgustingly stale and prosy, and fundamentally false and perverse." Not to be outdone, Wagner himself weighed in with an essay entitled *Über das Dirigieren* (1869) in which he sarcastically referred to Brahms as, among other things, "a Jewish czardas player" (Geiringer 1961, 143, 77). (The possibility that Brahms might actually have been Jewish was frequently raised during the early Nazi period in Germany: see Beller-McKenna 2004, 178–82.)

It should be noted that Brahms neither sought nor wanted this controversy. With the exception of an early publication (1860, co-signed by Joachim, Grimm, and Scholz), bemoaning the influence of Liszt and other composers of "new" music, Brahms never—either publicly or privately—offered any criticism of Wagner. It should also be noted that, in terms of harmonic language, the mature Brahms was anything but old-fashioned. Still, Brahms became the darling of the musical conservatives in Germany— even the Caecilians were thrilled with his unaccompanied Latin pieces—and a lightning rod for criticism by Wagnerites. The situation was not helped when the conductor Hans von Bülow, who became a friend of Brahms after he was cuckolded by Wagner, coined the phrase "the three Bs"—Bach, Beethoven, and Brahms. Through all of this Brahms maintained a typical modesty in regard to his own place in history. Late in life he said, "I know very well the place I shall one day have in music history: the place that Cherubini once had, and has today" (Brockway and Weinstock 1958, 469). While the controversy with the Wagnerites had no direct bearing on Brahms's music, it did affect how his music was perceived: criticisms of it, even into the twentieth century, abound with Wagnerian references.

Brahms composed no choral music during the earliest part of his career, and it was not until he had experienced the chorus firsthand as a conductor in Detmold and then in Hamburg that he began writing for it. In the same way that Bruckner pursued opportunities revealed through study of Wagner's ideas, Johannes Brahms gleaned from the models of Bach, Beethoven, and other old masters. Bach's shadow, particularly, is evident in Brahms's choral music.

Even in his most unassuming choral pieces, the twenty-six *German Folk Songs* (without opus number, completed 1864) for unaccompanied mixed chorus, Brahms relied heavily on the example of Bach's chorale settings. This was only natural: Brahms had begun collecting folk songs (or at least, tunes he thought to be of folk origin) while a teenager and had absorbed them in the same way that Bach had absorbed all facets of Lutheran congregational song. Most of these settings were made when the composer was in his twenties, the first fourteen being published in 1864 (the others were published posthumously). The folk texts are strophic, and Brahms does not vary the setting from verse to verse. Most are homophonic, with carefully conceived, grateful vocal lines. Counterpoint is

mostly reduced to passing tones and brief quasi-canonical passages, such as the opening of "Vom heiligen Märtyrer Emmerano,
Bischoffen zu Regensburg" (The Holy Martyr Saint Emmeran,
Bishop of Regensburg). The Renaissance German polyphonic lied
provides inspiration for the five pieces with more prominent contrapuntal writing: "Von edler Art" (The Ardent Suitor), "Täublein
weiss" (The White Dove), "Morgengesang" (Morning Song), "Der
englische Jäger" (The Heavenly Hunter), and the second setting of
"Wach auf!" (Wake Up!).

This pendulous movement between Renaissance and baroque
models is a typical feature of Brahms's other choral compositions
as well. His earliest surviving choral work is a collection of Mass
movements (Kyrie, Sanctus, Benedictus, and Agnus Dei) that
dates from 1856–57. It is obvious from Brahms's correspondence
with Joseph Joachim and Julius Grimm that he was not only just
learning the craft of choral composition, but also hoping for a performance by Grimm's choir in Münster. Brahms finally responded
to Grimm's suggestions for rewriting by saying only that he did
not "want to go on with the mass" (Otto Biba, in Brahms 1984).
As with other pieces he considered unsatisfactory, Brahms may
have destroyed his manuscript, keeping only the Benedictus. But
the copy sent to Grimm survived and was eventually published
as *Missa canonica* in 1984. It has since been recorded. Clearly a
youthful study, its primary value is in observing how Brahms later
adapted the Benedictus for use in the motet Op. 74, No. 1.

Es ist das Heil uns kommen her, the first motet of Op. 29 (c. 1860,
on text by Johann Jakob Schütz), is a prelude and fugue based on
an old German chorale tune (although there is some disagreement
as to the exact form of the second part: is it really a fugue or a line-
imitating chorale motet?). *Schaffe in mir*, Op. 29, No. 2 (Create in
Me a Clean Heart, 1857, text from Psalm 51) is a three-movement
study of Renaissance and baroque forms: the first movement a
canon in augmentation, the second a four-voice fugue, and the
third a harmonized canon at the seventh followed by a fugue.

Lass dich nur nichts nicht dauren, Op. 30 (Let Nothing Ever
Grieve Thee, 1856, on text by Paul Flemming), for mixed chorus

and organ, is a double canon at the ninth. The motets of Opp. 109 and 110, which are mostly for double choir, pay homage to Gabrieli and Heinrich Schütz.

The two motets of Op. 74, for unaccompanied mixed chorus, explore old forms in other ways. The second, *O Heiland reiss die Himmel auf* (O Savior, Throw the Heavens Wide, c. 1860–65, on an anonymous Lutheran chorale text first published in 1631) is a set of variations on an original chorale tune. Variation form, in Brahms's hands, is an evolutionary process wherein each variation takes on some aspect of its predecessor. This is obviously a technique best suited to a large number of variations. In this case, where the variations are limited to the five stanzas of text, the evolutionary process can still be observed as contrapuntal procedures become more complicated with each successive verse, culminating in the last, a strict double canon in inversion.

On the other hand, the first motet of this set, *Warum ist das Licht gegeben?* (Wherefore Has the Light Been Granted?, 1877), is a multimovement structure similar in form to Bach's late Leipzig cantatas. Texts from Job, the Lamentations of Jeremiah, St. James, and Martin Luther attempt to reconcile humankind's painful existence and ultimate death with the concept of a loving God. The architectural concept is brilliantly ambiguous: the opening movement, sections of which are separated by homophonic declamations of "Warum?" (Why? or Wherefore?), begins as a four-voice fugal exposition in D minor that—like life, in many cases—evaporates before it can fully develop (Geiringer 1961, 273, refers to the opening movement as "a peculiar rondo-like structure"); the second is a brief canon at the fifth in F major (a reworking of material in Brahms's early *Missa canonica*); the third begins in the style of a Renaissance motet and runs headlong into an abbreviated reprise of the F major canon on the text "Now of Job's patience ye have been hearing"; the fourth is a four-voice chorale on an original tune of Brahms, in the style of Bach, that ends on a D major chord. Setting aside unanswered questions raised by the first movement, the structural ambiguity is more apparent on paper than to the listener (who may not hear the third movement as a

separate entity from the second) and is created by the separation
of movements according to the text source:

1. Wherefore hath the light been granted to those lost in woe, and
   the lifeblood to the sore afflicted? Who for death are longing, that
   comes not; they dig for it more than for great treasure hid; yea,
   they are glad, and go rejoicing when they their grave see open.
   Wherefore? To the mortal whose way is darkly hid, and whom
   the Lord for ever hath hedged in? Wherefore? (Job 3:20–23)

2. Let us lift up our heart, let our hands be uplifted to God in
   heaven. (Lamentations 3:41)
3. Lo now, we count them happy who, enduring, fail not. Now of
   Job's patience ye have been hearing, and the outcome of God ye
   have been seeing: that the Lord hath great pity and tender mercy.
   (James 5:11)

4. In peace and joy I near my goal, if God is willing,
   And faith fills all my heart and soul, calm and stilling.
   The Lord God hath promised me
   That death is but a slumber.
   (Martin Luther; all translations by Willis Wager)

Brahms was more reliant on the traditions of homophonic song
in his secular part-songs, although appearances of Renaissance
antiphonal polyphonic technique—primarily presenting treble
and male voices in opposition—provide effective variety of texture within the sets of Op. 42 (*Three Songs*, 1859–61), Op. 62 (*Seven
Songs*, 1874), Op. 93a (*Six Songs*, 1883–84), and Op. 104 (*Five Songs*,
1886?–88). Brahms, true to his own instincts, also could not avoid
the occasional foray into canonic writing, as in "Beherzigung," Op.
93a, No. 6; and "Verlorene Jugend," Op. 104, No. 4. There is variety
within the homophonic songs themselves, too. For example, the
folk-song tradition is clearly audible in "Rosemarin," Op. 62, No. 1;
the Lutheran chorale is alive and well in "Vergangen ist mir Glück
und Heil," Op. 62, No. 7; an awareness of Mendelssohn is obvious

in "Vineta," Op. 42, No. 2; and Brahms's own dark romantic voice is heard in "Im Herbst," Op. 104, No. 5.

Brahms produced a significant number of compositions for women's voices, including the *Ave Maria*, Op. 12 (1858), with organ or orchestra; *Songs for Female Chorus*, Op. 17 (1860), with two horns and harp; Psalm 13, Op. 27 (1859), with organ or piano (strings ad libitum); *Geistliche Chöre*, Op. 37 (1859–63), for unaccompanied women's choir; *Twelve Songs and Romances*, Op. 44 (1859–63), for unaccompanied women's choir; and *Thirteen Canons*, Op. 113 (composed at various times), also for unaccompanied women's choir. Of these, Opp. 17, 27, 37, and 44 were composed specifically for Brahms's women's chorus in Hamburg. The influence of folk music is apparent throughout Op. 44, while contrapuntal forms are prominent in Op. 37. For instance, all three movements of Op. 37 contain canons: the first two ("O bone Jesu" and "Regina coeli") in contrary motion, the third ("Adoramus") a four-voice canon at intervals of a fourth, a fifth, and an octave below. As in the mixed-voice *Begräbnisgesang*, Op. 13 (Funeral Song, 1858, on text by Michael Weisse), with winds (oboes, clarinets, bassoons, horns, trombones, tuba, and timpani), Brahms's primary interest in the accompanied pieces of Opp. 12, 17, and 27 seems to be the exploration of new and interesting tone colors.

The set of small pieces for male chorus, *Five Songs*, Op. 41 (c. 1862) is less well-known than the various works for mixed and women's choir but are just as finely wrought, looking to medieval polyphony and folk song for inspiration.

The quartets that Brahms composed for SATB soloists and piano have simply been absorbed into the choral repertoire. Among these are the *Three Quartets*, Op. 64 (1862–74); *Four Quartets*, Op. 92 (1877–84); *Six Quartets*, Op. 112 (1888); eleven *Zigeunerlieder*, Op. 103 (Gypsy Songs, 1887); eighteen *Liebeslieder Walzer*, Op. 52 (Lovesong Waltzes, 1868–69); and fifteen *Neue Liebeslieder*, Op. 65 (New Lovesong Waltzes, 1874).

With the exception of the two sets of *Liebeslieder Walzer* (selections of which had been released in choral octavo format by the firm of E. C. Schirmer in 1928), the popularity of the quartets as choral works was promulgated largely by Robert Shaw in the late 1950s. Shaw did not perform them according to opus number, but instead selected individual pieces from different sets, recorded them together, and published them in choral octavo format. They quickly became well-known to American high school and college choirs. Notable among these are "Der Abend," Op. 64, No. 2; and "Nächtens," Op. 112, No. 2. "Der Abend" impresses with the richness of its harmonic language and its incessant three-against-two accompaniment figure, while "Nächtens"—one of Brahms's more melancholy utterances—creates an unsettled feeling with its 5/4 meter and nervously busy piano part.

Zigeunerlieder are settings of Hungarian folk-song texts. Although Brahms retains the 2/4 meter typical of Hungarian folk song, the music is his alone.

The *Liebeslieder Walzer* and *Neueliebeslieder*—both for piano four-hands—are by far the most popular of Brahms's quartets. The freshness of each successive waltz creates the sensation of unending inspiration. Brahms maintains variety through various means, including variations in tempo and occasional reductions in the number of voice parts. With the exception of the closing movement of the second set, all the texts are by Daumer. The finale of the *Neueliebeslieder*, however, sets a text by Goethe ("Zum Schluss" [To Close]), and is altogether different in form and character: "This number is a Chaconne with a canon-like middle movement; and it is just here, where he is turning from a light to a more serious mode of writing, that Brahms gives of his best" (Geiringer 1961, 254). In 1870 Brahms created the *Liebeslieder Suite* of nine waltzes by orchestrating eight from Op. 52 and composing a new one, which would eventually be incorporated into the *Neueliebeslieder*. The four voices are retained; the orchestration consists of pairs of flutes, oboes, clarinets, bassoons, and horns, and full strings.

The *Liebeslieder Suite* is part of a genre of brief works for voice (or voices) and orchestra, approximately ten to thirty minutes in duration, which may have developed from the concert arias of Mozart (examples include Beethoven's *Meeresstille und glückliche Fahrt*, Mendelssohn's *Hear My Prayer*, and Schumann's *Requiem für*

Mignon). Brahms excelled in this genre, and although the majority of his large works for chorus and orchestra are now infrequently performed (see below), virtually all his shorter pieces for chorus and orchestra have remained in the repertoire. These include the *Rhapsody*, Op. 53 (1869, on text by Goethe), for contralto solo, male chorus, and orchestra; *Schicksalslied*, Op. 54 (Song of Destiny, 1871, on text by Hölderlin), for mixed chorus and orchestra; *Nänie*, Op. 82 (1880–81, on text by Schiller), for mixed chorus and orchestra; and *Gesang der Parzen*, Op. 89 (Song of the Fates, 1882, on text by Goethe), for mixed chorus and orchestra.

The *Rhapsody*—popularly called *Alto Rhapsody*—is the composer's best-known work for male choir. A profound setting of selected stanzas from one of Goethe's more problematic poems, *Harzreise in Winter*, it is structured as a lengthy recitative, three-section aria, and concluding aria with chorus. The intensely emotional music magically avoids any hint of sentimentality.

Schicksalslied was premiered on 18 October 1871 in Karlsruhe, in a concert conducted by the composer. In that program, Brahms placed the *Schicksalslied* between the overture and Garden Scene of Schumann's *Faust*. The most frequently performed of the brief works for chorus and orchestra, it represents an unusual solution to a compositional and philosophical problem. At least as early as Op. 27 Brahms had been fascinated, not with death per se, but with the end of life in death. Here he was faced with a text presenting two extremes: the comfort and peace of the gods resting in Elysian Fields, as opposed to the anguish, uncertainty, and pain of mortals on Earth below. The opening two sections aptly depict both by way of a serenely beautiful opening Andante, followed by a driven and tortured sonata form in the tempo of a Scherzo—a devilish kind of *Todtentanz* (Dance of Death)—which eventually dies away in hopelessness. In spite of the composer's personal view of death as the ultimate finality, he was unable to end his piece on this note, solving the problem by repeating the serene opening music, without chorus, in a new key. Whatever symbolism may attach to this, it is unique among Brahms's compositions as the only one to end in a key different from its beginning.

In *Nänie* Brahms chose a text that approaches death as a kind of gift. It was composed after the death of the painter Anselm Feuerbach, who was a friend of Brahms's. Its long melodic lines and taut structure are supported by harmonies of unusual warmth and richness. A particularly sensitive stroke, especially because the work is dedicated to the artist's grieving mother, is Brahms's substitution of text at the end, finishing not with Schiller's last line about ignoble death, but rather with a repeat of the penultimate line of text: "Yet a sad song is sweet, and sung by a loved one is glorious."

In spite of two episodes in major keys, *Gesang der Parzen*, Brahms's last composition for chorus and orchestra, is the most unrelentingly gloomy of Brahms's works. Brahms had by this time achieved a remarkable ability to compress his thought into music without extraneous notes. In this case the compactness accentuates the subject matter, creating an exceptionally forceful presentation of Goethe's text. Unlike *Schicksalslied* or *Nänie*, Brahms here makes little or no effort to soften the harsh blow delivered by Goethe regarding the randomness of life and death and the indifference of the gods. Brahms never feels the need to contrapuntally embellish his straightforward rondo form; the choral writing is homophonic virtually throughout. The modulations used to achieve the final return to the home key of D minor are so remarkable that Anton Webern referred to them as "the path to the new music."

Brahms composed three large works for chorus and orchestra: *Ein deutsches Requiem*, Op. 45 (1867, 1869), for soprano and baritone soloists, mixed chorus, and orchestra; the cantata *Rinaldo*, Op. 50 (1863, final chorus completed 1868, on Goethe's reworking of the legend of Rinaldo and Armida), for tenor solo, men's chorus, and orchestra; and the patriotic ode *Triumphlied*, Op. 55 (1870–71, on text from Revelation 19), for baritone solo, eight-part mixed chorus, and orchestra.

The workmanlike though generally uninspired *Rinaldo* is the closet Brahms came to opera, and the results suggest that any attempt on his part to write for the stage would not have met with success. The raucous and rousing *Triumphlied* is more interesting. Brahms was an outspoken German patriot. When Prussia defeated the French in 1871, firmly establishing what we now know as modern Germany, Brahms composed a fitting song of triumph. Geiringer sees this work primarily in musical terms, comparing it with Handel's great "Dettingen" Te Deum (1743), which was one of Brahms's favorite pieces (Geiringer 1961, 287–88). Beller-McKenna sees it more in a political context, with Brahms quoting "God Save the King" (which was then also the German national anthem) and "Nun danket alle Gott" for purely patriotic reasons, and correctly asserts that its unfamiliarity is a result of the desire in most countries, since the end of World War I, to avoid programming anything that touts German military prowess.

The largest work composed by Johannes Brahms is *Ein deutsches Requiem*. He may have begun consideration of such a project after the death of Schumann in 1856, but it was his mother's death in 1865 that spurred him to creative action. Within the space of a few months Brahms had completed the first and fourth movements and revised part of a piece begun after Schumann's suicide attempt in 1854 as the second movement (the rest of the aborted 1854 work had been incorporated into the First Piano Concerto, Op. 15, in 1857). During the next year and a half he completed the third, sixth, and seventh movements; and after the first two performances in Bremen in the spring of 1868 he added the fifth. The *Requiem* was published later that year, and the final version was premiered in Leipzig in February 1869.

Brahms himself chose texts from the Lutheran Bible, and he was certainly aware of earlier funeral pieces by north German composers—specifically the *Musikalische Exequien* of Heinrich Schütz and the early Cantata No. 106, *Gottes Zeit ist die allerbeste Zeit*, of J. S. Bach—which did not rely on the Latin *missa pro defunctis* text. But although all these works share some common texts and are similar in spirit, Brahms avoids any mention of Christ and focuses on comforting the living (a Christological reference in the most popular English translation—that of a Miss E. M. Traquair, revised by R. H. Benson, c. 1871—results from an attempt to simply overlay the English of the Authorized King James Version of the Bible; see Hoggard 1984, xiii).

Brahms ends the third and sixth movements with great fugues, and there is substantial contrapuntal writing at the end of the second and fourth movements and in the middle of the third as well. Geiringer (1961, 282) pointed out the work's symmetry: most movements are in three parts, and outer movements—moving toward the center—correspond in some way, with the famous fourth movement ("How Lovely Is Thy Dwelling Place") acting as the centerpiece of the arch. Geiringer also astutely observed that this symmetry would not exist without the inserted fifth movement. In addition, Daniel Beller-McKenna acknowledged another key contribution of the fifth movement:

> Musically it provided a more gradual progression of keys from the middle to the end of the work. . . . Textually, movement five reinjected comfort (*Trost*) as a main theme of the piece. "Trost" is presented in the opening phrase of the *Requiem*: "Selig sind die da Leid tragen, denn sie sollen *getröstet* werden." Although the baritone soloist of movement three briefly takes up the question of *Trost* in his last utterance ("Nun, Herr, wes sol ich mich *trösten*?," bars 142–144), he does so as an expression of doubt and anxiety. Only in movement five does the anticipation of comfort, in fact its promised delivery, become the central theme of the work. (Beller-McKenna 2004, 66)

It is curious, perhaps, that Brahms did not realize the catalyst was missing until he heard the performances in Bremen. It is also possible that he knew something else was needed but did not know what it was until he heard the first performance. In any case, he quickly corrected the situation in such a way as to draw unmistakable attention to the fifth movement: it marks the only appearance of the soprano soloist.

In keeping with the practice of the day (before recorded sound), Brahms made a piano four-hands arrangement of his *Requiem*, which omitted the voice parts. Whether or not he intended it for anything other than home edification, the first performance in England (1871) was given in this manner (omitting the fifth movement). The English translation sung at that time (Traquair/Benson) was eventually published in the United States by the firm of G. Schirmer. Not only has this translation become the most widely used (even though there are better, more recent ones), but the piano four-hands version is now recorded and occasionally performed by smaller choruses in settings more intimate than a large concert hall. Incidentally, the English premiere omitted the fifth movement. Although the four-hands version included this movement, the first edition of the piano-vocal score did not. An interesting copy of the first-edition vocal score, owned by Morten Lauridsen, actually contains movement 5 in a handwritten manuscript, sewn into the published score.

Ein deutsches Requiem became popular immediately. Most of Brahms's close friends and family were present at one or another of the first performances, and many of them wrote to the composer expressing their deep sense of emotional fulfillment. The work was obviously close to Brahms's heart, too, and he was not above expressing his ire when told of a performance planned by an inadequate choir in Hamburg:

My very esteemed sir:

Permit these few hasty lines which surely seem permissible about a poor concert of your friend.

You write: the perform[ance] of the Requiem is to "take place with the participation of the *Bach*-Society."

Maybe that is just inadvertence, a slip of the pen!?

The planned perf. makes sense only if it is an especially good one; heading the list for that is the choral group and we have every reason to be cautious.

The choral group for participation I found and still find most desirable is the Cecilia-Society. It did perform the R. less than a year ago and I am surely able to completely rely upon its choirmaster Spengel. If that society either is unwilling or unable, then I would take a chance doing the thing with the combined theatre choruses of Hbg. and Schwerin—but it is really quite a lot to ask of these people for them, in addition to their daily chores, also to practice so difficult a piece, etc!

The Hbg. Bach-Society on the other hand never sang my R.—I need not describe to you at length how utterly impossible that outfit is!

I lack the time and this pointed steelpen makes writing almost impossible for me. But you can imagine what goes on at the Hamb. Choral Society: The Cecilian Society is the only one where they practice, etc.

I just hope you merely made a mistake as you were writing!!

As concerns England I will not be able to make up my mind in the affirmative—but more of that from Vienna where I am going on Tuesday.

Forgive the scrawlmarks!

Sincerely yours J. Brahms

The favorable popular reaction to the *Deutsches Requiem* made it not only newsworthy but a likely target for the press as well, and lengthy comments appeared in papers and journals throughout Europe and Britain. Among favorable reviews were those of Maitland, who called it "the greatest achievement of modern sacred music in Germany," and Louis Kelterborn, who thought that "the German Requiem is of such great importance that without a knowledge of it neither a full estimation of Brahms's individual genius, nor of the significance of the latest epoch of music in general can be obtained" (Thrall 1908, 201).

There were detractors, too. For example, George Bernard Shaw, in one of his kinder reviews, wrote: "Brahms' Requiem has not the true funeral relish: it is so execrably and ponderously dull that the very flattest of funerals would seem like a ballet, or at least a *danse macabre*, after it" (*World*, 9 November 1892; quoted in Slonimsky 2000, 77).

Critics still resisted it as late as the mid-twentieth century. For example, Wallace Brockway and Herbert Weinstock thought that

the outstanding musical feature of this vast work is that it is a veritable compendium of technical effects. Every contrapuntal resource

Letter from Johannes Brahms to unknown recipient in Hamburg, c. 1882 (see pp. 63–64). Courtesy of the Roy E. Atherton Collection.

is laid under contribution, often to excess, chiefly in certain fugal passages, which though marvels on paper are confusing in performance. Here, again, Brahms draws out some of his best effects to the point of boredom. The result is a general amorphousness that is not sufficiently compensated for by many passages of real beauty. The whole *Requiem* is instinct with earnestness, with a genuine reverence for the sacred texts that makes one wish the results were better. Yet the total effect is one of noble dreariness. There are factors quite independent of Brahms' musical limitations that had their part in flawing the *Requiem*. No soul-lifting faith in the transcendental aspects of religion shines from it. Brahms had no such faith. At best, he had a homely respect for the Good Book. He repeatedly stated, for instance, that he had no belief in life after death. Without absolutely echoing the brash Shaw of the early [eighteen] nineties, who said that listening to the *Requiem* was a sacrifice that should be asked of a man only once in his life, it may be said that the reputation of this interminable work is, among critics, justifiably waning—with no especial loss to Brahms' position. Perhaps quite the contrary. (Brockway and Weinstock 1958, 483)

In the approximately sixty years since Brockway and Weinstock offered their opinion, the reputation of Brahms's *Requiem* has certainly not waned. Otherwise, their view that "no soul-lifting faith in the transcendental aspects of religion shines from it" is true, and that may, in fact, be the most compelling reason for its continuing popularity. It does not matter that unnumbered choirs in churches where such music is still welcomed on Sunday morning, unaware of Brahms's lack of conventional faith, still wallow in the beauties of "How Lovely Is Thy Dwelling Place." What matters is that in a world polarized by an increasingly atheistic, humanistic view on one hand, and a fundamentalist view demanding uncritical acceptance of scripture and dogma on the other, the *Requiem* offers some neutral common ground. *Ein deutsches Requiem* does not pretend to know anything about an afterlife. It simply comforts the living and honors the dead: those ancestors who went before us and, for better or worse, helped create the world we inherited.

And perceptive listeners on hearing it understand that they are connected not only to these ancestors, but also to the present and the future. It is a view consonant with the evolutionary processes in Brahms's variation forms.

Other works by Johannes Brahms include *Marienlieder*, Op. 22 (1859), for unaccompanied mixed choir; several canons; two works for mixed chorus with piano accompaniment, *Tafellied*, Op. 93b (1884) and *Kleine Hochzeitskantate* (1874, on text by Gottfried Keller); and some arrangements of Schubert songs for unison chorus and orchestra.

The great majority of choral conductors will never conduct a note of music by Gustav Mahler. And yet they should study Mahler as if their lives depended on it. Richard Strauss said that Mahler's Second Symphony was the one score he kept on his piano at all times, and conductors today can still learn much from it.

Mahler was born in Bohemia but went to Vienna in 1878 for study at the conservatory. A gifted student, he was apparently excused from counterpoint classes. In 1880 he accepted a conducting post for the summer outside of Vienna and, later the same year, completed his first major work, *Das klagende Lied* (1880, on text adapted by the composer after the Brothers Grimm), for SAT soloists, mixed chorus, and orchestra. Thereafter he focused his energies on conducting and the composition of symphonies and orchestral song cycles.

Whereas Brahms represented the logical extension of Beethoven in terms of classical form and reliance on tradition (as exemplified by Beethoven's Symphonies No. 1–5, 7, and 8), Mahler extended Beethoven's influence through the filter of Wagner, freely assigning extramusical meanings to melodic fragments, expanding the music's structural and emotional universe, and relying heavily on music as a vehicle for the presentation of text (as exemplified by Beethoven's Symphonies No. 6 and 9). Before the century came to a close Mahler had completed three symphonies, two of which require chorus, pointing the way to many of the twentieth century's most important developments.

The Symphony No. 2 in C Minor, "Resurrection" (1894, on texts from *Das Knaben Wunderhorn*, Klopstock, and the composer), for soprano and alto soloists, mixed chorus, and large orchestra, presented a new concept for the still evolving form of the vocal symphony. Mendelssohn's "Lobgesang" had expanded Beethoven's finale concept into a full-blown cantata. Berlioz, in *Roméo et Juliette*, had created an unstaged opera squeezed into a vestige of symphonic structure. Liszt had simply tacked a soloist and chorus onto the finales of his *Dante* and *Faust Symphonies*. But Mahler integrated voices into the overall fabric without weakening the integrity of traditional symphonic form, even while stretching it almost beyond recognition. Mahler's Second is seventy-five minutes long, and though the expansiveness may have been unusual, the results are heavenly; few works have such impact in performance.

The context of the Second Symphony's purely orchestral movements, especially the opening giant funeral march ("Todtenfeier" [Funeral Rites], which Mahler had offered for publication as a separate work) and central Scherzo ("Die Welt wie im Hohlspiegel" [The World as Seen in a Concave Mirror]) are best understood by examining the texts Mahler chose for the concluding movements. As Mahler said: "Whenever I conceive a large musical form, I always arrive at the point where I have to turn to the word as a bearer of my musical ideas. Beethoven must have had a similar experience with his Ninth, only at that time the appropriate material was not yet at hand" (Floros 1993, 67).

The fourth movement ("Urlicht" [Primeval Light]) sets one of the *Wunderhorn* poems for alto:

Oh, little red rose
Mankind lies in great need,
Mankind lies in great pain,
Rather I would heaven claim.
. . . I am from God, I want to return to God.

This theme is expanded and sealed in the finale (following "Urlicht" without pause), which Mahler divided into two great

programmatic sections, "Der Rufer in der Wuste" (The One Calling in the Wilderness) and "Der grosse Appell" (The Great Roll
Call), requiring a number of theatrical effects, including offstage
brass. The texts are two quatrains by Klopstock, followed by six
additional stanzas of commentary, in freer verse, by Mahler:

Arise, yes you will arise,
Dust of my body, after a brief rest!
Immortal life
Will he, who called you, grant to you.

You are sown that you might bloom again!
The Lord of harvest goes
And gathers sheaves,
Gathers us, who died.

Oh, believe, my heart, nothing is lost for you!
Yours, yes, yours alone is what you longed for,
What you loved, and what you fought for.
Oh believe, you were not born in vain,
Nor have you lived and suffered in vain!

That which was created must perish,
What perished will arise!
No longer tremble!
Prepare to live!

Oh agony, you piercing pain,
From you I have escaped!
Oh death, all-conquering claim
Now you are defeated!

With wings that I have gained,
In seeking to perfect my love
Will I ascend
Into the light which no eye has ever reached.

With wings that I have gained
Will I ascend.
I will die to be alive!

Arise, you will arise,
My heart, within a moment!
What you have conquered,
To God, to God it will bear you up.

Initial choral entrance in finale of Gustav Mahler's "Resurrection" Symphony.

In addition to the finale's concluding section, which is overpowering, to say the least, the initial unaccompanied pianissimo entrance of the choir is one of the most thrilling passages in the repertoire. The gorgeous, ethereal homophony of this "Resurrection Chorale" helped establish a lingering misconception of Mahler as primarily a composer of vertical sonorities. But in spite of the obvious influence of Berlioz and Wagner, Mahler was no less a student of Bach and other baroque masters and, as his art matured, proved himself to be essentially a linear composer. The orchestral writing in the Second Symphony is shot through with contrapuntal intricacies, and the movement to the relative major at the work's conclusion further reveals Mahler's awareness of older style (such awareness would culminate in the Eighth Symphony; see Strimple 2002, 16–18).

One line of text "constitutes the central thought" of Mahler's Second: "Sterben werd' ich, um zu leben!" (I will die to be alive; Floros 1993, 55). This idea, and an important secondary one ("O glaube: du wardst nicht umsonst geboren / Hast nicht umsonst gelebt, gelitten" [Oh believe, you were not born in vain / Nor have you lived or suffered in vain!]), must have been very much on the mind of Rudolf Israel Schwarz when notified early in 1941 that the Berlin Jüdische Kulturbund, of which he was music director, would be disbanded and the members "relocated" in the east. The Kulturbund's last concert, on 25 February 1941, was Mahler's "Resurrection" Symphony.

All of Mahler's symphonies create their own universe, and the Third Symphony, in D Minor (1898), for soprano and alto soloists, boy's choir, women's choir, and orchestra certainly occupies a world vastly different from the "Resurrection," even though both utilize texts from *Des Knaben Wunderhorn*. In Mahler's words: "My symphony will be unlike anything the world has ever heard! All of nature speaks in it, telling deep secrets that one might guess only in a dream!" (Floros 1993, 83). The movement titles as found in the autograph tell all:

1. Introduction: Pan Awakes; Summer Marches In (Bacchus's Parade)

2. What the Flowers in the Meadow Tell Me
3. What the Animals in the Woods Tell Me
4. What Mankind Tells Me
5. What the Angels Tell Me
6. What Love Tells Me

So, after composing a monumental work chiefly concerned with getting out of the world, Mahler writes another monumental work, this time concerned with living in the world—here and now—and absorbing all that nature and the angels have to offer. Besides the folk poetry, Mahler includes text by Friedrich Nietzsche, whose works had made a great impression on him. In addition to birdcalls, a commonplace feature in much of his music, Mahler attempts to invoke the sounds of nature by scoring instruments in unusual ranges (very high trombones, very low piccolos, for instance) and calling for harmonics in the strings. The opening theme is disquietingly similar (in contour, at least) to the main theme of the finale of Brahms's First Symphony; but its intent is completely different. Michael Kennedy wisely advises listeners to focus on

> absorbing its atmosphere, its astonishing creation of a mood of protean energy unleashed. Its impressive and portentous opening theme for eight horns symbolizes the force of nature but gives way at once to a long mysterious prelude, another example of potent Mahlerian scene-setting, with eerie brass *glissandi*, declamatory trumpet solos, exhortatory trombones—all the fingerprints which the kleptomaniac Mahler impresses on his score, pressing their emotional connotations into his service and rendering them Mahlerian. (Kennedy 1990, 126)

The introduction of boy's voices and bells into the fifth movement is tone painting at its best. And the innovative Adagio closing movement—the prototype for succeeding Mahlerian Adagios—provides an excellent example of successful risk-taking. Still, the Third Symphony is problematic: in spite of its expansiveness, it is too intimate to impact listeners with the same force as the "Resurrection"; the D major ending can easily seem overwrought; and in the wrong conductor's hands it can be interminably long.

The Singakademie, "Berlin Academics," and the Sternscher Gesangverein

The Berlin Singakademie was established in 1791 with Johann Friedrich Fasch as its first director. Focusing on study and performance of sacred music, succeeding directors, Carl Friedrich Zelter, Carl Friedrich Rungenhagen, and Eduard Grell solidified its reputation, making it the most important choral organization in the city, its influence extending throughout Germany. Originally the Singakademie's outlook was progressive: giving the first performances by a mixed choir in a Berlin church (1791) and the first Berlin performances of Mozart's Requiem and Mendelssohn's *St. Paul.* Toward the middle of the century, however, it became much more conservative, promoting the neo-Renaissance view of sacred music as promoted by the Caecilians.

In 1847 Julius Stern formed a choir that was somewhat opposed to the Singakademie's strictly conservative views in that it consciously sought to perform new works by composers whose outlook was not confined to the neo-Renaissance ideal. The resulting Sternscher Gesangverein flourished until 1911 and after Stern was conducted by Julius Stockhausen and Max Bruch. Affiliated with both the Singakademie and the Sternscher Gesangverein were several anti-Wagner, pro-Brahms composers who, by either natural inclination or training, gravitated toward the neo-Renaissance ideal. These became known as the "Berlin academics."

Eduard Grell (1800–1886) was a prominent organist and composer associated with the Berlin Singakademie for almost sixty years, as either student, conductor, teacher, or director. An ardent and accomplished practitioner of the old contrapuntal school of church composition, he influenced a number of talented younger composers whose natural inclinations were equally conservative.

Grell composed several highly complicated psalm settings, motets, cantatas, a Te Deum, and the oratorio *Die Israeliten in der
Wüste* (1838), for soloists, mixed chorus, and orchestra. His Mass
(c. 1861), for unaccompanied sixteen-part mixed chorus, is particularly impressive.

Martin Blumner (1827–1901), while a student in Berlin, began
singing in the Berlin Singakademie under Eduard Grell in 1845,
eventually becoming Grell's assistant conductor and, in 1873, principal conductor. An accomplished and respected choral conductor, Blumner also served as conductor of the Berlin Men's Chorus
originally begun by Zelter. Blumner's compositions are exclusively
for the voice. One of the Berlin academics and totally devoted to
the nineteenth-century neo-Renaissance ideal in church music, he
composed many small unaccompanied choral works, both sacred
and secular, and two oratorios: *Abraham*, Op. 8 (1859), and *Der
Fall Jerusalems*, Op. 30 (1874), both for soloists, mixed chorus, and
orchestra. Blumner's compositions are undistinguished; his most
significant contribution was the book *Geschichte der Singakademie
Berlin* (1891).

Max Bruch (1838–1920) was best-known during his lifetime as
a composer of pieces for chorus and orchestra, even though he is
mostly remembered now for his violin concertos and *Kol nidrei* for
cello and orchestra. Indeed, the continued popularity of *Kol nidrei*
has led many to believe Bruch was Jewish, although in reality he
was north German Protestant through and through. His first big
success was the cantata *Frithjof: Szenen aus der Frithjof-Sage*, Op.
23 (1864, on text by Esaias Tegnèr), for soprano and baritone soloists, male chorus, and orchestra. This was not his first choral work,
but its success set the stage for an almost continuous outpour-
ing of choral music, both sacred and secular, a catalog that would
eventually include thirty large compositions, seven smaller pieces
with orchestra, and eight sets of part-songs (in various vocal configurations) ranging from folk-song arrangements to settings of
Schiller and Goethe.

Most of the orchestral works are for mixed chorus, but three
are for female voices and six are for male voices. Among the more

interesting are *Das Feuerkreuz*, Op. 52 (1889, text adapted by H. Bulthaupt from Sir Walter Scott's *The Lady of the Lake*) for soloists, mixed chorus, and orchestra; *Hebräische Gesänge*, without opus number (1888, on text by Byron), for mixed chorus, organ, and orchestra; *Moses: ein biblisches Oratorium*, Op. 67 (1895, on text by L. Spitta) for soprano, tenor, and bass soloists, mixed chorus, and orchestra; *Das Lied von der Glocke*, Op. 45 (1879, on text by Schiller) for soloists, mixed chorus, organ, and orchestra; and the two pieces of Op. 31, *Die Flucht nach Ägypten* (text by R. Reinick) and *Morgenstunde* (1870, text by H. Lingg), for soprano solo, female chorus, and orchestra.

Works without orchestra include *Nine Lieder*, Op. 60 (1892, various texts), for mixed chorus; *In der Nacht*, Op. 72 (1897, on text by G. Tersteegen), for male chorus; and the very late *Sechs Christkindlieder*, Op. 92 (n.d., on text by Margarethe Bruch), for female voices and piano.

When Bruch died his most famous compositions were the big secular oratorios on librettos from Greek mythology, *Odysseus*, Op. 41 (1872, on text by W. P. Graff), and *Achilleus*, Op. 50 (1885, on text by H. Bulthaupt), both for solo voices, mixed chorus, and orchestra. The reason for his music's fall into disuse was that "the strength of his talent lay not in dramatic but in epic expression . . . [his pieces'] characteristic melodiousness and technically excellent choral writing won them immediate favor with Bruch's contemporaries. It was his inclination to compose music which could be easily assimilated by the public and not a lack of proficiency or invention that caused his larger works to date" (Horst Leuchtmann, "Max Bruch," in Sadie 1980, 3:349). But attitudes change. Now there are excellent recordings of *Moses* and *Das Lied von der Glocke*. Given the revival of interest in the choral music of Hugo Wolf and Josef Rheinberger, perhaps some enterprising conductors will rediscover Bruch's part-songs as well.

Heinrich von Herzogenberg (1843–1900) and his wife, Elisabeth, were close friends of Brahms's, although Brahms never considered him a good composer. Early on he attempted to follow Wagner's example but soon realized it was not for him. In 1871, after lengthy studies of J. S. Bach, he founded, with Philipp Spitta, the Leipzig Bach Society and served as its director from 1875 to 1885. In 1886 he became professor of composition at the Berlin Hochschule für Musik. His own works have been viewed as pedantic in the extreme but have gained favor in recent years. In addition to cantatas, oratorios, and liturgical works great and small, he also composed a significant number of part-songs for mixed, men's, and women's choirs. *Vier Notturnos*, Op. 22 (1876), for unaccompanied mixed chorus, may be taken as representative, with its idiomatically confident part-writing and occasional stylistic references to Brahms.

Another of the Berlin academics, Wilhelm Berger (1861–1911), excelled in the composition of choral music, including *Meine Göttin*, Op. 72 (1898), for chorus and orchestra. Other works include eight additional pieces for chorus and orchestra, seven sets of part-songs for mixed chorus and piano, eight sets of part-songs for unaccompanied mixed chorus, eight sets of part-songs for women's chorus, and three sets of part-songs for unaccompanied male chorus.

Other Composers Active in the Second Half of the Century

The Austrian August Wilhelm Ambros (1816–1876) composed an imposing *Missa solemnis*, which received numerous performances between 1857 and 1889. His most important contributions to choral music, however, are found in his four-volume *Geschichte der Musik* (1862, 1864, 1868, 1878), in which he places music into its cultural context and lavishes individual attention on Ockeghem, Josquin, Palestrina, and Monteverdi.

Franz Wilhelm Abt (1819–1885) was an exceptionally distinguished choral director whose fame reached well beyond the German-speaking areas of Europe. His remarkably successful tour of the United States in 1872 helped generate interest in choral singing in America. He composed many choral pieces, primarily works for male chorus, in a style akin to folk music: straight forward and simple.

Franz Xaver Witt (1834–1888), in addition to founding the Caecilian Society, was also the Society's most active composer. In a list compiled in 1893 of some 1500 works approved by the Caecilian Society, Witt composed sixty-six and arranged fifty-one by other composers. A mediocre talent, his works were an attempt to reflect his liturgical views. In reality they simply reveal glaring inadequacies as a composer: flagrant parallel fifths, predominance of root-position triads, weak progressions between root-position chords, and so on. Most of his compositions promote the a cappella ideal; but his Te Deum, for mixed chorus and organ (or orchestra of flutes, oboes or clarinets, horns, trumpets, trombones, and strings), exemplifies a precept of the Caecilian Society that allowed for instruments in certain situations as long as the spirit of the service and the purity of the music remained intact.

Josef Gabriel Rheinberger (1839–1901) was rediscovered (by American choral conductors, at least) toward the end of the twentieth century. He enjoyed a very productive career as music director of the Munich Oratorio Society, director of sacred music at the court of Bavaria, and professor of composition in Munich, in which capacity students came from all over the world to study with him. Outstanding among his works are the Mass in E-flat Major, Op. 109 (1878), for double mixed chorus; and the *Drei geistliche Gesänge*, Op. 69 (Three Sacred Part-songs, published 1873), for unaccompanied six-part mixed chorus.

The Mass, dedicated to Pope Leo VIII, is a thorough repudiation of the ideals of F. X. Witt and the Caecilian Society. Also, it represents only the tip of the iceberg in regard to Rheinberger's production of Masses: he composed thirteen more, including *Missa Sanctissimae Trinitatis*, Op. 117, for unaccompanied mixed chorus; Mass in A, Op. 126, for three-part women's chorus; Mass, Op. 155, for three-part women's chorus and organ; Mass in F Minor, Op. 159, for mixed chorus and organ; Mass, Op. 169, for soloists, mixed chorus, and orchestra (or strings and organ); Mass, Op. 172, for male chorus and organ (or wind instruments); and Mass in F Major, Op. 190, for male chorus and organ.

Drei geistliche Gesänge was not composed as a single work, but is rather a compilation of three of Rheinberger's more attractive vernacular pieces on religious texts. The first, "Morgenlied," was composed in 1858. The second, "Dein sind die Himmel" (Thine Are the Heavens), is a *contrafactum* of an offertory in Latin (*Tui sunt coeli*) which was first published in 1864. The third, "Abendlied"— the most famous of the three—was most likely composed as early as 1855. Each can be performed alone, of course, and together they do make an attractive set; but enterprising conductors should be warned that Rheinberger's rich harmonic vocabulary can be treacherous in performance.

Other works include the cantata *Daughter of Jairus* (*Das Töchterlein des Jairus*), Op. 32, for children's chorus; the cantata *Star of Bethlehem* (*Der Stern von Bethlehem*), Op. 164, for soloists, mixed chorus, and orchestra; and many part-songs, including at least thirteen sets for male chorus (each set containing at least three songs)—seven sets for mixed chorus, and two for treble chorus, including *May Day*, Op. 64, a set of seven songs for three-part treble chorus and piano.

Hugo Wolf (1860–1903) was an Austrian composer known not only for his exquisite art songs, but also for his rabid criticisms of Johannes Brahms. A disciple of Richard Wagner, Wolf found his niche not in opera or other large forms, but in the vocal miniature. He composed a few choral works with orchestra, for example *Elfenlied* (1889–1891, on text by Shakespeare), for soprano solo, women's choir, and orchestra; and the impressive *Der Feuerreiter* (1892, on text by Mörike), for mixed chorus and orchestra, as well as a couple of arrangements for chorus and orchestra of his solo songs. But the gold is in the part-songs. Most of them are unaccompanied and exhibit much of the emotional sweep and confident craftsmanship of his other songs. There are seven for male chorus (all composed in 1876), representative examples being "Die Stimme des Kindes" (on text by Lenau), with piano; and "Mailied" (on text by Goethe), for unaccompanied chorus. There are nine part-songs for mixed chorus (most composed in 1881), including "Aufblick" and "Resignation" (on text by Eichendorff); and "Im stillen Friedhof" (1876, on text by Ludwig Pfau), with piano.

Other composers in the second half of the century include Ferdinand Hiller (1818–1885), a distinguished conductor and writer on music who contributed the oratorios *Die Zerstörungs Jerusalems* (1840) and *Saul* (premiered 1858), both for soloists, mixed chorus, and orchestra, as well as other choral works; Johann Baptist Weiss (1813–1850), whose liturgical works provided models for the young Anton Bruckner; Robert Volkmann (1815–1883), who wrote several sets of part-songs and a couple of Masses for male voices, as well as a few pieces for mixed chorus that were quite popular in Europe during his lifetime; Jean Baptiste Andre (1823–1882), son of Johann Anton Andre, who composed numerous choral works, some published under the pseudonym "de St. Gilles"; Peter Cornelius (1824–1874), who composed part-songs for mixed and male choirs; Julius Otto Grimm (1827–1903), a prominent choral conductor and friend of Brahms, who contributed an ode for chorus and orchestra, *An die Musik* (n.d.); Woldemar Bargiel (1828–1897), who contributed several psalm settings for mixed chorus and orchestra; Carl Goldmark (1830–1915), who composed several part-songs for mixed chorus, a couple of pieces for chorus and orchestra, and several interesting works for men's chorus, including *Frühlingsnetz* (Op. 15) with four horns and piano, and *Meeresstille und glückliche Fahrt* (Calm Sea and Prosperous Voyage, Op. 16, on text by Goethe), with horns; Heinrich Bellerman (1832–1903), a student of A. E. Grell, whose Palestrina-like unaccompanied choral works reflect strict adherence to the principles of his teacher and the Caecilian Society; Max Zenger (1837–1911, conductor of several prominent choirs in Munich (including the Munich Oratorio Society, 1878–1885), whose several choral works include *Zwei Konzertstücke* for mixed chorus and strings; the philosopher Friedrich Nietzsche (1844–1900), who composed, in addition to several anti-Wagner monographs, *Hymne an die Freundschaft* (1874) and *Weihnachts Oratorium*, both for mixed chorus and piano, as well as *Hymne an das Leben* (1887), for chorus and orchestra; Constanz Berneker (1844–1906), a choral conductor, organist, and composer whose works include part-songs, small sacred pieces, at least one cantata, and the oratorio *Judith* (1877), for soloists, mixed chorus, and orchestra; August Bungert (c. 1845–1915) who composed a number of part-songs for male chorus and a large cantata on biblical texts, *Warum? Woher? Wohin?*, Op. 60 (n.d.), for soloists, mixed chorus, and orchestra; Ignaz Brüll (1846–1907), a friend of Brahms's who wrote numerous part-songs, with and without piano accompaniment; Adalbert von Goldschmidt (1848–1906), an Austrian composer whose secular oratorio *Die sieben Todsünden* (1870, on text by Robert Hamerling) was thought by many to have been influenced by Wagner's *Ring* cycle until research established it as the earlier work; and Anton Beer-Walbrunn (1864–1929), who contributed part-songs and a large cantata, *Mahomets Gesang* (c. 1896, on text by Goethe), for soloists, mixed chorus, organ, and orchestra.

3

France, Switzerland, and the Low Countries

France

Revolutionary music—that is, music written in honor of or reflecting the French Revolution in some way—held sway in France at the beginning of the century. As a result, French composers were forced to deal with two unusual situations. First, audiences had become accustomed to hearing performances at civic festivities that were held outdoors. Following the lead of the Belgian François Joseph Gossec (1734–1829)—specifically his Requiem (1760), which called for a second orchestra (of winds) placed outside the church and otherwise enlarged brass sections, and his Te Deum, which called for three hundred wind instruments, including fifty serpents and as many snare drums as possible—composers provided pieces that required both enormous numbers of performers and also, because of their often inflated length, immense patience on the part of listeners. Observed J. H. Elliot:

> All this vastly inflated choral music, though it had historical influence of some moment, is not undeservedly neglected today. Turning over its copious and innocuous pages, one has the impression that it was all made plain and simple "by order." It is almost fanatically diatonic, as though the use of accidentals had been forbidden

on pain of the guillotine. A diminished seventh, cropping up in the introduction to a battle hymn (1794) by Méhul, seems like an impious stain on a page of otherwise virginal innocence, justified only by the belligerence of the subject. (Jacobs 1963, 202)

Second, in 1794 Robespierre, attempting to establish a middle ground between the militant atheists on the revolutionary Left and the church on the Right, had decreed a new holiday, a religious observance of a nondescript, pantheistic type. Even though Robespierre was guillotined some weeks after the decree, the holiday stuck around, and composers had to write music for it. Again, Gossec led the way with *Hymn to the Supreme Being*, and others followed, among them Jean François Lesueur (1760–1837), Etienne Nicolas Méhul (1763–1817), André Gretry (1741–1813), and, to a lesser extent, Luigi Cherubini, who, because he was living in Paris, was forced to conform to the same governmental whims and decrees as everybody else. With the exception of Cherubini (who is discussed in chapter 7), these were mature men who had already made their mark by the beginning of the century. Still, they continued to contribute to the choral repertoire.

Henri-Montan Berton (1767–1844) was a prominent composer and teacher. He composed several sacred cantatas for performance at the *concert spirituel* prior to the French Revolution but afterward changed his emphasis to the stage. He cultivated the reputation of being a musical reactionary but, at the same time, introduced forcefully innovative ideas into his operas, the most successful of which involved the dramatic use of chorus. In addition to a substantial number of cantatas, including the *Cantata for the Marriage of Napoleon and Marie-Louise* (1810), for tenor and baritone soloists, mixed chorus, and orchestra, Berton also contributed a requisite number of liturgical works.

Marie Désiré Beaulieu (1791–1863) organized both the Association Musicale de l'Ouest and later, in 1860, the Société des Concerts de Chant Classique. The former produced music festivals in the provinces that presented the first French performances of oratorios by Handel, Haydn, Mendelssohn, and others; the latter produced the same kind of choral and orchestral repertoire for audiences in Paris. Also a composer, Beaulieu was particularly adept at sacred music. Among his works is a Requiem in memory of Méhul (c. 1819), for SATB soloists, mixed chorus, and orchestra. He also composed several oratorios which are, unfortunately, lost.

Jacques-François-Fromental Halévy (1799–1862) was an outstanding opera composer who scored a lasting hit with *La juive* (1835). He was also a fine teacher who counted Gounod, Bizet (his future son-in-law), and Saint-Saëns among his pupils. His choral works include *Prométhée enchaîné* (1849) and *Ave verum* (1850), both for soloists, mixed chorus, and orchestra; an Agnus Dei and Sanctus (1851) for men's chorus, soprano soloists, and organ (his contribution to the *Messe de l'Orphéon*, composed jointly with Adam, Clapisson, and Ambroise Thomas); and a couple of cantatas and some slight pieces for men's chorus.

Adolphe Adam (1803–1856) wrote a considerable amount of choral music, even though his enduring success was achieved through his ballets and operas. He studied with Boieldieu and Rejcha and as a student won the Prix de Rome in 1825 for his cantata *Ariane à Naxos* (later incorporating this music into the opera *Le chalet*). He composed several other secular works, including the earlier cantata *Agnes Sorel* (1824); several pieces for four-part male chorus (*Les métiers, Les enfants de Paris, La garde mobile, La marche républicaine,* and *La muette,* all 1848 except the last, which is not dated). The cantatas *Les nations* (1851, on text by Banville), *La fête des arts* (1852, on text by Méry), *Victoire* (1855, on text by Carré), and *Cantata* (1856, on text by Pacini), were designed for the stage and were all presented either at the Paris Opéra or the *opéra-comique.* In addition, he composed a number of sacred works, including the *Messe solennelle* (1837), for four soloists and chorus; the *Messe de Ste. Cecile* (c. 1850), for four soloists, chorus, and orchestra; and the large motets *Domine salvum* (c. 1860), for three soloists, chorus, and organ, and *O salutaris* (n.d.), for chorus, organ, and orchestra. The very famous *Cantique de Noel* (1858, known in English as "O Holy Night"), was composed as a solo: the various arrangements

for chorus, or combination of soloist with chorus, were not made
by the composer.

Hector Berlioz (1803–1869) was not only gripped by the work of
his teacher, Lesueur, but was also very impressed by the operas
of Méhul and the choral and orchestral extravaganzas of Gossec.
His early *Messe solennelle* (1824), for soloists, mixed chorus, and
orchestra, was obviously influenced by these men (even though it
was written two years before he began official study with Lesueur).
It was withdrawn by the composer, who forbade its performance.
But because he did not destroy the manuscript, it was—for better
or worse—recorded in 1993. Full of exuberance and sprawl, it contains some good ideas that Berlioz would use later in his Requiem
and more than hints at the grandiosity of his mature works.

Berlioz's first important choral composition, the *Grande messe
des morts* (1837), for tenor solo, mixed chorus, and very large orchestra, was composed the year of Lesueur's death, seven years
after the 1830 revolution. Its reputation is one of complete self-
indulgence, but its dimensions were really nothing new to listeners
who remembered the music that sprang from the 1789 revolution.
In addition to a huge orchestra, Berlioz asks for a chorus of eighty
women, sixty tenors, and seventy basses, numbers that, according
to the composer, "are only relative, and one can, space permitting,
double or triple the vocal forces and increase the orchestra propor-
tionately. If one had an immense chorus of 700 or 800 voices, the
entire group should sing only in the 'Dies irae,' the 'Tuba mirum,'
and the 'Lacrimosa,' using no more than 400 voices in the rest of
the score" (Steinberg 2005, 61–62). The choral writing is mostly for
divisi STB chorus; altos are called for only in the "Quarens me,"
Sanctus, and Agnus Dei. (It should be noted here that neither
gargantuan choruses nor standard configurations such as SATB
are the norm in Berlioz; for example, his Prix de Rome cantata of
1830, *La mort de Sardanapale*, called for a three-part men's chorus
[TTB] of only nine singers [Bloom 1981, 289].)

For its imposing size, the overall effect of Berlioz's Requiem is
not one of bombast, nor even the kind of edgy psychological dra-

UN CONCERT DE LA SOCIÉTÉ PHILHARMONIQUE.

(Gustave Doré, *Journal pour rire*, 1850.)

Caricature of Hector Berlioz conducting. Courtesy of Monir Tayeb and Michel Austin (www.hberlioz.com).

ma found in Mahler's Eighth Symphony. There is instead a strange kind of lyricism throughout, with the extended brass sections used only sparingly but with fantastic results. For instance, the build-up to the entrance of the four brass choirs surrounding the performers in the "Tuba mirum" is almost leisurely; likewise, the terror of the Dies irae is not immediate, but incremental. On the other hand, the Lacrimosa is a kind of *danse macabre* throughout, in an angular, almost hypnotic compound meter that plays against type. Said Ronald Kean, who posited a number of medieval sources of inspiration for Berlioz:

> The Lacrimosa is the quintessential picture of Gothic sublimity. It portrays the agony of resurrection as man rises from the dust to be judged for his sins. It is the representation of the violent, wild, and more awesome aspects of human nature, and a fantastic vision of medieval churchmen's most admired book of the Bible, the Revelation, with its visions of the Apocalypse. It is a stroke of genius that Berlioz accompanies the prayer for mercy to Jesus . . . with a figure similar in composition to the accompaniment of "Te Decet hymnus" [in the opening movement]. In so doing, Berlioz subtly portrays the distance between heaven and hell. (Kean 2002, 15)

Berlioz's Requiem is the first of the great nineteenth-century Requiems composed by nonbelievers. Michael Steinberg pointed out that Berlioz, like Verdi, found the stuff of drama in religion and approached his sacred texts in that way. Steinberg also pointed out that the other two great sacred works of Berlioz, the Te Deum, Op. 22 (1850), for tenor soloist, double soprano, alto, and bass chorus, children's chorus, and large orchestra; and *L'enfance du Christ*, Op. 25 (1854), for soloists, mixed chorus, and orchestra, were not written on commission (Steinberg 2005, p. 64). Rather, Berlioz somehow felt compelled to compose them. The Te Deum shares much with the Requiem: considerations of direction and space, large number of performers, and so on. But *L'enfance du Christ* is different in many respects: it requires several soloists who are characters in the story, the orchestra and chorus are of standard size, and the duration (about ninety minutes) is not unusual for a work designed to be the sole substance of an evening's concert. And although the incredible multilayered sense of urgency propelling the drama at the work's beginning gradually dissipates, the music is often glorious, especially Hérode's soliloquy aria and the dance (in 7/4) and ruminations of the soothsayers. "The Shepherd's Farewell" is often excerpted for Christmas concerts, and herein is the only troubling aspect of this marvelous piece: when should it be performed? It deals not with Christmas, but rather with the Slaughter of the Innocents by King Herod and the Holy Family's flight into Egypt.

Berlioz's third symphony, *Roméo et Juliette*, Op. 17 (1839, on text by Emile Deschamps, after Shakespeare), for ATB soloists, double mixed chorus (without altos), and orchestra stretches symphonic structure almost beyond recognition. Although individual scenes are certainly operatic, Berlioz is consciously exploring musical form, with a clearly defined introduction, first movement, slow movement, scherzo, and finale. In this case the finale is "a complex sequence of movements, scarcely symphonic in the traditional sense, but drawing the listener out from the inner drama to the world of action and resolution" (Hugh MacDonald, "Hector Berlioz," in Sadie 1980, 2:596).

Another work based on a literary masterpiece is *La damnation de Faust*, Op. 24 (1845–46, on text by Goethe, adapted by Berlioz and others), for mezzo-soprano, tenor, baritone, and bass soloists, eight-part mixed chorus, and orchestra. Even the composer was not sure what this was, calling it first an *opéra de concert* before finally settling on *légende dramatique*. It is a pastiche of new music, revisions of his earlier *Huit scènes de Faust* (1828–29) and his arrangement of the traditional Rákóczy March. Berlioz's decision not to turn this into a full-blown opera was correct: because he took isolated scenes from Goethe's book, the sequence of events is sometimes jarring, rather like a very long film trailer; but the effect in concert is superb.

Other choral works include *Lélio, ou Le retour à la vie*, Op. 14 (Lelio, or the Return to Life, 1831–32), for orchestra with chorus, a sequel to *Symphonie fantastique*; several works with piano accompaniment (including *Le ballet des ombres*, Op. 2 [1828], for STTBB chorus; *Chant guerrier* [1829] and *Chanson à boire* [1829], for tenor solo and men's chorus; and *Prière du matin*, Op. 19, No. 4 [c. 1848] for two-part children's choir); two motets, *Veni creator* (1861) for SSA soloists, three-part treble choir, and optional organ, and *Tan-*

tum ergo, for SSA soloists, three-part treble choir, and organ; and numerous cantatas and occasional pieces.

Ambroise Thomas (1811–1896) contributed two interesting pieces to the choral repertoire: *Messe des morts* (c. 1840) and *Messe solennelle* (1857), both for mixed chorus and orchestra. Typically melodious and deftly orchestrated, they clearly demonstrate his gift for idiomatic vocal writing and felicitous text setting. The Requiem is still popular with French choral societies. Thomas also composed other sacred and secular works.

Charles-Valentin Alkan (1813–1888) was one of the most underappreciated composers of the nineteenth century. Alkan rarely performed or even appeared in public, although he was considered a leading piano virtuoso, was a close friend of Chopin, and was highly respected by Liszt and Busoni. His compositional style was completely original, incorporating old and new, and was, furthermore, somewhat out of step with his era: he refused to admit the use of rubato; pedal points and ostinati sometimes create a feeling of bi- or polytonality; and his music is often conceived linearly, with no harmonic or notational adjustments made for tonal considerations, leading to occasionally biting dissonance and strange, difficult-to-read notation (for example, he had to invent a notation for a triple sharp). Such intellectual rigidity is not again encountered until the twentieth century in certain works by Bartók, Sessions, and others. Although most of his compositions are for piano, he did contribute a few interesting vocal pieces. In addition to two early cantatas written for the Prix de Rome competition and never published, he composed four works that can be performed either with soloists or chorus: *Etz chajjim hi*, for SSTB, unaccompanied (1847, in Hebrew); *Halelouyoh*, for SATB with piano or organ (1857, in Hebrew); *Marcia funebre sulla morte d'un papagallo*, for SSTB, three oboes, and bassoon (1859); and *Stances de Millevoye*, for SSA and piano (1859).

Samuel Naumbourg (1815–1880)—like Sulzer in Vienna and Lewandowski in Berlin (see chapter 5)—reformed Jewish liturgical music in France. His collection of liturgical pieces for cantor and mixed chorus, *Zemriot Israel*, relied heavily on traditional melodies. Naumbourg, however, modified them to accommodate the popular expression of French opera, using Meyerbeer as his primary model. Further, because Naumbourg's project was sponsored by the French government, his collection was disseminated throughout the French colonies, thus introducing choral music to Sephardic communities in North Africa and the Near East. Another extremely important contribution of Naumbourg's, in conjunction with Vincent d'Indy, was the first modern edition of works by Salomone Rossi (c. 1570–c. 1630).

Charles Gounod (1818–1893) was an exceptionally important figure in nineteenth-century choral music, not for his compositions, which for the most part have not lasted, but rather for the immense influence his work exerted (in tandem with that of Mendelssohn) on English music during the latter part of the century. A good example is the oratorio *La rédemption* (1881, on text compiled by the composer), for soloists, mixed chorus, and orchestra, which was renowned in England. Although it can be easily argued today that the popularity of this and his other choral works helped further stagnate a musical culture already mired in the shallow pretense of the Victorian age, contemporaries did not see it this way. Wrote Josephine Thrall in 1908:

> The Redemption is perhaps the best of modern oratorios. Expressing, as it does, in music both majestic and melodious, the deep, warm color of religious fervor, it appeals as strongly to the emotions as to the intellect. And in giving us this masterpiece of sacred music Gounod has added to the world's best composition a tone picture so beautiful in its harmony, and so profound in sentiment, that for ages it will arouse the sincerest sympathy of all who hear it. (Thrall 1908, 221)

Gounod was a man of the theater as well as faith, and a superb craftsman, too. But his lyric muse was not sufficient to plumb the intellectual and emotional depths of his oratorio topics. Further, his dramatic and religious impulses were sometimes confused, so

that his music seems to be "hovering between mysticism and vo-
luptuousness" (Gustave Chouquet and Adolphe Jullien, "Charles
Gounod," in Blom 1954, 3:731). Hearing his oratorios today has the

Above and opposite: Climactic moment in the Sanctus of Charles Gounod's
St. Caecilia Mass.

same effect as watching an old, very long silent movie: we recognize the technical brilliance but understand the drama and sentiment as obvious and calculated.

Even though he approached oratorio text with a missionary's zeal, he seems to have been more at home with the liturgy. The *St. Caecilia Mass* (1850), for STB soloists, mixed chorus, and orchestra stands out because of its continued popularity. It demonstrates Gounod's talent to its best advantage without melodramatic excess: the melodies are natural, the harmonies warm, the lyricism genuine, and the climaxes fulfilling. All these attributes are particularly noticeable in the Sanctus, independently popular as a church anthem, which is direct expression at its best.

Among Gounod's other choral works are several Masses (some written for the Orpheon Men's Choir, which he conducted) and many other liturgical works; some dramatic scenes for chorus and orchestra; and the oratorios *Tobias* (c. 1866) and *Mors et vita* (1884), both for soloists, mixed chorus, and orchestra. Gounod's reputation does not seem to have been enhanced by early twenty-first-century recordings of *The Redemption* and *Mors et vita* (which some consider a masterpiece).

Like Gossec and Grétry, César Franck (1822–1890) was born in Belgium, but he lived and worked mostly in Paris and is generally considered a French composer. During his life he had little success as a composer, and even his best works are marred by strange lapses of taste and forays into banality. This is true of his most impressive choral work, the oratorio *Les Béatitudes* (1872–79), for soloists, mixed chorus, and orchestra, and is an omnipresent characteristic of his sacred music. A review of his Mass for Three Voices (not, incidentally, a choral work) by the Italian critic Ricciotto Canudo is telling: "Full of inequalities, the Mass, like all Franck's church music, is a curious dream, half mystic, half secular, in which the flow of ecstatic sentiment is sometimes complete and superb, and sometimes interrupted by rhythms and affectations which are essentially theatrical" (Blom 1954, 3:468).

His famous *Panis angelicus* was composed for tenor solo, organ, harp, cello, and double bass; the version for mixed chorus, solo voice, and organ was arranged at a later date by someone else. Among Franck's other choral works are Psalm 150 (1888), for mixed chorus, organ, and orchestra; the symphonic poem *Psyché* (1886–88), for orchestra with mixed chorus; and *Trois offertoires* (1871), for soloists, mixed chorus, organ, and double bass.

Georges Bizet (1838–1875) was thoroughly a man of the stage and is remembered now primarily for the operas *Carmen* and *Les pêcheurs de perles* (The Pearl Fishers), from which choruses are often extracted. He did, however, flirt with other kinds of choral music, leaving at least five cantatas unfinished. He also considered writing an oratorio on text by Louis Gallet, but there is no evidence he ever began work on it. The few surviving choral pieces include the cantatas *David* (1856, on text by Gaston d'Albano) and *Clovis et Clothilde* (1857, on text by Amédée Burion) and a Te Deum (1858), all for soloists, mixed chorus, and orchestra. The Te Deum, which has been revived and recorded, is, in the words of Winton Dean, "a compound of the trivial and the complacently sanctimonious" (Dean, "Georges Bizet," in Blom 1954, 1:729). That the composer felt comfortable transferring the music he had written for the Pleni sunt coeli into *The Pearl Fishers* for "O Brahma divin" seems to corroborate Dean's conviction that Bizet had virtually no affinity for religious music. But, perhaps all religions were the same to the composer.

Alexis Castillon (1838–1873) was a controversial figure in French music during the nineteenth century. His own inclinations were toward absolute music, as defined by Beethoven, Schumann, and other German composers of symphonic and chamber music. And although many French musicians recognized his promise as a composer, as well as what the development of his musical impulses could mean for French music, he was not appreciated at all by the French public. He was ahead of his time, and Duparc, Chausson, and d'Indy all benefited from his influence. He died just as his own authentic compositional voice was beginning to assert itself. Among his last are two very interesting choral works, *Paraphrase du psaume 84* (1872, on text by Louis Gallet), for soloists, mixed chorus and orchestra, and a Mass (1872), left incomplete.

Gabriel Fauré (1845–1924) did not compose much choral music, but what he did leave us is excellent. His best-known choral work, the unassumingly beautiful Requiem, Op. 48 (1886–88), for soprano and baritone soloists, mixed chorus, and orchestra, is not only a fixture in the repertoire, but also inspired later Requiems by Maurice Duruflé and John Rutter. It is notable among Roman Catholic Masses for the dead in that fear of divine judgment is lacking entirely: the music is comforting in the extreme. Fauré was uniquely suited to write such a piece, for a large part of his originality lies in the ability to turn restraint into a constant virtue. Because his music functions on such an even keel, all the subtleties of harmony and texture are made readily apparent, and the peculiarities of his melodic arches are placed in bold relief. The composer originally produced a five-movement version (for chamber ensemble) in 1888, after the deaths of his parents, and a seven-movement version adding the baritone solos (also for chamber ensemble) in 1893. The seven-movement version for full orchestra appeared in 1900.

Other works by Fauré include the early *Messe basse* for female chorus (originally three soloists) and organ; the charming and popular *Cantique de Jean Racine*, Op. 11 (c. 1873), for mixed chorus, harmonium, and string quartet (or orchestra); and three exquisite settings of *Tantum ergo*, one for solo voice and mixed chorus (Op. 55, c. 1890), one for three-part female chorus (Op. 65, No. 2), and one for soprano and tenor soloists, mixed chorus, organ, and harp (c. 1905).

Camille Saint-Saëns (1835–1921) remains one of the more popular French composers of the nineteenth century, noted for various orchestral works, piano and violin concerti, and *Samson et Dalila*, Op. 47 (1877, on text by Ferdinand Lemaire), an opera that began life as an oratorio. It is still occasionally performed in concert version and contains some attractive choral moments. His Mass, Op. 4 (1856), for mixed chorus and orchestra, was one of his earliest successes. He followed it with the still popular *Oratorio de Noël*, Op. 12 (1863), for SATB soloists, mixed chorus, string orchestra, and organ, particularly notable for its lovely concluding chorale; the cantata *Les noces de Prométhée*, Op. 45 (1867); and the oratorio *Le déluge*, Op. 46 (1876).

Saint-Saëns's Requiem Mass, Op. 54 (1878), for SATB soloists, mixed chorus, and orchestra, has garnered interest in recent years and provides an illuminating glimpse into the freedom and mastery of his orchestrations. In Jean-Gabriel Gaussens's words:

> The orchestration is notable for its lack of percussion, trumpets and clarinets, which places the work on a plane more meditative than brilliant, and when the unison trombones enter, their impact is all the greater for being unexpected, especially when they echo, *tutti forza*, the great organ. It is equally notable that Saint-Saëns wished to show the difference between the Light of Eternal Life and the Darkness of Death by multiplying the high pitched instruments (i.e., 2 harps, 4 flutes, 2 oboes) and reinforcing the low-pitched ones (i.e., 2 English horns, 4 bassoons). (Gaussens 1972)

Saint-Saëns wrote additional liturgical pieces, part-songs, cantatas and oratorios, many of which were composed well into the twentieth century (see Strimple 2002, 53). His style is centered in French classicism. In the early 1970s the eminent composer and pedagogue Halsey Stevens told his graduate students at the University of Southern California (the author among them) that when he heard a composition obviously from the nineteenth century, but without any other identifying characteristics, he assumed it to be by Saint-Saëns. This assessment, although entertaining, does not take into account Saint-Saëns's consummate skill and technique, nor the continuing attractiveness of his straightforward harmonic language, which generally avoids augmented sixths and other progressions stereotypical of French music.

Gustave Charpentier (1860–1956) was a successful and promising composer before becoming a prisoner of his bohemian lifestyle: he did not compose (or at least finish) any new works after 1913, even though he lived past the middle of the twentieth century, and after World War II he was a recluse until his death. A man of the stage, his style was a blend of Berlioz, Wagner, and Gounod. In addition to his operas, of which the most famous is *Louise* (1896), he also composed a number of highly dramatic cantatas, often designed for outdoor performance. These include the "symphony-drama" *La vie du poète* (1888–89, revised 1892, on text by the composer), for soloists, mixed chorus, and orchestra; *Sérénade à Watteau* (1896, on text by Paul Verlaine), for soloists, mixed chorus, and orchestra; and the impressively large *Le chant d'apothéose* (1902, on text by the composer and Saint-Georges de Bouhélier), for soprano, tenor, and baritone soloists, mixed chorus, and orchestra. Charpentier also made choral and orchestral arrangements of several of his songs for solo voice and piano.

Pierre de Bréville (1861–1949), a student of Franck and Théodore Dubois, was also deeply influenced by Wagner and, in his later works, by Fauré and Debussy. His gifts peaked early, and by his own account, his most important choral work was the cantata *La tête de Kenwarc'h* (1890, on text by Leconte de l'Isle), for baritone solo, mixed chorus, and orchestra; however, it was never published. Much of his sacred music follows Liszt's example in calling for somewhat unusual instrumental forces. These include the Mass (1883–86), for soprano, tenor, and bass soloists, mixed chorus, string quartet, harp, and organ; and *Laudate Dominum* (1889), for baritone solo, mixed chorus, harp, double bass, and organ. He was naturally inclined toward the female voice and composed several large works, including *Médeia* (1892, on text by A. F. Herold), for soprano, female chorus, and orchestra; and *Chant des divinités de la forêt* (1896, adapted from his incidental music for *L'anneau de Çakuntala*, a play by Kâlidâsa, in translation by Herold), for soprano, tenor, female chorus, and orchestra. In 1889 he composed a work entitled *Hymne à Venus*, for an ensemble of viola, flute, oboe, clarinet, bassoon, and harp accompanying two female voices, either soloists or chorus. This voicing, for one or more on a part, became a peculiarity of his late music, and in his last years Bréville composed a lengthy series of small pieces for two, three, or four female voices, either unaccompanied or with piano.

Charles Bordes (1863–1909) contributed several motets and some part-songs. His great achievement, however, was the establishment, in 1894, of a society for the study and performance of sacred music. In 1896 this became a school known as the Schola Cantorum, in which students learned Gregorian chant and works by Renaissance masters. Bordes also formed a touring choir that performed this repertoire, and other early French music, throughout France.

Other French composers include François Aimon (1779–1866), who contributed choruses to Egidio Duni's opera *La fée Urgèle* (libretto by Charles-Simon Favart, 1821); Felice Biangini (1781–1841), a Frenchman of Italian birth, who somehow managed to find time for composing four Masses for mixed chorus and orchestra, several motets, and other church music when he wasn't busily involved in his love affair with Napoleon's sister Pauline Borghese; Pierre-Auguste-Louis Blondeau (1784–1865), who composed a couple of Masses, three Te Deum settings, and at least thirty cantatas; François Benoit (1794–1878), who composed a Mass (1861) for mixed choir, organ, and orchestra, and a few small liturgical works; Auguste Bottée de Toulmon (1797–1850), a student of Cherubini and Rejcha who contributed an oratorio and some Masses; Félicien David (1810–1876), whose oratorios for soloists, mixed chorus, and orchestra, including *Moïse au Sinai* (1846), and symphonic odes, such as *Le désert* (1844), for male chorus and orchestra, are now completely forgotten; Louis-Désiré Besozzi (1814–1879), a rival of Gounod, whose works include a number of sacred pieces for women's chorus published collectively under the title *La chapelle du convent* (1857); François Bazin (1816–1878), a conservative composer and opponent of Franck, who, while conductor of Les Orphéons, a male choir in Paris, wrote many pieces for men's voices; Samuel David (1836–1895), who served as music director in a Paris synagogue and composed the cantata *Le génie de la terre* (1859) for male chorus and orchestra, performed in Paris by a choir numbering six thousand; Louis Bourgault-Ducoudray (1840–1910), who composed several cantatas, among them the interesting *Stabat mater* (1868, on text by G. Benedetti), for soloists, mixed chorus, cello or double bass, harp, trombone, and organ, and whose modally harmonized collections of French, Greek, and Celtic folk songs foreshadow the work of Vaughan Williams and Bartók; Jules Massenet (1842–1912), the celebrated opera composer whose choral works include the impressive oratorio *La terre promise* (The Promised Land, 1899), for soloists, mixed chorus, and orchestra; Albert Cahen (1846–1903), whose "biblical drama" *Jean le Precurseur* was performed at the Concerts Nationals in 1874; Camille Benoit (1851–1923), who contributed *Eleison* (1890), for soloists, mixed chorus, and orchestra, arranged Berlioz's *Roméo et Juliette* for piano duet (1878), and even provided a Latin translation of Beethoven's *Elegischer Gesang* (n.d.); Ernest Chausson (1855–1899), whose works include Three Motets, Op. 12 (1886), for mixed chorus, cello, harp and organ, as well as the lyric scene *Jeanne d'Arc* (c. 1880) for soloists, female chorus, and piano; and Alfred Bruneau (1857–1934), who wrote choral pieces large and small, including a particularly adventuresome Requiem (c. 1884–88, vocal score published 1895), for soloists, children's choir, mixed chorus, organ, and orchestra.

Switzerland

Wilhelm Baumgartner (1820–1867) was a pianist and choral conductor who was responsible for several choirs in Zurich, including the Zurich Male Chorus, which he founded and for which he composed about forty pieces, the best-known being *O mein Hei-matland*, Op. 11, No. 1 (n.d., on text by Gottfried Keller).

Charles Samuel Bovy-Lysberg (1821–1873) was a concert pianist whose many works (mostly for piano) also include a cantata, *Le Alpes* (1860, on text by A. Richard), for male chorus and orchestra.

The Netherlands

In 1796 a concert organization called Eruditio Musica was formed in Amsterdam for the purpose of giving Sunday concerts. In 1801 it presented Haydn's *Creation*. The Toonkunst Choir was founded in 1829, and the Maatshappij Caecilia was founded in 1841.

The first important Dutch composer of the century was Johannes Bernardus van Bree (1801–1857). Known primarily as a conductor, he was instrumental in introducing oratorios and Masses by recent German masters to Dutch audiences. The German influence can be heard in his three Masses and other works for male chorus and orchestra.

Gijsbertus Johannes Bastiaans (1812–1875) was an organist who was instrumental in promoting J. S. Bach's music in Holland. He also wrote many works for organ himself. Paradoxically, he strove to eliminate organ interludes from worship, preferring to use instead a combination of choral music and congregational singing. He composed a number of cantatas and smaller works for mixed choir, in addition to several chorale books for four-part mixed chorus that retained the tunes in their original forms.

Charles-Louis-Joseph André (1765–1839) was an organist and priest at the Cathedral of St. Rombout in Mechelen. In 1797 he was exiled for political reasons but returned in 1801. He composed church music with various instrumental accompaniments.

Anton Berlijn (1817–1870) was one of the most acclaimed Dutch composers of the century. He received honors from the Dutch King Wilhelm II, the Saint Cecilia Society in Rome, and several other international awards and commendations. He was for a brief time director of the Municipal Theater in Amsterdam, and for many years he served as the director of various choirs and music director in one of Amsterdam's synagogues, where he also taught Hebrew. Berlijn was primarily known for his operas and other theatrical music, but Dutch audiences were also very aware of his cantata *Die Matrosen am Ufer* (1848) and his oratorio *Moses auf Nebo* (1843), both for soloists, mixed chorus, and orchestra. Berlijn composed many part-songs for male choir; and—given the tolerant nature of Amsterdam society, coupled with the esteem in which he was held—it is not surprising that Berlijn also composed a Mass. Most of his works remain in manuscript.

Ludwig Felix Brandts Buya (1847–1917) was an organist and ethnomusicologist who composed two very popular part-songs for male voices: *Avondrood* (n.d.) and *Zegepraal* (n.d.).

Alphons Diepenbrock (1862–1921), who would have a great impact on Dutch music in the early twentieth century, developed a "striking individual style of composition, in which Wagnerian elements curiously intertwine with impressionistic modalities" (Slonimsky 1992, 432). Among his early works are a *Stabat mater*, for male chorus; *Missa in die festo* (1891), for tenor solo, male chorus and organ; and *Les elfes* (1896), for soprano and baritone soloists, women's chorus, and orchestra.

Other Dutch composers include Samuel de Lange (1840–1911), an organist and conductor who composed an oratorio, *Mozes*, for soloists, mixed chorus, and orchestra, as well as other choral works; and Charles Smulders (1863–1934), who contributed many part-songs for male chorus and mixed chorus.

Belgium

Peter Benoit (1834–1901) was the most important Belgian composer of the century. Responsible for the rejuvenation of Flemish music, he was also an ardent nationalist who fought, and won, the battle for teaching and producing music in Flemish rather than French. This resulted in the eventual establishment of the Royal Flemish Conservatory of Music in 1898. As a young composer Benoit was impressed with the music of early nineteenth-century German composers, but these influences were gradually superseded by an ever-increasing interest in Berlioz, Meyerbeer, and Wagner, and his application of principles he learned from them resulted in music that was often shockingly modern. As his interest in Flemish nationalism increased, Benoit simplified his style considerably in an attempt to make his music more accessible. Benoit was particularly adept at writing for large choral forces, pioneered the composition of cantatas for children, and also created a form he called lyric drama, in which actors on the stage spoke in exactly notated rhythm with orchestral accompaniment. His most important choral compositions are the *Quadrilogie religieuse* (1864; a quartet of large works consisting of a *Messe solennelle*, a *Cantate de Noel*, a Te Deum, and a Requiem, composed in succeeding years beginning in 1860), for mixed chorus and orchestra; and the oratorio *Lucifer* (1865), for soloists, mixed chorus, and orchestra. Other works include a Mass for male chorus and organ (1873); several oratorios, including *Prometheus* (1867) and *De Rhijn* (1889), both for soloists, mixed chorus, and orchestra; male choir pieces, including *De Maaiers* (1864) and *Aan Antwerpen* (1877); several cantatas; and numerous small choral pieces for various vocal configurations.

Jan Blockx (1851–1912) was a composer most recognized for his operas. He studied with Peter Benoit at the Flemish Music School (soon to become the Royal Flemish Conservatory of Music) but found Benoit's strictness confining and went to Leipzig, where he studied with Carl Reinecke. Nevertheless, Benoit's clearly articulated nationalism found fertile ground in Blockx, and he developed a style enriched by the German romantic aesthetic while remaining firmly planted in the soil of Belgian folk music. His choral works include *Licht* (1895), for soloists and male choir; *De Heide* (1899), for male choir; *Vredezang* (1877), for women's choir and orchestra; *De kleine bronnen* (1878), for women's or children's choir and orchestra; the cantatas *Klokke Roeland* (1888, on text by A. Rodenbach) and *Antwerpen's schutsgeest* (1888, on text by A. Wouters), both for mixed chorus and orchestra; the oratorio *Een droom van't paradijs* (1881–82, on text by J. van Beers), for soloists, mixed chorus, and orchestra; and a few additional works composed after the turn of the century.

Other Flemish composers include Laurent-François Boutmy (1756–1838), an organist and harpsichordist who contributed a lightweight "lyric scene" called *Le naufrage* (1806) for mixed chorus and orchestra; Jean Ancot (1779–1848), who composed two Masses and other church music (now lost); François van Campenhout (1779–1848), who composed a Requiem and several Masses that survive in manuscript, as well as the Belgian national anthem; Hendrik Waelput (1845–1885), who contributed some cantatas; François-Joseph Gevaert (1828–1908), a respected scholar and composer who produced much valuable research on early music and composed several interesting choral works, including an important Requiem for male chorus and orchestra; and Edgar Tenel (1854–1912), who would significantly impact Roman Catholic music in the next century (see Strimple 2002, 69), and whose oratorio *Franciscus* (1888) for soloists, mixed chorus, and orchestra, was very successful in Belgium during his lifetime.

4

The British Isles

Nineteenth-century English music is often simply dismissed. Still, music making thrived at all levels of society, and new music was needed for these endeavors. Most towns in England had organizations, as well as churches, in which local amateurs could perform music. And, since Handel, the favorite performance vehicle had been the oratorio. The oldest English music festival, Three Choirs, had begun around 1715, and others had sprung up by the 1780s. Their importance declined, and, indeed, their relevance was questioned during the Napoleonic Wars. But interest was rekindled after Napoleon was defeated in 1814; not only were the old festivals—Three Choirs and Birmingham, for instance—revived, but also many other cities and large religious establishments rushed to create annual music festivals in which oratorio and other choral music was featured. Thus the festivals at Manchester, Norwich, Leeds, and other places began. Choral societies, which had been formed as necessary appendages to festivals, became so powerful by the 1850s that often they no longer needed the festivals in order to survive. So the smaller festivals waned, with a new batch at seaside resorts springing into existence in the 1870s (see Smither 2000 for more information).

In the largest cities choral organizations that had nothing to do with festivals were also popular. For example, the Vocal Association was established in London in 1856, based on the model of the German singing societies. It was essentially a choir of about two hundred amateurs, conducted first by Julius Benedict and then Charles E. Horsley. Its first concert in 1857 included Mendelssohn's *First Walpurgis Night.*

In addition, the appreciation of English choral music was furthered late in the century by the publication of several studies, including William Alexander Barrett's (1834–1891) *English Glee and Madrigal Composers* and *English Church Composers,* both published in 1877.

Composers

John Wall Callcott (1766–1821) studied with Franz Joseph Haydn and composed anthems, catches, and glees. Considered one of the finest glee composers, most of his almost three hundred are still unpublished. He also helped compile a collection of harmonized psalm tunes, designed for use in small parishes, and authored a theory textbook that remained popular well into the nineteenth century.

Samuel Wesley (1766–1837) was the son of the extraordinary hymn writer Charles Wesley. His musical and intellectual gifts manifested themselves early: by the age of eight he had already composed an oratorio on the book of Ruth. He forsook the Methodist church of his father and uncle, John Wesley, and joined the Roman Catholic Church in 1784. Three years later Samuel Wesley fell into a pit at a construction sight, severely injuring his head. He was incapacitated for several years, and even after resuming his career, he continued to suffer occasional debilitating relapses for the remainder of his life. Still, he became one of England's finest organists and was paramount in creating an appreciation of Bach's music there. He was not as prolific as many of his contemporaries, and his choral music is generally of very high quality. He composed a number of glees for three and four voices and other secular pieces as well, in addition to sacred works for both the Anglican and Roman Catholic rites. Among his Anglican works are a Morning and Evening Service in F major for mixed chorus, several anthems (some with organ obbligato), and other service music. For the Catholic church he composed several Masses, of which the most interesting may be the Gregorian based *Missa solemnis* for unaccompanied mixed chorus. He left a sizable number of impressive Latin motets, of which *In exitu Israel*, for double choir, is particularly outstanding. Unlike the music of his English contemporaries, it compares favorably with virtually any European choral work of the time. It is wonderfully eclectic, though mostly modeled on Bach, beginning with a Gregorian incipit, a spectacular and difficult fugue, frequent classical turns of phrase, and a surprisingly understated conclusion.

Henry R. Bishop (1786–1855) was an exceptionally prolific and highly popular composer during his day. Famous for his operas and songs, he is now remembered only for "Home, Sweet Home." He composed over three hundred glees, of which some might still be successfully performed, as well as cantatas, odes, a large funeral anthem, and an oratorio. Bishop published about half of his glees in 1839 as *A Complete Collection of Glees*. His other choral works remain in manuscript.

John Barnett (1802–1890) was the son of Hungarian and German Jewish immigrants. His talent manifested itself early, and by the age of eleven he was singing professionally on the stage. He became one of the leading innovators in English opera but gave up composition for the stage in 1841 after serious public arguments with several leading theatrical producers. He had a demanding, cantankerous personality and seemed to enjoy provoking controversy. A successful voice teacher, he managed to exclaim publicly, at one point, that singing could not be taught (Nicholas Temperley, "John Barnett," in Sadie 1980, 2:168). He was a supporter of Charles Darwin's theory of evolution. His choral works consist of

Fugue subject from Samuel Wesley's motet *In exitu Israel*.

two Grand Masses (designed for concert use rather than religious services), one in G minor (1823) and one in C minor (sometime before 1827), the cantata *Abraham on the Altar of his Son* (1823), and two oratorios, *The Omnipotence of the Deity* (1829, on text by R. Montgomery) and *Daniel in the Den of Lions* (1841); all are for soloists, mixed chorus, and orchestra. He also composed many glees, madrigals, and part-songs.

The Irishman Michael William Balfe (1808–1870) was the most famous composer of opera in the British Isles. Balfe composed one motet, *Save Me, O God* (1846), for mixed chorus, which was published in England in an arrangement with organ accompaniment by W. A. Burnett. This edition claims that the English text is also by Burnett but does not indicate what the original text, accompaniment (if any), or purpose may have been. He wrote two cantatas, *Nelly Gray* (1859, on text by J. Oxenford), for soloists, mixed chorus, and piano, and the more well-known *Mazeppa* (1862, on text by Jessica Rankin, after Byron), for soloists, mixed chorus, and orchestra. In 1887 George Upton included it in his study of famous cantatas but, excepting the first two choruses and a canonic ensemble piece toward the end, did not seem to think much of it. According to Upton, the libretto was particularly weak: "It is but a feeble transcript of Byron's glowing verse, and in its diluted form is but a vulgar story of ordinary love, jealousy, and revenge" (Upton 1887, 46).

Samuel Sebastian Wesley (1810–1876), the son of Samuel Wesley (see above), composed exclusively for the church. According to early twentieth-century commentators, his works showed "an independence of thought and a mastery of climax which was well above the heads of his listeners. He was little touched by the Mendelssohn fever, and preserved to the full the traditions of his own country. . . . He proved that the spirit of Henry Purcell was not dead in England" (Stanford and Forsyth 1925, 301). Noteworthy pieces include the anthems *The Wilderness* and *Let Us Lift Up Our Heart*, both for soloists, mixed choir, and organ.

George Alexander Macfarren (1813–1887) edited Purcell's *Dido and Aeneas* (1840) for the Musical Antiquarian Society and later made editions of Handel's *Belshazzar*, *Judas Maccabaeus*, and *Jephtha*

for the Handel Society (1843). A prolific composer, he produced a
number of cantatas for soloists, mixed chorus, and orchestra, including *Leonora* (1851), *May Day* (1856, for the Bradford Festival),
Christmas (1859), and *The Lady of the Lake* (1877, for the Glasgow
Festival). His oratorios, also for soloists, mixed chorus, and orchestra, include *St. John the Baptist* (1873, for the Bristol Festival), *The
Resurrection* (1876, for the Birmingham Festival) and *Joseph* (1877,
for the Leeds Festival). Among his smaller sacred works are a service, anthems, chants, psalm tunes, and a set entitled *Introits for the
Holy Days and Seasons of the English Church* (1866); secular works
include *Shakespeare Songs for Four Voices* (1860–64), for unaccompanied mixed choir. Some of his best works—the oratorio *St. John the
Baptist*, for instance—were composed after he became blind. The
universal acceptance (in England, at least) of *St. John the Baptist* not
only demonstrates Macfarren's place in British musical life at the
time, but also reflects the immediacy of his language. According
to Howard J. Smither, it "is a breakthrough work for oratorio. It
is an original and imaginative piece in which the shadow of Mendelssohn, so prominent since the appearance of *Elijah* in 1846, is
only occasionally perceptible" (Smither 2000, 340). Reviewing the
premiere at the Bristol Festival, an English critic remarked:

> it is a strange thing that John the Baptist has not often attracted
> the notice of musical composers in search of a subject. No more
> remarkable personage, with one great exception, figures in Bible
> history. . . . At length, however, in that "fullness of time" which ever
> brings forth the best results, the Man and his Life have found a mu-
> sical illustrator. There is now an oratorio of "John the Baptist,"—a
> work worthy of its theme, and to which the stamp of enthusiastic
> approval has been affixed by the unanimous verdict of an audience
> competent to judge. (Upton 1886, 197)

Henry Thomas Smart (1813–1879) was a great organ builder
who, like George Macfarren, lost his sight. He is best remembered
today for a couple of widely used hymn tunes, "Regent Square"
("Angels from the Realms of Glory" or "Christ Is Made the Sure

Handel Festival concert in London's Crystal Palace, 1859. Courtesy of the *Illustrated London News*/May Evans Picture Library.

Foundation") and "Lancashire" ("The Day of Resurrection!" or "Lead On, O King Eternal"). A popular composer, Smart contributed several cantatas (for soloists, chorus, and orchestra) for the English festivals. Usually on secular subjects, these include *The Bride of Dunkerron* (1864, for the Birmingham Festival), *King Rene's Daughter* (1871), *The Fishermaidens* (1871, female voices), and *Jacob* (1873, for the Glasgow Festival). He also composed two large anthems for soloists, choir, and organ for the London Choral Choirs' Association Festivals of 1876 and 1878, as well as many part-songs.

William Sterndale Bennett (1816–1875) was, in the words of Nicholas Temperley, "the most distinguished English composer of the Romantic school" (Temperley, "William Sterndale Bennett," in Sadie 1980, 2:499). It is certainly true that his contemporaries—on both sides of the Atlantic—held him in high esteem. The American writer George P. Upton in 1887 said of Bennett's cantata *The May Queen* (1858, on text by Henry F. Chorley), for SATB soloists, mixed chorus, and orchestra:

The music of the cantata is divided into ten numbers, which are characterized by exquisite refinement and artistic taste. The solos . . . are very melodious and well adapted to the individual characters. The concerted music is written in the most scholarly manner, the choruses are full of life and spirit, and the instrumentation is always effective. There are few more beautiful cantatas than "The May Queen," though the composer was hampered by a dull and not very inspiring libretto. Poor words, however, could not affect his delightful grace and fancy, which manifest themselves in every number of this little pastoral. It is surprising that so excellent a work, and one which is so well adapted to chorus singing and solo display, without making very severe demands upon the singers, is not more frequently given in this country. (Upton 1887, 65–66)

However an early twenty-first-century reader (or listener) might respond to Upton's praise, it is true that the criticism of Chorley's text is appropriate. More often that not Victorian librettists and translators were much inferior to the composers with whom they worked. Many, if not most, cantata and oratorio texts from this period are so insipid and cloying that an objective appraisal of the music is exceptionally difficult. Be that as it may, Bennett did not seem really comfortable writing choral music, and his single oratorio, several cantatas, and a handful of anthems and part-songs are now forgotten. He did, however, remain successfully involved in various aspects of choral performance, founding the Bach Society in 1849 and arranging Bach's *St. Matthew Passion* and *Christmas Oratorio* in 1854.

Henry David Leslie (1822–1896) organized the famous 100-voice Leslie Choir in 1855, which took first prize at an international competition in Paris in 1878. His compositions include a Te Deum and Jubilate in D (1846), for mixed chorus and organ; the oratorios *Immanuel* (1853) and *Judith* (1858, for the Birmingham Festival), both for soloists, mixed chorus, and orchestra; the cantatas *Holyrood* (1860) and *The Daughter of the Isles* (1861), both for soloists, mixed chorus, and orchestra; many anthems, including *Let God*

Arise (1849), for mixed chorus and organ; and part-songs, madrigals, and other works for his choir.

John Francis Barnett (1837–1916), nephew of John Barnett (see above), established an international career as a pianist before he turned his hand to composition. His first choral work was a cantata, *The Ancient Mariner* (1867, based on Samuel Taylor Coleridge's poem), for soloists, mixed chorus, and orchestra. Its premiere at the Birmingham Festival that year was so successful that he was invited, over time, to produce large choral works for almost all the English festivals, even though his abilities were better suited to the composition of small pieces. In addition to *The Ancient Mariner*, his most successful choral work was the oratorio *The Raising of Lazarus* (1873), for soloists, mixed chorus, and orchestra, which received frequent performances in churches throughout England.

Joseph Barnby (1838–1896) became one of the most important choral musicians in nineteenth-century England, successfully establishing his own choir in 1864 and inaugurating daily concerts at Albert Hall in 1874. He composed a large amount of sacred music, of which the anthems are forgotten. Several of his hymn tunes, however, are still sung on both sides of the Atlantic, most notably "Laudes Domini" ("When Morning Gilds the Skies"), and "Merrial" ("Now the Day Is Over").

Alexander Campbell MacKenzie (1847–1935) was an important Scottish composer, conductor, and administrator. He had a particular fondness for choral music. Appointed conductor of the Scottish Vocal Music Association in 1873, he also conducted Novello's oratorio concerts during the 1885–86 season and appeared often as a guest conductor with the Royal Choral Society. His reputation as a composer rests largely on his early works, primarily the oratorio *Rose of Sharon*, Op. 30, for soloists, mixed chorus, and orchestra, composed for the Norwich Festival in 1884. Its success catapulted MacKenzie to the first rank of British composers. He served as principal of the Royal Academy of Music from 1888 to 1924. In addition to *Rose of Sharon*, he composed another fourteen large choral and orchestral works, including the cantata *The Story of Sayid*, Op. 34 (1886, for the Leeds Festival, on text by Edwin Arnold), which became very popular in America as well; *A Jubilee Ode*, Op. 36 (1887, on text by Joseph Bennett), for Queen Victoria's jubilee; and *Veni creator spiritus*, Op. 46 (1891, English paraphrase by John Dryden), for mixed chorus, optional SATB soloists, and orchestra. Although he composed several anthems, MacKenzie's heart was not in church music. Rather, he was a gifted composer of part-songs, of which excellent examples may be found among the *Seven Partsongs*, Op. 8 (1879), for mixed chorus; and *Two Toasts for Male Voices* (1893, on texts by S. S. Stratton).

By the middle of the century English music had sunk up to its neck in a vapid style with little to recommend it. Because England was not at that time producing composers capable of overcoming banalities, this style remained dominant for the duration of the century. It was aptly described (and succinctly skewered) by the American critic Daniel Gregory Mason, writing about an English cantata composed in 1893:

> How this [music] calls up the atmosphere of the typical English choral festival: the unwieldy masses of singers, the scarcely less unwieldy orchestra or organ, the ponderous movement of the music, half majestic, half tottering, as of a drunken elephant, the well-meaning ineptitude of the expression, highly charged with good nature but innocent of nuance! There is the solid diatonic harmony, conscientiously divided between the four equally industrious parts. There is the thin disguising of the tendency of this hymn-tune type of harmony to sit down, so to speak, on the accent of each measure, by a few conventional suspensions. There is the attempt to give the essentially stagnant melody a specious air of busyness by putting in a triplet here and a dot or short rest there. And there is the sing-song phraseology by which a phrase of four measures follows a phrase of four measures as the night the day. In short, there is the perfectly respectable production of music by the yard, on the most approved pattern, undistorted by a breath of personal feeling or imagination. (Mason 1918, 101–3)

Fortunately, English musical fortunes began to revive during the last quarter of the century with the maturation of the four great Victorian composers, Arthur Seymour Sullivan (1842–1900), Charles Hubert Hastings Parry (1848–1918), Charles Villiers Stanford (1852–1924), and Edward William Elgar (1857–1934). Each was born within a few years of the century's midpoint, each was knighted by Queen Victoria, and each, in his own way, helped extricate British music from the sentimental and formulaic quicksand into which it had fallen.

Arthur Seymour Sullivan was perhaps the most famous English composer of the century. His continuing fame was secured by the series of comedic stage masterpieces he wrote with William S. Gilbert. It is not unusual today to hear choruses (or scenes) from these operettas in choral concerts, delighting listeners. But Sullivan also composed a significant number of other choral pieces, all popular and highly regarded in their day. His concert music was in demand at the English choral festivals, which commissioned several of his best works, including the oratorios *The Prodigal Son* (1869, for Worcester), *The Light of the World* (1873, for Birmingham), and *The Martyr of Antioch* (1880, for Leeds); and the cantata *The Golden Legend* (1886, also for Leeds). All of these are for soloists, mixed chorus, and orchestra. He also composed part-songs and other small works, wrote anthems and service music for the Anglican church, and edited *Church Hymns with Tunes* (1872) for the Christian Knowledge Society. Many of his part-songs are still viable; of the larger works, *The Light of the World* and *The Golden Legend* (on text by Longfellow) might deserve revival.

Charles Hubert Hastings Parry was particularly known to English audiences for his large choral and orchestral works. But he was virtually forgotten outside of England until 1981 when his hymn tune to William Blake's poem "And Did Those Feet in Ancient Time" became popular through its use in the Academy Award–winning film *Chariots of Fire* (thereafter his music was reconsidered on both sides of the Atlantic with generally favorable conclusions). This hymn, known as "Jerusalem," was originally one of the several songs Parry wrote for unison children's choir.

Whereas Stanford's music often seems coldly objective, Parry's is warm and inviting, but usually without the cloying sentimentality typical of most Victorian music. Many of his best works were composed after the turn of the century, among them the brilliant coronation anthem *I Was Glad* (1902), for mixed chorus and organ (or orchestra); the six motets *Songs of Farewell* (1916–18, on texts by Vaughan, Davies, Campion, Lockhart, and Donne); and *An Ode to the Nativity* (published 1912), for soprano, mixed chorus, and orchestra. He understood how to set text effectively and clearly, and his mastery of the choral idiom is obvious in his part-songs, anthems, and larger works as well, most notably the *Ode at a Solemn Music: "Blest Pair of Sirens"* (1887, on text by Milton), for chorus and orchestra; and *Ode to Music* (1901), for STB soloists, mixed chorus, and orchestra. These works are the equal of anything by Stanford or Elgar. J. A. Fuller-Maitland observed:

> There is apparent the same mastery of accentuation that was noticed in his songs; besides this, the composer shows a wonderful power of handling large masses with the utmost breadth and simplicity of effect, and of using the voices of the choir in obtaining climax after climax. This is the secret of Parry's power over the musical people of his time, and it is a power that is felt not only by the educated listener, but even by the untrained listener. Without the smallest trace of the actual influence of Handel, there is a grandeur which is commonly called "Handelian" about many of Parry's choruses. The more delicate side of his choral writing is beautifully shown in the various partsongs, and several of these are among the most expressive and tender things in music. ("C. H. H. Parry," in Blom 1954, 6:562)

Of his four oratorios, *Judith* (1888, on text by the composer), for soloists, mixed chorus, and orchestra may be taken as representative. In addition to the odes discussed above, Parry composed several others, as well as large works that do not fit neatly into a common choral genre, such as *Scenes from Shelley's "Prometheus Unbound"* (1880), for contralto, tenor, and bass soloists, mixed chorus, and orchestra.

Charles Villiers Stanford was born in Dublin and received his early musical training there. He was sent to London to study when he was ten years of age and entered Queen's College, Cambridge, eight years later as an organ student. In 1883 he became professor of composition at the Royal College of Music, and in 1887 he was named professor of music at Cambridge. He held both appointments concurrently until his death. Late in life he coauthored, with Cecil Forsyth, *A History of Music*, which is valuable for its many astute observations on European music in the nineteenth century, as well as its appreciation for English music. In addition to Stanford himself, six of his contemporaries are singled out for praise: Sullivan, Mackenzie, Parry, Goring Thomas, Cowen, and Elgar. His own paragraph reads:

> Stanford is the man of widest achievement in this group. He has an opus-series that approaches 150. This includes nearly a dozen operas, seven symphonies, a mass of chamber music, several church-services that have become standard works, and more than a dozen "choral and orchestral works." He has dealt with subjects as far removed from each other as *The Eumenides*, *The Canterbury Pilgrims*, *Shamus O'Brien*, *Much Ado about Nothing*, and *The Critic*. Of all his works perhaps his *Irish Symphony* and *Irish Rhapsodies*, his choral ballad *The Revenge*, and his *Cavalier Songs* are at present most esteemed. But it may be questioned whether his *Stabat mater* and his colossal *Requiem* will not eventually hold a higher place than any of these. An earnest collector, editor, and arranger of Irish folk-song, he has always shown himself an upholder of his national artistic ideals—purity, clarity, and beauty of expression. (Stanford and Forsyth 1925, 316)

Perhaps Forsyth wrote this paragraph. But regardless of who actually concocted the thumbnail biography, it is true that Stanford was a particularly hardworking composer who took great care in shaping his music. There is often an academic quality that, in his hands, is quite becoming: not stuffy or dry but, rather, thoughtful and well crafted. He was tirelessly prolific: more than thirty large choral works (cantatas and oratorios) flowed from his pen. His church music included six complete Anglican services, three Masses, and the *Stabat mater*, Op. 96 (1907), for soloists, mixed chorus, and orchestra. Several anthems and much of his service music are still, deservedly, in the repertoire. Other interesting compositions include *Three Motets*, Op. 51 (1905, in Latin), for unaccompanied mixed chorus; *Three Cavalier Songs*, Op. 17 (1880, on text by Robert Browning), for baritone solo and men's choir; and *Nine Songs for Children*, Op. 30 (1888, on text by Robert Louis Stevenson), for unison or two-part treble chorus and piano. Of his large works, the Requiem, Op. 63 (1896), for soloists, mixed chorus, organ, and orchestra, is particularly interesting: composed in memory of a friend and influenced by Richard Wagner, it effectively employs a devise he would use again in the *Stabat mater*: a leitmotiv to represent human mortality (Chase 2003).

Edward William Elgar—when able to extricate himself from the Victorian platitudes described above by Daniel Gregory Mason—was a great composer. He enjoyed a long career, and some of his best-known works, the oratorios *The Apostle* (1903) and *The Kingdom* (1906), were written in the new century. But he had composed enough by the nineteenth century's end to be more than highly regarded. Early in the twentieth century Josephine Thrall wrote that "Elgar ranks with the best of the modern European composers in the orchestral field, but his greatest work has been done in the oratorios *The Dream of Gerontius*, *The Apostles*, and *The Kingdom*. It has been said that Elgar is doing for oratorio what Wagner did for opera" (Thrall 1908, 252–53).

Indeed, *The Dream of Gerontius* (1900), for alto, tenor, and bass soloists, mixed chorus, and orchestra, on text by John Henry Cardinal Newman, has come to symbolize all that might have been achieved (rather than what actually was achieved) by nineteenth-century English composers. It should be understood, however, that *Gerontius* is not a perfect work. The choral movements are brilliant. Each soloist is given memorable and idiomatic music. But Cardinal Newman's lengthy poem in defense of purgatory makes it very difficult for any non-Catholic listener to achieve that temporary suspension of disbelief necessary for the oratorio to convince, and the music is sometimes overbearing, stuffy, and dull. But it is also packed full of magnificent moments, and the overall musical effect is wonderful. Particularly thrilling are the scene in hell and the scene of angels glorifying God ("Praise to the Holiest in the height"). There is no greater—nor more fully realized—contrast in the repertoire. And it must be admitted, too, that the complete success of these scenes is due not only to Elgar's management of choral forces, but to his absolutely brilliant orchestration.

Elgar was out of fashion for thirty years or so after his death. His reputation was rejuvenated largely through the efforts of the conductor William Steinberg in the late 1960s. Still, excepting *Gerontius*, Elgar's large choral and orchestral works have not come back into vogue. These include the cantata *The Black Knight* (1893), for mixed chorus and orchestra, and the oratorios *Lux Christi* (1896) and *Caractacus* (1898), both for soloists, mixed chorus, and orchestra. It may be that current and perhaps future audiences will remain satisfied with only one large work from Elgar's pen. However, there is much gold to be mined from his catalog of smaller pieces, which include numerous anthems, Latin motets, and part-songs. Especially worthy are the Te Deum and Benedictus, Op. 34 (1897), for mixed chorus and organ; *Five Partsongs*, Op. 45 (1903, on translations of Greek texts), for four-part male chorus; *Four Partsongs*, Op. 53 (1907), for mixed chorus; *Christmas Greeting*, Op. 52 (1907, on text by C. Alice Elgar), for two soprano soloists, optional male chorus, two violins, and piano; and *Two Partsongs*, Op. 26 (c. 1895, on text by C. Alice Elgar), for women's voices, two violins, and piano (which includes the exquisite and justly popular "The Snow"). Additionally, the ode *The Music Makers* (1912, on text by Arthur O'Shaughnessy), for contralto solo, mixed chorus, and orchestra; and the heartfelt *Spirit of England*, Op. 80 (1916, three movements on text by Laurence Binyon), for soprano and tenor soloists, mixed chorus, and orchestra, might be successfully revived.

Other British composers include Matthew Camidge (1764–1844), a famous organist and conductor of oratorio at St. Michael-le-

Choral parts at a climactic moment in Edward Elgar's *The Dream of Gerontius*.

Belfrey church in York, who contributed a morning and evening service and other liturgical music; Thomas Attwood (1765–1838), an important opera composer who also made fine contributions to English liturgical music, including several services and anthems, of which two coronation anthems with orchestral accompaniment, *I Was Glad*, and *O Lord, Grant the King a Long Life*, are still held in high regard; George William Chard (1765–1849), a composer of twenty-eight anthems and other service music who became mayor of the city of Winchester in 1833 after being officially reprimanded for neglecting his duties as organist at the cathedral and college; John Addison (c. 1766–1844), who adapted music by one P. Winter into a sacred music drama called *Elijah Raising the Widow's Son*, which was performed as one of the Drury Lane Lenten Oratorios in 1815 and promptly lost; William Beale (1784–1854), a popular and prolific composer of glees and madrigals; John Fane Burghersh (1784–1859), a founder of the Royal Academy of Music, who composed a Grand Mass (1858) for mixed chorus and orchestra, as well as some other service music and part-songs; Thomas Adams (1785–1858), who managed to compose a hymn, an anthem, and, in the words of Nicholas Temperley, a "satirical harmonization" of 'Old 100th' Psalm Tune" ("Thomas Adams," in Sadie 1980, 1:101); Zechariah Buck (1798–1879), an organist and outstanding organ teacher, who contributed an evening service and a few anthems; John Goss (1800–1880), who wrote a significant number of choral works—large and small—for the Anglican church that were very popular in their day and now are largely forgotten; Joseph Wade (1801–1845), an Irish composer who settled in London, where his oratorio *The Prophecy* (1824), for soloists, chorus, and orchestra, was produced at Drury Lane Theatre; Julius Benedict (1804–1885), a great conductor and popular composer of German birth, who authored an important biography of Weber and contributed numerous cantatas—in a style greatly influenced by Rossini—for the Birmingham and Norwich Festivals; John Liphot Hatton (1809–1896), whose cantata *Robin Hood* (1856), for soloists, mixed chorus, and orchestra, enjoyed fleeting popularity; William Richard Bexfield (1824–1853), a student of Zechariah Buck, who had modest success with his oratorio *Israel Restored* (1851), for soloists, mixed chorus, and orchestra; John Baptiste Calkin (1827–1905), a respected composer of anthems, glees, and part-songs; Samuel Butler (1835–1902), a music critic and amateur composer whose adoration of Handel resulted in some dramatic cantatas that are exceptional copies of Handel's style; John Stainer (1840–1901), who wrote many works for the Anglican church, as well as cantatas and oratorios, the most famous being *The Crucifixion* (1887), for soloists, mixed chorus, and organ (from which comes the redoubtable setting of "God So Loved the World," for unaccompanied mixed chorus); Frederick Bridge (1844–1924), who composed numerous liturgical works and occasional pieces for the Birmingham and Three Choirs Festivals; Alfred Cellier (1844–1891), an occasional collaborator with Arthur Sullivan, who wrote the little cantata *Grey's Elegy* (1883), for mixed chorus and orchestra, for the Leeds Festival; Arthur Goring Thomas (1850–1892), whose cantata *The Swan and the Skylark* was found in piano score after his death, orchestrated by Stanford, and successfully produced at the Birmingham Festival in 1894; Frederick Corder (1852–1932), who contributed the popular cantatas *The Cyclops* (1880) and *The Bridal of Triermain* (1886, both for soloists, mixed chorus, and orchestra); Jamaican-born Frederic H. Cowen (1852–1935), who drew on his Jewish heritage for the oratorio *Ruth* (1887) and on his English heritage for the popular cantata *The Sleeping Beauty* (1885), both for soloists, mixed chorus, and orchestra; Dame Ethyl Smythe (1858–1944), whose Mass in D (1893), for soloists, mixed chorus, and orchestra, and other works were deservedly praised by her peers; Hamish MacCunn (1868–1916), a Scottish composer who composed cantatas and a few part-songs that are still occasionally performed in Scotland; and John McEwen (1868–1948), another Scottish composer and important music educator who contributed the *Scene from "Hellas"* (1894, on text by Shelley) , for soprano, women's chorus, and orchestra; as well as a couple of cantatas for mixed chorus and orchestra.

5

The Czech Lands, Slovakia, Hungary, and Poland

The Czech Lands (Bohemia and Moravia)

Antonín Rejcha (1770–1836) is known today primarily for his woodwind quintets and other chamber music that includes wind instruments. He became a professor at the Paris Conservatory in 1818, and his impact there, as a teacher and an author of theoretical treatises, was great: his students included Berlioz, Adolphe Adam, Liszt, Gounod, and Franck. Before settling in Paris, however, he lived for several years in Vienna (1802–8), and it is during this time that most of his choral music was composed.

These works include an impressive Requiem (1806), for soloists, mixed chorus, organ, and orchestra, and *Der neue Psalm* (1807, on text by Siegfried Augustus Mahlmann), also for soloists, mixed chorus, and orchestra. The Requiem was Rejcha's initial artistic reaction to the Napoleonic Wars, specifically the French invasion of Vienna in 1805 and the subsequent Battle of Jena in 1806. The composer happened to be in Leipzig when the French were occupying it after Jena and translated this experience into music of the first order. As might be expected, wind instruments are prominent, as is the chorus. Rejcha's mastery of contrapuntal form is evident in the "Quam olim Abrahae" fugue as well as the final movement. *Der neue Psalm* sets Mahlmann's paraphrase of the Lord's Prayer to music that is both intimate and grand, effectively marrying elements of classical and baroque style.

Rejcha's best choral work is his magnificent Te Deum (1825), for SATB soloists, mixed chorus, and orchestra. A product of artistic maturity, it showcases the songlike qualities of his best woodwind quintets, his considerable abilities as a contrapuntist, and his inter-

Above and opposite: The concluding measures of Antonín Rejcha's Te Deum.

est in new harmonic developments. Also, a good sense of dramatic timing—not always present in Rejcha's music—manifests itself, a good example being the final unison statement of the concluding fugue subject. As always, the woodwind writing is brilliant, but here Rejcha bows to practicality by providing an optional obbligato organ part as a substitute.

František Doubravsky (1790–1867) was the music director and choirmaster at the Church of St. Nicholas in Lomnice nad Popelkou, in northern Bohemia. In that position he composed nearly three hundred sacred works, including Masses, litanies, a *Stabat mater*, a Te Deum, and thirteen Masses for the Dead (two of which are in Czech). Most are written for mixed chorus, soloists, and small chamber orchestra usually consisting of some combination of flute, clarinets (2), trumpets (2), strings, timpani, and organ. Notable among his works are the *Missa pastoralis* (1822, for Christmas), the Te Deum in C Major (1836), the *Missa solemnis* in D Major (1840), and the Requiem in E-flat Major (1830). All of these were composed for liturgical situations, so the longest (*Missa solemnis*) is still under a half hour in duration. His works may be considered typical of the small-town Kapellmeister laboring in the Czech lands during the first half of the century: the technical demands are slight, the orchestrations reflect viable options, and Doubravsky's mastery of classical style is evident.

Jan Hugo Voříšek (1791–1825) was highly regarded in Prague and Vienna during his life but never achieved real prominence. A pianist, choral conductor, and composer, he worked as a civil servant in Prague to make ends meet between appearances as a performer. In 1818 he moved to Vienna, securing the position of conductor of the Gesellschaft der Musikfreunde, a job he would hold until his untimely death. His songs and small piano works are quite important because of the influence they had on his friend Franz Schubert, and his excellent Symphony in D returned to the repertoire during the last quarter of the twentieth century. His Mass in B-flat Major for mixed chorus (with incidental solos) and orchestra is unjustly ignored and deserves performance. While sitting squarely in the classical tradition, it exhibits an expressive restraint more in keeping with Cherubini than with Haydn or Mozart, and it exudes a harmonic warmth that clearly establishes the composer's Czech ancestry, suggesting later developments that manifest themselves in the music of Smetana and other Czech composers.

František Škroup (1801–1862) was, according to Rosa Newmarch, "the moving spirit" behind the first opera produced in Czech (Joseph Weigl's *The Swiss Family* [*Švýcarska rodina*], originally in German). Škroup, attorney by trade and composer and opera singer by avocation, then set his hand to write the first Czech opera, *Dratenik* (The Tinker, 1826, on text by Chmelensky). He wrote another in 1834, which was not successful. These and other early attempts at establishing a national style failed because "[Škroup dropped] too easily from the national style to the idiom of Italian opera, with which he was familiar. The inconsistencies of his style are such as we find in nearly all the early attempts to create a national art by the mere *imitation of folk-song*" (Newmarch 1942, 53). Škroup's imitations of folk music hit pay dirt, however, with the song *Where Is My Home?* (*Kde domov můj?*, 1833, from one of his later operas), which became the national anthem. He composed not only opera but also a quantity of sacred (for both church and synagogue) and secular choral pieces.

Pavel Křížkovský (1820–1885) is not currently known outside the Czech Republic, but he should be. As a child he was forbidden to speak of music, even though he demonstrated talent. Through the patient intervention of a teacher he was allowed to sit with a church choir in rehearsal. When his singing talent was discovered he received a paid position in the choir. He fell on very hard times after his voice changed but eventually succeeded in completing a Ph.D. at the university in Brno; in 1845 he entered the Augustinian monastery in that city.

He was introduced to the study of Moravian folk music by a member of the Augustinian community, F. Sušil, a prominent collector of Moravian tunes, and was further encouraged by the monastery church's music director, Gottfried Rieger. Through his study of and immersion in Moravian folk tunes, Křížkovský came to understand this music as the authentic artistic voice of his people (the "Music of Truth," as Leoš Janáček would later call it). He began to make arrangements for four-part male chorus at about the time he took his ordination vows in 1848. He also composed original pieces and, like Bela Bartók and Ralph Vaughan Williams after him, so absorbed the essential elements of his native folk music that it is impossible for someone unfamiliar with the tunes to recognize which pieces are arrangements and which are newly composed.

The first arrangements were possibly made for the monastery choir to sing recreationally. It is certain, however, that many of his later works were composed for the choir of the Moravian Teacher's College, an ensemble with such a high standard of excellence that pieces written for it (by Křížkovský, Janáček, and others) make up an unparalleled body of work for virtuoso male choir.

Křížkovský's best-known male chorus is the heart-rending *Utonulá* (The Drowned Maiden, 1860), which became standard repertoire in the Czech lands. Other compositions for unaccompanied male chorus include *Odvedeného prosba* (The Recruit's Prayer,

1861, revised 1862), much admired by Smetana; *Odpadlý od srdca* (also known as *Divka* [Fallen Away from the Heart, Lassie], 1849); *Dar za lásku* (The Love-gift, 1849, revised 1861); and *Zaloba* (The Plaint, c. 1859). Additional works include *Zatoč ze* (Turn Round, 1851, revised 1860, original music to a folk text), for solo quartet and male chorus; *Modlitba Sv. Cyrilla na sotnach* (Prayer of Saint Cyril on His Deathbed), for male chorus and three trombones; and a sacred cantata in honor of Sts. Cyril and Methodius, *Hvězdy dvě se z východu* (Two Stars from the East, 1850), for male chorus and piano or organ (revised for piano and brass, 1861).

Czech folk texts tend to be gritty, often with changing points of view and intense emotions. Also, these texts are frequently narratives requiring music of much longer duration than the average part-song. Křížkovský had no problem meeting the various emotional and technical challenges inherent in such texts. Furthermore, his relatively simple, homophonic settings are as satisfying as his polyphonic ones, such as the humorous *Vyprask* (Threshing, 1866), for tenor solo, male chorus, and piano.

Eventually Křížkovský's interest in folk music got him into insurmountable trouble with the Caecilians, and he was transferred to Olomouc in 1872 (just out of convenient reach of his students, including Janáček). There he served as music director at the cathedral and composed a number of liturgical works in a style deemed appropriate by the authorities that conformed to the principles of Franz Xaver Witt (leader of the Caecilian movement). Among these are a Requiem and a Te Deum. He brought to these compositions his accustomed high standard of compositional excellence (it must be remembered that Křížkovský was a good clergyman who took his ordination vows seriously, including the vow of obedience).

Křížkovský apparently composed no secular music after 1872. Fortunately, he was able to pass on everything he knew to his devoted student, Leoš Janáček, who, having no binding ties to the Roman Catholic church, was free to compose whatever and however he wanted. Unfortunately, much of Křížkovský's music is lost, possibly because he held it in low regard, and possibly because he was not allowed to keep copies in the monastery or in Olomouc.

In any case, his pattern was to send the finished manuscript to the choir for which it was written; he kept no catalog or list of his compositions, and only a few were published.

If not the authentic founder of Czech national style, Pavel Křížkovský is certainly a creator of the venerated Czech male choir tradition, which had profound impact on both Janáček and Smetana. In the words of Smetana's biographer Brian Large, Křížkovský "was one of the first composers whose understanding of music and profound insight into the spirit and traditions of folk idiom enabled him to reconcile the two. In a way, he was a precursor of Smetana, who confessed that only through Křížkovský's scores had he grasped the true significance of folk melody" (Large 1970, 123).

Rosa Newmarch summed up his contribution succinctly: "Smetana's observation that it was not until he heard Křížkovský's choruses that he really understood the full significance of the Czech folk-melody sets these works in the light of a revelation" (Newmarch 1942, 50).

Bedřich Smetana (1824–1884), the generally acknowledged father of Czech opera, was from a very poor family and became a musician only through great difficulty. His first job was as head of household music for Count Leopold Thun. In 1846, while still in the count's employ, the struggling young composer first tried his hand at choral music, composing six works as exercises, four for unaccompanied mixed chorus based on Lutheran models (*Jesu, meine Freude* [chorale], *Ich hoffe auf den Herrn* [fugue], *Lobet den Herrn* [introduction and fugue], and *Heilig, heilig, ist der Herr Zabaoth* [for double chorus]), followed by settings of two Roman Catholic offertories, *Scapulis suis* and *Meditabitu in mandatis tuis*, both for mixed chorus, organ, and chamber orchestra. These texts were chosen certainly not for religious reasons—Smetana was not a believer—but most likely because he was familiar with the languages. His primary language was German. Having been raised in the German educational system, he undoubtedly knew Latin as well, and at this time spoke very little Czech.

A Czech patriot, he entered into a kind of voluntary exile after the failure of the Revolution of 1848, finally obtaining a conducting position in Göteborg, Sweden, in 1856. While there, Smetana began to study Czech seriously. He composed choral pieces in Czech in 1848 and again in 1860, but his unfamiliarity with the language and ignorance of the choral idiom doomed both to well-deserved failure.

Italian victories over Austria caused the Czech political situation to relax in 1859, and after rather aimlessly concertizing around Europe, Smetana returned home in 1862. On arrival in Prague he assisted with the formation of the Czech Provisional Theatre (1862), helped found the Society of Artists, and accepted a conducting position with the Hlahol Choral Society. In addition to acquiring the Czech language, he had another life-changing experience at this time: he became acquainted with the music of Pavel Křížkovský.

Smetana's mature choral pieces, almost entirely for unaccompanied male voices, are largely inspired by Křížkovský. The finest of these were composed for Hlahol: *Tři jezdci* (Three Horsemen, 1863, on text by Jiljí Jahn); *Odrodilec* (The Renegade, 1863, on text by Ambrož Metlinský, translated from Ukrainian by Čelakovský); and *Rolnická* (The Peasant, 1868, on text by Václav Trnobranský). In general they exhibit a careful approach to text and a refined use of vocal color. In a letter to his best friend, Josef Srb-Debrnov, in 1880, Smetana described his approach to setting text: "I read the poem many times then I declaim it—simply pacing to and fro in my room until words change into rhythm and melody" (Large 1970, 122).

Tře jezdci tells the story of three Czech noblemen returning home with the news that Jan Hus had been burned at the stake. Their conversations are transmitted in dramatic fashion by three soloists from the choir accompanied by humming chorus, an effect that would be successfully copied eighty years later by Gideon Klein in *Prvni hřich* (The First Sin, 1942).

Odrodilec was composed immediately after the successful first performance of *Tře jezdci*. For eight-part male chorus, it is a virtuoso piece in every respect, utilizing the full potential of the double chorus. Smetana's music vividly portrays the response of the people on learning that a traitor in their midst has been captured and executed: the finale is a Czech polka. However, this obviously nationalistic element was overlooked by one critic, who wrote that the composer filled his piece with "an indigestible German and Italian artificiality covering the disease of a dried-up imagination. All praise, then, to Mr. Smetana for having used in his *Renegade* all the filth of the German style" (Large 1970, 124). Throughout his career Smetana would be hounded by critics who were offended by perceived German—primarily Wagnerian—influences in his music. These critics did not carry the day, of course, and the following year Smetana made an arrangement of *Odrodilec* for four soloists, mixed choir, and optional brass, in which version it was successfully performed by a choir of fifteen hundred singers (Large 1970, 125).

Rolnická was composed some years later, after the success of *The Bartered Bride* and just before the disaster of *Dalibor*. Its highly descriptive music portrays the joys of peasant life throughout the seasons of the year, a message that fell on particularly receptive ears just as the rural population was breaking free of the feudal restraints under which they had lived during two centuries of Austrian oppression. Laid out like a four-movement symphony, its tonal scheme, A–D–G–A, projects just a hint of modality. In his comments on *Rolnická*, Brian Large reminds us that Smetana's operas are another rich resource for choral repertoire: "*The Peasant* develops the rich, lyrical choruses in *The Brandenburgers* and *The Bartered Bride*, and is imaginatively worked out with delightful pictorial touches" (Large 1970, 192).

Smetana's only choral work with orchestra, the forceful and exuberant cantata *Česka piseň* (Czech Song, on text by Jan Jindřich Marek) went through two abortive versions before reaching the final one in 1878. The first, a vocally awkward—if not impossible—version for male chorus, was written in 1860. The second, for mixed chorus and piano, was written in 1868 and performed with a chorus of some three hundred singers in 1870. Smetana realized immediately that an orchestra was necessary to balance such large choral forces but did not get around to including it for several years. The final version follows the scheme of a classical four-movement symphony with introduction. The opening section is for mixed chorus, the second for women, the third for men, and the rousing, patriotic finale—which recalls music from the introduction—is again for mixed chorus.

Other works include *Slavnostni sbor* (Festive Chorus, 1870), *Piseň na moři* (Sea Song, 1877), *Veňo* (The Dower, 1880), *Modlitba* (Prayer, 1880), and *Naše piseň* (Our Song, 1883). Unlike Janáček, who would transfer the emotional wallop of his male choruses into his works for women, Smetana's *Three Choruses for Women's Voices* (1878, on text by Sladek) are slight, lovely, and somewhat superficial.

After graduating from the Prague Organ School in 1858, Karel Bendl (1838–1897) devoted several years to composing before traveling to France and the Low Countries, where he became established as a conductor and choirmaster. Returning to Prague in 1865, Bendl assumed Smetana's post as conductor of the Hlahol Choral Society. He served in this capacity for the next twelve years, exerting considerable influence on Czech choral music. His own style is a mixture of nationalism (derived from Smetana) and lyric romanticism (his affinity to Mendelssohn was so obvious that one Czech wag labeled him "Bendlssohn"). He was an important opera composer and also composed over a hundred songs; still, his approximately three hundred choral works stand out. Perhaps his most significant compositions are the cantata *Švanda dudák* (Švanda the Bagpiper, 1881, on text by Vrchlický), for soloists, mixed chorus, and orchestra; and the pieces dealing with the Hussite revolution of 1419: *Umírající husita* (The Dying Hussite, 1869), for mixed chorus and orchestra; *Smrt Prokopa Velikého* (The Death of Prokop the Great, 1871, revised 1894), for baritone solo, mixed chorus, and orchestra; and *Pochod Táborů* (March of the Taborites, 1880), for unaccompanied male chorus. Other important works include the cantata *Štědrý den* (Christmas Eve, 1885, on text by K. J. Erben), for soloists, mixed chorus, and orchestra; *Four Songs* (n.d.) for female chorus; and a couple of Masses.

Zdeněk Fibich (1850–1900) was an exceptionally important composer of opera and melodrama. In spite of his abilities as a vocal composer, he was not particularly adept at choral writing. Of his several choral works, all written early in his career, only one is worthy of notice, the little cantata *The Bride of the Wind* (*Meluzina*, 1872–74, on text by Kinkel), for soloists, mixed chorus, and orchestra.

Joseph Foerster (1833–1907) was a church musician and teacher who counted Antonín Dvořák among his pupils. He wrote a respected harmonic treatise, and his son, the composer Josef Bohuslav Foerster, would have great impact on Czech choral music in the twentieth century. Virtually all of his choral pieces are sacred and, because he was influenced by the Caecilians, tend to be modest in technical demands and straightforward in expression. Foerster was also a better composer than most of the Caecilian hacks, and his best works still speak agreeably to modern audiences. The charming *Missa Bohemica*, for two-part chorus and organ, can be taken as representative: the harmonic language is warm, the diatonic vocal lines sing easily, and the two-voice texture is written to accommodate any combination of high and low voices (SA, TB, or ST with AB).

Antonín Dvořák (1841–1904) is primarily known as a composer of symphonic and chamber music. He believed, late in life, that his operas were his greatest achievement. Between the instrumental and operatic genres reside a number of important choral works, most of which were initially received with enthusiasm and performed regularly throughout Europe and the United States until World War II. In the middle of the twentieth century, though, performances of his music outside Czechoslovakia became rare.

Reasons for this vary and often have nothing to do with the music itself. For one thing, some of his works have been seen as too narrowly nationalistic (see Brahms's comments on this in Beckerman 1993, 83–84). On the other hand, there have been those who considered Dvořák nothing more than a slightly exotic, watered-down Brahms. The mixture of Slavic and German elements was particularly grating to some Czech critics, such as the Moravian musicologist František Bartoš (1837–1906), who wrote: "our national style is something far deeper than his sonorous exoticism; therefore, for the sake of truth, we must be prepared to renounce before future generations even so distinguished a musical personality" (Robertson 1945, 88). Soviet-era authorities, copying this line, accused Dvořák of a fraudulent nationalism, a sham when compared to Smetana (whose atheism, by the way, fit nicely into the Marxist aesthetic). Zdeněk Nejedlý, the Communist minister of education and, later, culture, developed a line of descent for Czech music that passed from Smetana through Fibich, Foerster, and Ostrčil, omitting Dvořák altogether. Dvořák's son Otakar, in his reminiscences, quotes an unnamed Communist-era critic: "Dvořák was a dead chapter in Czech music, where there is nothing for a searching and creative spirit to do" (Dvořák 1993, 111). Further, although four of Dvořák's major works are in Latin, there are also several in Czech, which can be a stumbling block for conductors of other nationalities who feel that every work should be performed in its original language. And existing English translations are often inadequate. Lastly, Dvořák's exceptional facility has been occasionally confused with superficiality, an error that tends to obstruct (or at least inhibit) a proper appreciation of his emotional depth, craftsmanship, and subtly conceived formal structures. For example, virtually all commentators view the *Stabat mater* as a succession of unrelated set-pieces, which, as we shall see below, is absolutely incorrect. John Clapham has shown definitively that Dvořák composed with painstaking care (Clapham 1966). A clear understanding of the exceptional nature of his achievement begins with the knowledge that his melodies, effortless though they seem, are actually the product of considerable sweat.

Dvořák's first big splash came with the cantata *Hymnus: Dědicové Bílé Hory*, Op. 30 (The Heirs of the White Mountain, 1872, revised 1880, 1884, on text by Vítězslav Hálek), for mixed chorus and orchestra, a heartfelt commemoration of the battle on the outskirts of Prague in 1620 that began both the Thirty Years' War and the subjugation of the Czechs under the iron fist of the Habsburgs' Austro-Hungarian Empire. Bohemia was still suffering under this oppression during Dvořák's time, and the cantata was appreciated not only as a poignant reminder of the value of freedom, but also as a beautiful and well-crafted work by a promising young composer.

Soon Dvořák's reputation grew beyond the borders of the Czech lands. Fritz Simrock began publishing his music, and he became very popular in England. The *Stabat mater*, Op. 58 (1876, orchestrated 1877), for soprano, alto, tenor, and bass soloists, mixed chorus, organ, and orchestra, was an immediate hit with the English when Joseph Barnby conducted it in the Royal Albert Hall in 1883. Indeed, since its premiere in Prague on 23 December 1880, it had already become quite popular on the European continent. Still Dvořák's most popular choral work, it underwent a revival of interest in the latter part of the twentieth century and is now often programmed instead of the Requiems of Brahms or Verdi. (Dvořák's published opus numbers have nothing to do with the actual chronology of his works. The *Stabat mater* is actually Op. 28, but because Simrock had already published pieces with numbers higher than that and did not wish customers to think the *Stabat mater* a youthful work, he assigned it the higher number and insisted on continuing the practice with everything he published by Dvořák.)

The *Stabat mater* begins with ascending octaves, followed by a descending chromatic scale: a musical visualization of Mary standing at the cross, gazing up and down at it (the opening of this motive is altered when the voices enter). But effective text painting is the least of the devices Dvořák brings to this work, which was for him a painful journey from despair to faith. Structurally the *Stabat mater* is unique. It is constructed in an axial symmetry similar to those found in *Die Weihnachtsgeschichten* of Heinrich Schütz and J. S. Bach's *Jesu, meine Freude*. But only the opening and closing movements share obvious thematic material; other than the archlike allocation of performing forces, connection among the other movements is linear, with motives, identifiable harmonic progressions, or rhythmic patterns evolving from one movement into the next, an example of Dvořák's highly personal application of Liszt's principle of thematic metamorphosis. For instance: the half–half–dotted quarter–eighth rhythm that dominates the ending of the first movement begins in the main theme of the second, the dotted rhythm now used as a pick-up into two longer notes. This rhythm—now in 4/4—permeates the third movement, too. The theme of the fourth movement is a slight variant of the introductory material in the second movement and will return again in the sixth movement. And so on.

Tonal movement is also key to Dvořák's understanding of the text: In the beginning, as the poem observes Mary at the cross, minor keys dominate; but during the fourth movement, when the text changes to first person in the writer's desire to identify with Mary, the prevailing tonalities shift to major. Also, at this moment the music has progressed from the original B minor tonality to the far distant key of B-flat minor. Now the progression reverses: E-flat major–B major (with modal inflection)–A major–D major–D minor (with a Picardy-third ending)–B minor–D major. Dvorak further cements the nature of his return home by repeating a dramatic build-up that in the opening movement had occurred five times, always ending on a diminished seventh chord. In the last movement, however, this music climaxes brilliantly in major on the words "paradisi gloria," leading into the D major finale. Considering that Dvořák composed this after the death of one child and orchestrated it following the deaths of his two surviving children, one understands that arriving at a point where he could return home with hope in his heart was a difficult process, indeed.

After the success of the *Stabat mater*, Dvořák was commissioned, in fairly quick succession, to compose three other large choral works for the English market: the cantata *Svatební košile*, Op. 69 (The Specter's Bride, 1884–85, on Erben's retelling of a Czech folk tale), for soprano, tenor, and bass soloists, mixed chorus, and orchestra; and the oratorio *Svatá Ludmila*, Op. 71 (St. Ludmila,

The initial choral entrance in Antonín Dvořák's *Stabat mater*.

1886, on a libretto by Jaroslav Vrchlický), and the Requiem, Op. 89 (1890), both for SATB soloists, mixed chorus, and orchestra.

The Specter's Bride (so called because the literal translation of the Czech, "The Wedding Slip," was deemed inappropriate by the Victorian translator) was written for the Birmingham Festival. However, it was first performed in Plzen on 28 March 1885, several months before the English premiere. It is a grand ghost story in which a young girl is carried off by her dead lover and eventually saved only through her fervid prayers to the Virgin. The soprano and tenor are the lovers, the bass the narrator. The chorus provides commentary in response to the narrator, much like children listening to a camp counselor telling scary stories around a campfire. It is very effective music and deserves frequent performance, even though the string writing is quite difficult and the original English translation, by the Rev. Dr. Troutbeck, is overwrought.

Svatá Ludmila was composed for Leeds and contains some of the composer's most thrilling music. The two soprano arias in Part I are especially fine, the choral writing equal to anything of Mendelssohn, and the sense of drama compelling. Dvořák even provides a rare glimpse of his considerable ability as a contrapuntist toward the end of Part I. But the work is much too long. Composed for a festival accustomed to concerts lasting three to five hours, Dvořák padded his oratorio shamelessly, but not without having very good ideas on how to make its length manageable. Almost immediately after the very successful premiere he suggested a variety of cuts to bring it in at around two hours. In this form the story of the first Christian princess of Bohemia is quite entertaining. Also, Part III—the baptism of Ludmila and her prince—contains some of Dvořák's best choral music and stands alone very nicely as a twenty-five-minute cantata.

Dvořák's Requiem was popular in England and the United States for many years. After World War II, however, it not only fell into disuse, but also came to be held in disrepute. One is inclined to believe that a motivating factor in Alec Robertson's study of various Requiem settings (1967) was the opportunity to refute the positive impression he gave of Dvořák's Requiem in his earlier biography of the composer (Robertson 1945). However, it must be admitted that now, especially in the United States, this grand piece has become an acquired taste. But in the Czech lands it has never fallen from favor. Czechs consider it one of Dvořák's greatest works, a national treasure. It has been traditionally held in such high esteem in Bohemia and Moravia that before the Communist regime, regular radio programming would be discontinued and the Requiem played, without comment, prior to any grave governmental announcements. During the Nazi era some composers in the Terezín (Theresienstadt) concentration camp found ways to fit its four-note headmotive into their pieces, a kind of unique communication to the other Czech inmates that German guards most certainly didn't recognize. This motive, the same notes that drive the second Kyrie in Bach's B Minor Mass, permeates the work. Free alternation of tonal and modal harmonies and the use of customary Czech rhythms are recognizable as coming from Dvořák's pen; in other aspects, however, the piece is atypical. It is, for instance, the most Italianate of his compositions, the trumpet writing in the "Tuba mirum" being quite Verdian. It also contains a complete fugue (at "Quam olim Abrahae"), which, as indicated above, is very hard to find among Dvořák's works. According to one of his students, Harry Rowe Shelley, Dvořák did not care for the fugues of Bach: "It is easy enough to write music like that; all that is necessary is the theme, then say it as many times as you wish. It tires me to hear it so often" (Shelley 1919, 541).

The last three large choral works are the Mass in D Major, Op. 86 (1887) for soloists, mixed chorus, and organ; Te Deum, Op. 103 (1892), for soprano and bass soloists, mixed chorus, and orchestra; and the cantata *The American Flag*, Op. 102 (1893, on text by Henry Rodman Drake) for soloists, mixed chorus, and orchestra.

The Mass in D Major was composed for the dedication of a private chapel. Shortly after the premiere Dvořák arranged the organ

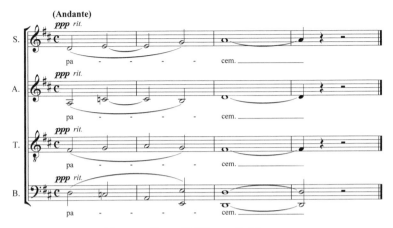

The final cadence of Antonín Dvořák's Mass in D Major.

part for four cellos, a version that unfortunately has not survived. Dvořák could not interest his publisher, Simrock, in the Mass, so he eventually submitted it to the English firm Novello for publication. Alfred Littleton, president of Novello, responded that he would happily publish the work if it were orchestrated, a task that Dvořák undertook in 1892. This version, which is quite different in details from the original, is scored for an orchestra of two oboes, two bassoons, three French horns, two trumpets, three trombones, timpani, organ, and strings. The woodwinds never play when the organ is used, and the original version's lengthy organ introduction to the Benedictus is retained (although Dvořák's manuscript clearly indicates that he considered having this played by strings). Novello published the parts and a vocal score with a piano reduction by Berthold Tours but never released the full score. This was unfortunate, because the piano score somehow omitted eight bars of accompaniment in the Credo, rendering the music useless. Now there are several good editions, clearly indicating the two version's frequent differences in choral voicing.

The Te Deum and *The American Flag* form a pair. Jeanette Thurber, who had just hired the composer as president of her newly organized National Conservatory in New York City, wanted Dvořák to compose a festive cantata for the Columbus Day celebrations in 1892. She promised to send an appropriate text, but when it did not arrive in time Dvořák proceeded with the Te Deum, thinking it fit the occasion. The resulting works were also attempts to deal with the problem of poetic text and symphonic form. Both works are organized as small symphonies; but whereas the Te Deum adjusts the text to fit the structure (ignoring its natural divisions and adding an Alleluia), *The American Flag* adjusts the formal structure to better accommodate the various progressions of the text (see Strimple 1993, 193–201). Still, the Te Deum is a minor masterpiece, while the cantata is barely an entertaining curiosity. That a wealthy American benefactor of the arts would think any foreign composer could identify with a preciously written American patriotic poem exemplifies the arrogance of America's upper class at the end of the century.

Dvořák was also an accomplished composer of part-songs. The two sets for mixed chorus, *Four Part-songs*, Op. 29 (1876), and *Amid Nature*, Op. 63 (*V přirodě*, 1883, five songs), are flawlessly crafted and charming. He also composed several sets for male chorus, including *From a Bouquet of Slavonic Folk Songs*, Op. 43 (*Kytice národních písní slovanských*, also known as *Three Slavic Folk Songs*, 1877–78), with piano, and the unaccompanied *Four Part-songs* (1877, without opus number), composed while journeying to Vienna to meet Brahms for the first time. His *Moravian Duets*, Op. 32 (1876) and Op. 38 (1877), for SA and piano, although written for solo voices, are often performed as treble-choir pieces. Leoš Janáček arranged six of the Op. 32 set for SATB chorus and piano, and Dvořák later arranged several for unaccompanied women's chorus (1880).

Other works include some small occasional pieces with orchestra; an arrangement of Stephen Foster's "The Old Folks at Home" (1893–94) for soprano and bass soloists, mixed chorus, and orchestra; and the vigorous *Psalm 149*, Op. 79 (1879, revised 1887), for male chorus (original version) or mixed chorus and orchestra, often performed with *The Heirs of the White Mountain*.

Leoš Janáček (1854–1928) would make his mark in the next century. Nevertheless, he composed a lot of choral pieces as a young man under the tutelage of Pavel Křížkovský. Among these are a few lovely motets for mixed chorus, either unaccompanied or with organ, several works for male chorus, including the unaccompanied *Three Male-voice Choruses* (1888), the *Choral Elegy* (1876), and *Ave Maria* (1883), as well as the *Festival Chorus* (1878), with piano. These works are much more accessible than the larger, more complex masterworks he composed for men's voices after the turn of the century.

In 1900 Janáček published his mixed-choir arrangement of Liszt's 1848 Mass for men's voices and organ. He was working from Liszt's 1872 Organ Mass version, which omitted the voice parts entirely. Janáček's version is therefore more than a simple restoration. The first work in which Janáček's unique personality was obvious is his virile setting of the old Czech hymn *Hospodine pomiluj ny* (Lord, Have Mercy, 1896), for SATB soloists, double mixed choir, harp, three trumpets, four trombones, and organ.

Other Czech composers include Jan August Vitásek (1770–1839), who was influenced by Mozart and contributed numerous respected Masses, motets, and other liturgical works; Václav Jan Tomášek (1774–1850), primarily known for his brilliant small piano pieces and songs, who contributed several Masses and a couple of Requiems; Leopold Eugen Měchura (1804–1870), an attorney who contributed the cantata *Christmas Eve* (on text by Erben); Vaclav Jindřich Veit (1806–1864), a judge who composed numerous part-songs for men's chorus and several large works, including a Mass in D Major (1858) and a Te Deum (1863), both for soloists, mixed chorus, and orchestra; and Jan Bedřich Kittl (1809–1868), an important symphonic precursor of Dvořák, who also composed a variety of choral works.

Slovakia

Johann Nepomuk Hummel (1778–1837) was born in Bratislava (then known as Pressburg in the Austro-Hungarian Empire). He was a celebrated pianist, composer, and teacher who served as Haydn's assistant at Eisenstadt during the last years of Haydn's life. Virtually all sources trace the origin of the romantic trill (that is, a trill beginning on the written note instead of its upper neighbor) to Hummel and his 1828 treatise on piano technique, *Anweisung zum Pianofortespiel* (Friddle 2006, ix). His Mass in E Major (1804), for soloists, mixed chorus, and orchestra, was composed for the Princess Esterházy's name day in 1804. In addition he composed four other Masses, an attractive Te Deum (1806) for soloists, chorus, and orchestra, and other smaller church works; a number of cantatas (most of which are occasional pieces); and several part-songs, including *Twelve Part-songs to Italian Texts* (1790s?), eight of which are for mixed chorus (four to six parts), one for treble chorus, and one for male chorus. Most of the other part-songs were written for specific occasions but are still of interest, namely "O ihr Geliebten" (c. 1810) for soprano solo and treble choir; the songs composed for Goethe's Weimar jubilee and birthdays, "Herauf Gesang" (1825), "Kehrt der frohe Tag" (1827), and "Wir steigen fröhlich" (1829), all for soloist and mixed chorus; and the two pieces on English texts, "Have" (1828), for men's chorus and brass, and "Think On Your Friend" (c. 1831), a canon for four-part mixed chorus.

Ján Levoslav Bella (1843–1936) was a teacher, priest, and friend of Richard Strauss, whose works he conducted. He was influenced by the Caecilian Society and composed accordingly until he left the priesthood in 1881 and took a position as organist at a Protestant church in Transylvania. Bella wrote many liturgical works for mixed chorus and a substantial number of works for unaccompanied male chorus, including the motets *Haec dies* (1865), *Tu es Petrus* (1869), and the secular *Drei ernste Gesänge* and *Vier heitere Gesänge* (both c. 1900). The efforts of his last years were devoted primarily to the composition of secular cantatas and songs.

Hungary

Ferenc (Franz) Liszt (1811–1886) was one of the most influential composers of the century. He was associated with Weimar for much of his adult life and had an international career as the leading pianist of his day. Vain in the extreme, he was the first to turn the piano sideways for concerts so that the audience could see his profile. Even though he had three children out of wedlock—one of whom, Cosima, later married Richard Wagner—by the Countess Marie d'Agoult (better known by her literary name, Daniel Stern), he still entered Holy Orders in 1865 and became Abbé Liszt. He composed an uncomfortably large amount of choral music, but although much of it is attractive and genuinely innovative, none of it comes up to the standard of his best piano or orchestral works. The church works show both sympathy with and revulsion against the Caecilian movement. He wrote a large number of liturgical works, large and small, including the simple *Missa choralis* (1865), for mixed chorus and organ; the Requiem (1867–68), for male chorus, organ, and brass; motets for male chorus and mixed chorus (some accompanied by organ); four settings of the *Pater noster* (one for unaccompanied male chorus, three for mixed chorus with organ); and many pieces accompanied by organ and other instruments such as harp or three trombones and timpani. Some of his later sacred works, such as *Via crucis* (1878–79), for soloists, mixed chorus, and organ, break new ground harmonically.

His secular works are equally diverse in concept and execution. They include the *Chorus of Angels from Goethe's Faust (Chor der Engel*, 1849), for mixed choir and harp or piano; and the various settings of *Ungarisches Königslied: "Magyar Kiraly-dal"* (1883): one each for male chorus, male chorus with piano, mixed chorus, mixed chorus with piano, male or mixed chorus with orchestra, and children's chorus.

Although they are not often performed, a handful of the large works with orchestra are fairly well-known. The oratorios *Die Legende von der heiligen Elisabeth* (1857–62, on text by Otto Roquette) and *Christus* (1855–66), both for soloists, mixed chorus, organ, and orchestra, are occasionally presented at European festivals with great fanfare and to mixed response. The *Dante Symphony* (1855–56) and the *Faust Symphony* (1854, chorus added 1857) both had their final choruses added as an afterthought. The *Missa solemnis*, also known as the *Granerfestmesse* (Gran Festival Mass, 1855, revised 1858), for soloists, mixed chorus, and orchestra, and the *Hungarian*

Coronation Mass (1867, Graduale added 1869), for soloists, mixed chorus, organ, and orchestra, are performed rather frequently in Europe but have not found receptive audiences or enterprising conductors in America. The Gran Festival Mass in particular contains fine music, although it is, like virtually everything else of Liszt's, uneven.

András Bartay (1799–1854) was a leader in the development of Hungarian musical life. A cofounder of Pest's first singing school and publisher of early collections of Hungarian folk songs as well as one of the first Hungarian music theory books, he was also for a time director of the Hungarian National Theater. In 1849, after the abortive revolution, Bartay emigrated, eventually settling in Germany. His compositions, which include Masses and oratorios, are the products of honest and competent effort to alleviate a need for national repertoire. His greatest contribution was in the overall development of Hungarian culture. His folk-song collections, along with those of his younger contemporary István Bartalus (1821–1899) helped to pave the way for Béla Bartók and Zoltán Kodály.

Ferenc Bräuer (1799–1871) studied piano with Joseph Czerny and composition with Hummel in Vienna. As an active pianist and violinist he played in several ensembles, including a gypsy orchestra. Although the gypsy influence is quite noticeable in his instrumental works, his choral works (all sacred, including two Masses for chorus and orchestra) remain firmly rooted in the classical tradition of his teacher Hummel.

Mihály Mosonyi (1815–1870) was one of the founders of Hungarian national music. Thoroughly schooled in German technique, he combined Germanic harmonies with typically Hungarian rhythms and scales, becoming an important precursor of Bartók and Kodály in the next century. He composed five Masses, some other church works, and several pieces for men's choir.

Kornél Ábrányi (1822–1903) wrote numerous small choral works but is of primary importance because of his efforts to improve music education in Hungary. To this end he wrote books on nineteenth-century Hungarian music that are still considered important sources, founded the National Association of Choral Societies (1867, serving as director until 1888), helped establish the Budapest Academy of Music (1875), and, as editor of *Zenészeti lapok* (the first Hungarian music periodical), encouraged composers to create an original Hungarian musical idiom.

August Adelburg (1830–1873) was born in Turkey of Italian and Croatian parents. His career as a violinist and composer took him throughout Europe. He eventually settled in Pest, marrying there in 1859, before eventually retiring in Vienna. He composed a Mass in 1858 and a Te Deum in 1864 and also published a pamphlet disputing Liszt's theories on the gypsy origin of Hungarian music.

Three other composers worth mentioning are Ferenc Erkel (1810–1893), Gyula Beliczay (1835–1893), and Károly Aggházy (1855–1918). Erkel, the creator of Hungarian national opera, also composed many small pieces for chorus. Beliczay contributed a number of sacred pieces and male choruses in the style of Schubert that were very popular during the latter part of the century. Aggházy was a concert pianist who eventually stopped performing in order to focus on teaching and composing. He composed a cantata (*Rákoczí*, 1905) and several other choral works that demonstrate a genuinely Hungarian style, strongly influenced by French elements, thereby establishing a bridge between Liszt and the nationalistic composers of the twentieth century such as Bartók and Kodály.

Poland

With the exception of Frédéric Chopin (1810–1849), one of history's greatest composers of music for piano, Polish composers focused on symphonic and operatic music during the century, and although many choral pieces for the Roman Catholic liturgy were produced, no large works gained an audience outside of Poland. Still, significant developments occurred, mostly in the realm of Jewish music. Beginning around the middle of the century, choirs for all ages were organized under the supervision of the Arbeiter

Ring (Workmen's Circle) in the ghettos of Warsaw, Krakow, and smaller cities. These choirs performed not only arrangements of Yiddish folk songs, but also standards from the European oratorio and secular repertoire, including opera (*Carmen* was a favorite). The tradition continued until these communities were destroyed by the Nazis in World War II.

Józef Elsner (1769–1854) was not only Chopin's teacher, but also an important composer in his own right. His choral works include seventeen Masses as well as several small pieces, sacred and secular. His two treatises on setting Polish texts (1818) were an important contribution to the literature.

Lewis Lewandowski (1821–1894) was born in the Polish town of Wreschen but moved to Berlin at the age of twelve, after his mother's death. There he sang in a synagogue choir, eventually attracting the attention of Felix Mendelssohn's cousin Alexander. With Alexander Mendelssohn's help, he became the first Jewish student to be accepted into the Berlin Academy of Arts. Although he showed promise as a composer of secular music, he eventually, after a long illness, devoted himself to service in the synagogue, working first as the choirmaster in Heidereutergasse Temple in Berlin before moving to the newly completed Oranienburger-strasse Temple in 1864. This new synagogue was one of the first to be equipped with an organ, and Lewandowski made full use of it. In 1882 he published *Todah W'Simrah* (Thanksgiving and Song), a complete liturgical cycle for cantor, mixed chorus, and organ. The most famous individual piece from this collection is surely Lewandowski's setting of Psalm 150, *Haleluyaw*, for four-part mixed chorus and optional organ, which is standard High Holy Day repertoire in synagogues throughout the world and is also very well-known to high school, college, and church choirs in America. Another worthy example of his work is the *Deutsche Kedushah*, for cantor (baritone), mixed chorus, and organ. Both of these energetic works project a sense of optimism, couched in the nineteenth-century German romantic language of Schubert and Mendelssohn. *Deutsche Kedushah* is particularly interesting because the primary text is in German, with Hebrew responses interspersed. Lewandowski is exceptionally important not only because he continued the pioneering work of Salomon Sulzer in Vienna, but also because he established a very high standard for the composition of Jewish choral music into the twentieth century. Owing to the nature of the liturgy, none of his pieces are of

The opening measures of Lewis Lewandowski's *Haleluyaw (Psalm 150)*.

extended length. Still, the best of them stand comparison to the motets of Schubert and the small sacred works of Mendelssohn.

Other Polish composers include Józef Baszny (?–c. 1862), who composed a number of liturgical works while serving as choirmaster at Lvov Cathedral; Josef Brzowski (1803–1888), who contributed *La foi messe* (1862), for male voices and organ, a Requiem (1845), other church music, and a couple of secular cantatas, one honoring Copernicus; Władysław Żeleński (1837–1921), who contributed a number of sacred works for men's chorus; Bohdan Borkowski (1852–1901), whose works include Masses and other liturgical works, a cycle of folk-song arrangements for mixed chorus, *Natarcie jazdy* (A Cavalry Charge, 1886) for mixed chorus, and the large *Hymn for the Feast of the Annunciation of the Blessed Virgin Mary* (*Hymn ne dzień Zwiastowania Najświętszej Marii Panny*, 1894), for tenor solo, mixed chorus, and orchestra.

6

Russia, Scandinavia, and the Baltics

Russian choral music at the beginning of the nineteenth century was dominated by the work of Baldassare Galuppi and Giuseppe Sarti—two Italians who had served the imperial Russian court for almost half a century—as well as Galuppi's prize pupil, Dmitri Stepanovich Bortniansky (1751–1825). During this Italian period a quasi-liturgical choral form, the sacred concerto, became popular. Its structure was derived from symphonic models of three or four movements that varied tempo and tonality. During the liturgy, sacred concertos were performed immediately before communion, usurping the role of the communion hymn—which should have been sung as the clergy took communion out of the congregation's sight—and simultaneously fulfilling the function of religious entertainment: a vehicle to edify the congregation while showcasing the abilities of the composer and choir. The use of sacred concerti in worship had become highly controversial by the second decade of the nineteenth century; but composers loved them because the form provided them freedom to compose substantial works to sacred texts of their own choosing.

Bortniansky was a Ukrainian who had the good fortune to become a member of the imperial court chapel at the age of seven, where he studied with Galuppi. When Galuppi returned to Italy in 1768, Bortniansky went with him in order to continue his musical education. There he composed his first sacred works, which, interestingly, were set to Roman Catholic and Lutheran texts.

Bortniansky returned to Russia in 1779. His ascension to the directorship of the Russian imperial court chapel, in 1801, provided him an opportunity to virtually monopolize Russian choral composition. In 1816 an imperial decree ordered that "everything sung in churches must be in printed form, and must consist either of the personal compositions of the Director of the Imperial Choir [Bortniansky] . . . or the compositions of other famous composers, but the compositions of the latter may only be printed with the approval of Bortniansky." The decree further stipulated that all music sung in worship must "correspond to the sort of singing that is acceptable in churches" (Morosan 1991, l).

Fortunately Bortniansky happened to be a very good composer. Thoroughly trained in the Italian style, he brought a lightness of texture and command of contrapuntal technique to compositions dominated by the principles of Viennese classicism. His new formal structure for the previously strophic or through-composed Cherubic Hymn—a tripartite adagio followed by an allegro with a treble-voice trio in the middle (at mention of the angels)—became the standard used by most composers thereafter.

He excelled in the sacred concerto, composing forty-five of them for unaccompanied mixed chorus (ten for double chorus), even though he had been a leader in the attempt to abolish or at least limit their use in worship. Thirty-five of these were published in a critical edition in 1881, edited by Tchaikovsky, who was particularly fond of the technical and expressive qualities found in *Lord, Make Me to Know My End*. Their popularity has never abated, and even today these concertos make excellent concert fare. According to Vladimir Morosan, the most frequently performed are the Christmas concerto *Glory to God in the Highest* and the Easter concerto *Let God Arise* (Morosan 1991).

Bortniansky was perhaps the first student of the Italians to make polyphonic arrangements of traditional church chants, and he occasionally incorporated elements of Russian and Ukrainian secular music, adapted in such a way as to be "acceptable in churches."

Still, his reliance on a Western European aesthetic established him as the leading composer of the St. Petersburg School (whose works were written in what came to be known as Common European Style), which would dominate Russian church composition for most of the century.

In addition to the sacred concertos, and his seven settings of the Cherubic Hymn (all for mixed chorus), Bortniansky composed ten settings of the Te Deum; a *Liturgy* for three male voices; eight sacred trios for SSA or TTB, of which the best-known is *Let My Prayer Arise, No. 2*; and a large number of other polyphonic hymn settings.

Aleksei Fyodorovich Lvov (1798–1870) became famous in 1834 when he composed the Russian national anthem. He was appointed director of the imperial court chapel in 1837, a post in which he served until 1861. During his tenure he strictly enforced the imperial decree of 1816 and established a nationwide system of education for church musicians. He supervised the compilation of the *Common Book of Music Singing*, a collection of sacred works for four-part mixed chorus, the use of which became mandatory throughout the country. Perhaps his most important contribution was a theoretical work, *Concerning Free or Unsymmetrical Rhythm* (1858), in which he asserted that choral music could be based on the natural rhythm of spoken text. Lvov's music, heavily influenced by German romanticism, is primarily driven by chromatically achieved vertical sonorities. He composed four multimovement sacred concertos as well as several smaller pieces whose sectional nature belies the influence of the concerto form. Seventeen of his forty-eight known works are composed in free rhythm. Among his best-known works are *Of the Mystical Supper*, the miniature sacred concerto *Standing Before the Cross*, and an arrangement of Greek chant, *It Is Truly Fitting, No. 3*, all for mixed chorus.

Mikhail Ivanovich Glinka (1804–1857) is universally recognized as the founder of the Russian national school of secular composition. He worked for the imperial court chapel for a couple of years beginning in 1837, an engagement that resulted in three sacred choral works. The first, a setting of the Cherubic Hymn (1837) for

Chromaticism and free rhythm in Aleksei Fyodorovich Lvov's *Standing Before the Cross*.

mixed chorus, does not follow the formal example of Bortniansky but rather looks to Palestrina for inspiration, albeit with romantic harmonies. The others, *Great Litany*, for male choir, and a setting of the Greek chant version of *Let My Prayer Arise* (both c. 1856), for three soloists and mixed chorus, were composed in a strictly consonant style. Other choral works include *Pleurons, pleurons sur la Russie* (Prologue on the Death of Alexander I and the Accession of Nicholas I, 1826), for mixed chorus, piano, and double bass; *Come di gloria al nome* (c. 1828), for mixed chorus and strings; *Molitva* (Prayer, 1828); *Velik nas Bog* (Our God Is Great, 1837), a polonaise for mixed chorus and orchestra; and a few incidental works.

Gavriil Yakimovich Lomakin (1812–1885) was a serf who as a child sang in the choir of Count Sheremetev. He received his freedom in 1831 when he became conductor of the choir. Although he served in other positions, such as voice teacher in the imperial court chapel, he maintained an association with the Sheremetev Choir until the end of his life, developing a reputation as one of the first and finest conductors of Western European Renaissance and baroque repertoire. He was also a competent composer, producing an *All-night Vigil* based on Znamenny chant (a type of fifteenth-century Russian chant), several secular choruses and folk-song arrangements, and numerous smaller works for the liturgy, including at least nine settings of the Cherubic Hymn.

Anton Rubinstein (1830–1894) was, after Franz Liszt, the greatest piano virtuoso of the century. He also composed in all genres, including choral works both large and small. Although he was a founder of the St. Petersburg Conservatory (1862) and served twice as its director, his musical sensibilities were international. He was not interested in the nationalism of Glinka or, later, the group known as the Five, but rather wanted to instill a love of German classical music in the hearts of his Russian students. He made many concert tours to Western Europe, England, and the United States and was appreciated—at least during his lifetime—as a composer as well as pianist. He thoroughly confused the genres of oratorio and sacred opera, composing many large dramatic works on biblical subjects that, although intended to be staged, were often performed in concert. Among these are *The Tower of Babel*, Op. 80 (1870); *The Maccabees*, (1875); *Paradise Lost*, Op. 54 (1855); *Moses*, Op. 112 (1887); *Christus*, Op. 117 (1888); and several others, all for soloists, mixed chorus, and orchestra. Smaller, nondramatic works include *Three Part-songs*, Op. 61, for male chorus; *Six Part-songs*, Op. 62, for mixed chorus; *The Water-sprite*, Op. 63, for contralto, female chorus, and orchestra; and *Songs and Requiem for Mignon*, Op. 91 (on text by Goethe), for soloists, mixed chorus, and piano. Rubinstein's music was generally forgotten after his death. Concerning his music, Frederick Corder's comment is astute: "Rubinstein's compositions may be considered as the legitimate outcome of Mendelssohn; they contain a fine broad vein of melody supported by harmony and sound, thorough technical skill; but they show also the fatal gift of fluency and the consequent lack of self-criticism and self-constraint" (Grove 1878, 4:296).

Konstantin Karl Albrecht (1836–1893) was the eldest son of the German conductor Karl Albrecht (1807–1863), who settled in Russia in 1838. Though a cellist, Konstantin Albrecht was particularly interested in choral music and singing. He founded the Moscow Choral Society in 1878 and wrote a book on choral singing that had some influence on the development of choral music in Russia.

Pyotr Il'yich Tchaikovsky (1840–1893) was one of the most prominent symphonic composers of the century. Considering his international stature, it is perhaps surprising that his substantial body of choral music remains virtually unknown in the West, but there are certainly reasons for this. His cantatas tend to be occasional pieces, honoring the birthday of a famous singer or the fiftieth anniversary of the imperial law school. In one case, the cantata *To Joy* (1865, on text by Schiller, translated by K. S. Aksakov), for soloists, mixed chorus, and orchestra, Tchaikovsky's effort does not fare well when compared to Beethoven's famous setting of the same text. Also, the issue of language has loomed over many Western European and American choirs, although this has become less of a problem in recent years as choristers and choral conductors familiarize themselves with multicultural world-music repertoire and eagerly learn to sing in languages that, only a few years ago, they may not even have known existed. In any case, Tchaikovsky's best-known choral piece, the charming "A Legend" (1889), as well as the "Our Father" (1884–85), both for unaccompanied mixed chorus, were introduced to American audiences by the composer during his famous appearances as guest conductor for the opening of New York's Carnegie Hall in 1992 and have long been available in translation.

Although he composed several secular pieces for male, female, and mixed choir, Tchaikovsky's greatest achievements in the choral genre are related to his involvement in church music. His settings of the two primary liturgical services of the Russian Orthodox church, the *Liturgy of St. John Chrysostom*, Op. 41 (1878), and the *All-night Vigil*, Op. 52 (1881–82), both for unaccompanied mixed chorus, are masterpieces of their kind. In these works the composer established, as Vladimir Morosan pointed out, "two fundamental stylistic directions followed by composers after him—free composition on the one hand (as in his *Liturgy*), and the polyphonization of traditional liturgical chants on the other (as in his *Vigil*)" (Morosan 1996, lxxxiii). He also edited the sacred works of Bortniansky, compiled *A Concise Textbook of Harmony, Intended to Facilitate the Reading of Sacred Musical Works in*

Russia, and, through his position on the supervisory council of the Moscow Synodal School of Church Singing, obtained important positions for his students Vasily Orlov and Alexander Kastalsky, a move that ensured the continued development of Russian church music. Because his publisher had sidestepped the imperial court chapel, both the *Liturgy* and the *Vigil* were banned from performance in worship for twenty years. However, both works enjoyed a healthy popularity in Russian concert halls during the intervening years, firmly establishing their styles in the minds and ears of younger composers. Tchaikovsky composed additional settings of liturgical texts for unaccompanied mixed chorus in 1884–85,

The opening measures of Pyotr Il'yich Tchaikovsky's "Dostóyno yest," with Protestant English text.

published together as *Nine Sacred Choruses*. In 1887 he wrote his last sacred work, a setting of the Easter hymn *The Angel Cried*. All of these, including individual movements of the *Liturgy* and *Vigil*, are fine additions to the concert repertoire and represent the best work of a master who was motivated to reestablish the primacy of traditional elements in Russian church music without allowing its growth to stagnate though the prohibition of everything new. For example, Tchaikovsky was quite comfortable with most aspects of the Common European Style, including the use of imitative counterpoint. However, he chafed at the inclusion of dominant seventh chords, which he believed did not fit into the modal aesthetic of the Russian liturgy (see Morosan 1996 for more on Tchaikovsky's reasons for his intense involvement with sacred music).

In addition to "Our Father" (from *Nine Sacred Choruses*) and "A Legend," other works that have long been available in translation—and thus popular outside of Russia—include two movements from the *St. John Chrysostom Liturgy*, "The Cherubic Hymn" and the Marian hymn "Dostóyno yest" (It Is Truly Fitting), which was outfitted with an English Protestant text early in the twentieth century and published in the United States by Oliver Ditson.

Sergey Ivanovich Taneyev (1856–1915) was Tchaikovsky's student, critic, and close friend. A brilliant pianist and teacher, he premiered Tchaikovsky's famous First Piano Concerto and became one of the most distinguished pianists and teachers in Russia at the end of the century. As a composer he was devoted to Bach and was therefore part of neither the international circle of composers, as represented by Rubinstein and Tchaikovsky, nor the nationalists, as represented by the Five. Appreciation for his compositions increased during the last quarter of the twentieth century, particularly the two great cantatas *John of Damascus*, Op. 1 (1884, on text by A. K. Tolstoy), and *At the Reading of a Psalm*, Op. 36 (1914, on text by Khomiakov). Taneyev was simply not interested in liturgical music. His other choral works, mostly for unaccompanied mixed chorus, set texts by Tyutchev, Khomiakov, Polonsky, and K. Balmont. The last of his cycle of sixteen pieces for men's choir, Op. 35

(1914), includes a solo violin (for brief discussion of Taneyev's style see Strimple 2002, 130).

Anton Stepanovich Arensky (1861–1906) studied with Rimsky-Korsakov and was influenced by Tchaikovsky. A choral conductor, he directed the Russian Choral Society for several years (1888–95), served on the council of the Synodal School of Church Music in Moscow, and eventually, on the recommendation of Balakirev, became director of the imperial court chapel in St. Petersburg, a post he held until his retirement in 1901. Except for his occasional exploitation of unusual meters, his music is unremarkable. Some of it, though, is attractive, especially the small choral pieces. Among his works are *Anchar*, Op. 14, for unaccompanied mixed chorus on text by Pushkin (n.d.); *Two Choruses*, Op. 31, for male chorus; *Four Sacred Choruses from the Liturgy of St. John Chrysostom*, Op. 40, for unaccompanied mixed chorus (n.d.); the cantata *The Fountain of Bakhchisaray*, Op. 46, for soloists, mixed chorus, and orchestra (1899; after Pushkin); and eight pieces for female chorus and piano entitled *Tsvetnik* Op. 69 (The Bed of Flowers, n.d.).

The Five

Mily Alekseyivich Balakirev (1836–1910) was opposed to foreign influences permeating Russian music: Common European Style in church music and German romanticism in secular music. Shortly after the middle of the century he organized a small group of like-minded composers whose artistic interests were guided by nationalism. This group became known as the Five and, in addition to Balakirev, included Alexander Borodin (1833–1887), César Antonovich Cui (1835–1918), Modest Mussorgsky (1839–1881), and Nikolai Rimsky-Korsakov (1844–1908).

Balakirev founded, with Lomakin, the Free Music School in St. Petersburg in 1862. At the school he trained the choir and conducted the choral and orchestral concerts. From 1883 to1894 he served as administrator of the imperial court chapel. Primarily a composer of instrumental music, he still contributed to the choral repertoire, including nine sacred works. Some of these are chant arrangements, including a lovely setting of the Kievan Chant from the Liturgy of Great and Holy Saturday, *Let All Mortal Flesh Keep Silence*, for mixed chorus. He also composed several part-songs for unaccompanied mixed chorus and choral arrangements of songs and instrumental works.

Alexander Borodin was a chemist whose avocation was composition. Although many of his large works were left incomplete (perhaps because he viewed composition as a hobby), he nevertheless made an impact on Russian music in the latter part of the century. His choral output was limited to choruses in his opera *Prince Igor* and two small four-part men's choruses on his own texts, *Serenade of Four Cavaliers to One Lady* (c. 1870) and *Song of the Dark Forest* (1868, originally a song for solo voice that was arranged by Aleksandr Glazunov for male voices and piano or orchestra). The choruses from *Prince Igor* (1869–87, left unfinished; completed by Rimsky-Korsakov and Glazunov, 1889) are substantial and often performed in concerts. These include the attractive and justly famous "Polovtsian Dances" for mixed chorus (with incidental male solo) and orchestra, which clearly demonstrate Borodin's considerable abilities as a choral composer. A last work is the curious Requiem (1877), a six-minute composition for tenor solo, men's chorus, and piano (or orchestra). Borodin had composed a children's polka for piano four-hands, utilizing the universally known "Chopsticks" (known in Russia as "Tati-tati") as an ostinato for the second piano. Several of his friends, including Rimsky-Korsakov, then wrote pieces based on "Chopsticks," prompting Borodin to put it to further use as an ostinato background for a setting of the Introit ("Requiem aeternam") of the Catholic *Missa pro defunctis*. It was orchestrated by Leopold Stokowski.

César Cui was the son of a French officer who, during the retreat of 1812, made it only as far as Poland, where he married a Lithuanian woman. He spent the rest of his life in Vilnius, teaching French. Cui, educated as a military engineer, was largely self-taught as a musician. Still, he proved to be a gifted and able music critic, a sphere in which he made his greatest contributions. Cui was one of the first to fall under the nationalistic spell cast by Balakirev, although native Russian elements are difficult to find in his own music. His lyrical style is marked by a refined elegance well suited to small, intimate forms, and it is in these that he excelled as a choral composer. Cui's name, easily recognizable as one of the Five, has only in recent years begun to appear on programs of enterprising conductors outside of Russia. Among his works are *Mystic Chorus*, Op. 28 (1885), for unaccompanied women's chorus; *Five Choruses*, Op. 46 (on text by Rimsky-Korsakov), for mixed chorus; *Two Choruses*, Op. 58, for unaccompanied male voices; and *Les oiseaux d'Argenteau*, for children's chorus.

Modest Mussorgsky was probably the greatest of the Five and was certainly the most original. Plagued throughout his adult life by emotional problems and alcoholism, he died of delirium tremens a few days after a very successful performance of his *The Destruction of Sennacherib* (1867, revised 1874, on text by Byron), for mixed chorus and orchestra. Many of his works were left in sketch form and completed by Rimsky-Korsakov, Cui, and others who, unfortunately, tended to "correct" his harsh, unapologetic harmonies (during the twentieth century there were numerous efforts by Paul Lamm, Boris Vladimirovich Asafiev, and others to rectify this situation with new editions faithful to the composer's uncorrupted manuscripts). Mussorgsky's music is extremely visceral. The great choral scenes from his opera *Boris Godunov* are frequently performed in concert. His other choral works are not well-known, but are certainly worthy of occasional performance. In addition to *The Destruction of Sennacherib*, they include *Shamil's March* (1859), for soloists, chorus, and orchestra; *Jesus Nevin* (Joshua, 1874–77), for contralto and bass soloists, mixed chorus, and piano; *Three Vocalises* (1880), for unaccompanied women's chorus; and *Five Russian Folk Songs* (1880, fifth song left incomplete), for four-part male chorus.

Nikolai Rimsky-Korsakov (1844–1908) was a major figure in late nineteenth-century Russian music. A leading exponent of new compositional techniques, a professor at the St. Petersburg Conservatory, and from 1883 to 1893 a composer at the imperial court chapel, he was a devoted friend and colleague to those in his

Above and opposite: Climactic moment in Nikolai Rimsky-Korsakov's
"Procession of the Nobles."

circle. He completed and/or orchestrated major works of Borodin and Mussorgsky after their deaths. He counted Taneyev and Igor Stravinsky among his pupils. Although his choral music has never been popular outside of Russia, a ceremonial chorus from the opera *Mlada*, "Procession of the Nobles" (1889–90), for mixed chorus and orchestra, was rejuvenated when it was included in John Rutter's fine collection of opera choruses, which appeared in 1995.

Rimsky-Korsakov's other choral works include part-songs, folk-song arrangements, occasional cantatas, and a substantial body of sacred works. His sacred choral music was written for the imperial court chapel during the early years of his tenure there. Balakirev, who was administrator of the chapel at the time, thoroughly disliked it and apparently managed to block both performances and publication. But the music, which was simply too modern for the prevailing church tastes at the time, does not deserve continued neglect. Rimsky's sacred works—some forty compositions—include polyphonic chant arrangements, sacred concertos such as *We Praise Thee, O God*, for double mixed chorus, which the composer thought was "better than anything by Bortniansky" (Rakhmanova 1999, xxxvii), and other freely composed pieces such as *The Lord's Prayer*, perhaps his most frequently encountered choral piece.

Other Russian composers include Archimandrite Feofan (c. 1785–1852), whose twenty-five surviving works—several of which remain standard repertoire in Russian churches—make up only a small fraction of his output; Alexander Alexandrovich Alyabyev (1787–1851), who wrote numerous small choral works that have been overshadowed by his operas and other stage music; P. Makarov (dates unknown, active in the first half of the century), whose *Angel vopiyáshe* (The Angel Cried Out, n.d.), for three soloists (SSA) and mixed choir, is still standard repertoire in Russian churches; Mikhail Aleksandrovich Vinogradov (1809–1888), whose thirty-seven known works—composed in a simple, straightforward, and unadorned style—were standard repertoire in Russian churches throughout the nineteenth and twentieth centuries; Vasily Starorussky (1818–1871), a conductor of the Novgorad Theological Seminary Choir (and other choirs as well) who contributed *Ot yúnosti moyeyá* (From My Youth) and other works that became popular with church choirs, even though they failed to meet the approval of the imperial court chapel censor; I. S. Dvoretsy (dates unknown; active in the middle of the century), whose *Svéte tíhiy* (Gladsome Light) is standard repertoire in Russian churches; Jacob Bachmann (dates unknown, active in the last half of the century), whose collection of Jewish liturgical pieces for solo voice and mixed chorus, *Shirat Jacob*, was published in Moscow in 1884; Nikolai Yakovlevich Afanas'yev (1821–1898), who composed a cantata, *Pir Petra Velikova* (The Feast of Peter the Great, 1860), for soloists, mixed chorus, and orchestra, as well as small choral pieces, including an anthology of folk-song arrangements for mixed chorus (1866) that became quite popular; Anatol Liadov (1855–1914), a brilliant composer of small piano pieces, whose few choral works include *Slava*, Op. 47, for women's chorus, two harps, and two pianos (each four-hands), and *Songs*, Op. 50, for women's chorus and piano; and Georgy Catoire (1861–1926), a minor composer of the Moscow school and an important teacher (numbering Dmitri Kabalevsky among his pupils), who composed part-songs and at least one cantata as well as making great contributions to the study of music theory in Russia.

The Society for Jewish Folk Music (the Petersburg Group) preserved, arranged, and edited much Yiddish choral music, from the Baltic countries as well as Russia, under the direction of the Russian Ethnological Society. The leading editor and arranger was Joel Engel (1868–1927).

Denmark

Andreas Peter Berggreen (1801–1880) was a folklorist, organist, educator, and self-taught composer who wrote several cantatas for chorus and orchestra, published a large collection of folk songs, and composed numerous part-songs and hymn tunes, some of which are still used in Denmark. His importance lies in the influence he was able to exert on the quality of singing in Danish churches and schools, the impact his folk-song collection had on public awareness of Danish musical traditions, and the higher international profile of Danish music achieved through the success of his student Niels Gade.

The distinguished organist and composer Johann Peter Emilius Hartmann (1805–1900) was the son of the composer, choral conductor, organist, and violinist August Wilhelm Hartmann (1775–1850). The younger Hartmann became renowned throughout Europe and was held in particularly high regard by Robert Schumann as a leader in the Danish romantic movement. With his son-in-law, Niels Gade, Hartmann founded the Copenhagen Conservatory in 1866. He composed in all genres, his numerous cantatas—often composed for university or governmental events—and part-songs comprising only a small percentage of his catalog.

Niels Gade (1817–1890) was the preeminent Danish composer of the nineteenth century. With his father-in-law, J. P. E. Hartmann, Gade brought Danish music squarely into the romantic age. A brilliant conductor, he served as Mendelssohn's assistant

in Leipzig and was named director of the Gewandhaus Orchestra after Mendelssohn's death in 1847. He returned to Copenhagen the following year, becoming director of the Copenhagen
Musical Society in 1850, in which capacity he conducted many
choral and orchestra concerts. Among these were the first Danish performances of Bach's *St. Matthew Passion* and Beethoven's
Ninth Symphony. As a composer Gade excelled in large forms,
primarily the symphony. Between 1846 and 1889, however, he
composed at least sixteen cantatas for chorus and orchestra, several of them as memorials to friends or famous Danish person-
ages. He was fond of the male choir, composing a set of *Five
Songs*, Op. 33, for unaccompanied male voices; *Choruses*, Op. 26
(1853), for male voices and orchestra; and a late cantata based
on a Norse legend, *Den Bergtagne*, Op. 52 (The MountainThrall,
1873), for solo voices, male chorus, and orchestra. Several of his
works, including the cantata *Elverskud*, Op. 30 (The Elf-king's
Daughter, 1853), for solo voices, mixed chorus, and orchestra,
are the first to incorporate Danish nationalistic elements into
an otherwise Germanic musical language. His last cantata, *Der
Strom*, Op. 64 (after Goethe's "Mahomet"), adds a solo piano to
the otherwise normal configuration of solo voices, mixed chorus, and orchestra.

Others Danish composers include Christian Barnekow
(1837–1913), an authority on Danish church music and editor of
the Danish hymnal (1878, with later supplemental editions), who
contributed several cantatas, part-songs, and hymn tunes; and
Victor Bendix (1851–1921), a prominent conductor and composer
whose choral works, including *Psalm 33*, Op. 7 (1874), for mixed
chorus and orchestra, reflect an inconsistent style influenced by
Gade, Liszt, and Wagner.

Finland

The first Finnish composer to impact choral music was the early
nationalist Bernhard Henrik Crusell (1775–1838), who contributed

a set of thirty-seven part-songs for four-part mixed chorus called *Den lilla slavinnan* (The Little Slave Girl), published in Stockholm in 1824.

The German-born Frederik Pacius (1809–1891), generally acknowledged as the Father of Finnish music, also contributed several part-songs as well as a fine setting of J. Runeberg's poem in Swedish, *Vårt land* (1843), which became the Finnish national anthem. His style is based on the early German romantic composers, especially Mendelssohn.

The most important Finnish composer in history is Jean Sibelius (1865–1957). Although his impact would be in the twentieth century, his first choral works were composed in the last decade of the nineteenth. These include the very large symphonic poem *Kullervo*, Op. 7 (1892), for soprano, baritone, and male chorus; *Rakastava*, Op. 14 (The Lover, 1893), for unaccompanied male chorus; and *Laulu Lemminkäiselle*, Op. 31, No. 1 (A Song for Lemminkäinen, 1900), for male chorus and orchestra.

Iceland

A primary exponent of choral music in Iceland was Sveinbjörn Sveinbjörnsson (1847–1927), who became a composer after pursuing theological studies. Eventually settling in Scotland, he composed many pieces for chorus and a hymn (1874) that later became the Icelandic national anthem.

Norway

In the first half of the century several composers who were inspired by Norwegian folk music became prominent. Among the leaders of this group was Halfdan Kjerulf (1815–1868), who excelled in small forms. A great influence on Edvard Grieg, he composed over forty part-songs for male chorus and made many choral arrangements of solo songs and Norwegian folk songs.

Johan Diderik Behrens (1820–1890) was a seminal figure in Norwegian choral music and was especially important in the development of male choirs. In 1846 he cofounded a student choral society at the Christiania Latinskole and thereafter founded additional male-voice singing societies for merchants (1847) and artisans (1848). He was instrumental in the establishment of several song festivals, including the Norwegian Choral Festival, first held in Christiania in 1849. Behrens was not a composer himself, but his editions and arrangements are the foundation of the Norwegian repertoire for male voices. Particularly important are the *Samling af flerstemmige mandssange*, published from 1845 to 1885 and containing some five hundred works for male voices, including new pieces by prominent Norwegian composers as well as folk-song arrangements and other pieces.

Edvard Grieg (1843–1907) was certainly the most celebrated Norwegian composer of the century. He studied in Copenhagen with Gade and also in Leipzig, where he learned all he wanted to know about German romanticism. On returning to Norway he and Rikard Nordraak formed the Euterpe Society, which sought to reduce German influences by promoting Scandinavian nationalism in music. Grieg composed a small but significant quantity of choral music, including *At a Southern Convent's Gate*, Op. 20 (1871, on text by Bjørnson), for solo voice, women's choir and orchestra; *Two Songs from "Sigurd Jorsalfar,"* Op. 22 (1870, on text by Bjørnson), for baritone, male chorus, and orchestra; *Album*, Op. 30 (1877), for male chorus; *Landsighting*, Op. 31 (1872, on traditional text), for male chorus and orchestra; *Scenes from "Olav Trygvason,"* Op. 50 (1873, revised 1889, on text by Bjørnson); *Ave maris stella* (c. 1899), for unaccompanied mixed chorus; and *Four Psalms*, Op. 74 (1906), for unaccompanied mixed chorus. One of his orchestral masterpieces also requires mixed chorus: the *Incidental Music to "Peer Gynt"* (1876, on text by Ibsen).

Other Norwegian composers included Martin Andreas Udbye (1820–1889), who composed a number of part-songs; Johan Svendsen (1840–1911), who contributed *Two Part-songs for Men's Voices*, Op. 2 (1865), as well as some cantatas; Rikard Nordraak

(1842–1866), a friend of Grieg's, who composed numerous part-songs (several to texts by his cousin, Bjørnstjerne Bjørnson), including the famous "Ja, vi elsker dette landet" for unaccompanied male chorus, which later became the Norwegian national anthem; and Christian Sinding (1856–1941), who composed part-songs and cantatas.

Sweden

The most important Swedish composer of the century was Franz Berwald (1796–1868), who was not only active as a composer, but also as a violinist, teacher, and successful businessman. His music was revived in the twentieth century, primarily through interest in his four symphonies. Although his music is shaped somewhat by the stylistic characteristics of older German contemporaries, it is permeated by a harmonic audacity not found in works by other composers of his generation. He helped edit the Swedish hymnal and composed occasional and commemorative cantatas. Some of his works are with full orchestra, such as the *Chorale* (1867), for mixed chorus; and *Apoteus* (1864), for soloists and male choir. A large number are with wind orchestra, including *Gustav Adolph the Great's Victory and Death at Lützen* (1845, on text by G. Ingelman), for soloists, mixed choir, and organ; *Larghetto, Allegro con Spirito* (no date, textless), for mixed chorus; and *Nordiska fantasibilder* (1846), for soloists, male chorus, and organ.

Carl Jonas Love Almqvist (1793–1866) was a largely self-taught composer. Primarily known for his literary achievements as well as for the various scandals subsequent to the publication and forced withdrawal of his book attacking the doctrine of free will and his embrace of free love and universal suffrage, he was forced to flee Sweden in 1851 after murder charges were brought against him. Nevertheless, his *Songes* (c. 1830), a series of some fifty small pieces on his own texts, for one to four unaccompanied voices, are considered miniature masterpieces. Designed to accompany tableaux vivants, their naiveté and direct expression are reminiscent of folk music. Later additions of piano accompaniments, by other composers, do nothing to enhance their charm.

As a conductor Jacob Axel Josephson (1818–1880) made Uppsala University a center of musical activity in Sweden. As a composer he was influenced by Mendelssohn. He was adept at composition for male chorus (which ensemble he conducted at the university), and several of the part-songs he wrote for men's voices are still widely used, among them *Stjänklart* and *Sjung, sjung, du underbara sång.* He also composed in larger forms, including the cantatas *Islossningen* and *Quando corpus,* both for mixed chorus and orchestra.

Erik Akerberg (1860–1938) was an important organist and choral conductor who also composed a significant amount of choral music. He served as organist at a synagogue in Stockholm from 1890 to 1928 and conducted a number of fine choirs, including the Bellamnska Sallskapet, which he founded in 1891. Of particular interest are the large choral ballads *Prinsessan och Svennen,* for soloists, chorus, and orchestra (1887); and *Der barde,* for soloists, male chorus, and orchestra (1895), which prominently display a style obviously reminiscent of Swedish folk music.

Wilhelm Stenhammar (1871–1927) was deeply influenced by the examples of Liszt and Wagner early in his career. But he later learned classical form and developed the ability to incorporate folk melodies into his otherwise romantic harmonic language. Stenhammar composed in all genres and excelled in choral music. Although his best work did not appear until the new century (see Strimple 2002, 156), he still produced several very worthy pieces in the last decade or so of the nineteenth century. Among them are *I rosengård* (1888–89), for soloists, mixed chorus, and orchestra; and *Three Choral Ballads* (c. 1890, on text by J. P. Jacobson), for unaccompanied mixed chorus.

Others include Olof Ahlstroem (1756–1835), a composer and music publisher who wrote two cantatas and the *Choralbok* (1832); Eric Gustav Geijer (1783–1847), who contributed various choral works; Eduard Brendler (1800–1831), whose *I de höjda toner skaller* (In the Heights the Tone Resounds, 1830), for double mixed chorus, and melodramas *Spastaras död* (1830) and *Edmund och Clara*

(1831), both for mixed chorus and orchestra, remained popular in Stockholm after his death; Peter Conrad Boman (1804–1861), an important historian and music critic, who published a cantata and several small choruses; Otto Lindblad (1809–1864), an esteemed choral conductor who composed a number of fine part-songs for male choir; Gunnar Wennerberg (1817–1901), who excelled in the composition of small pieces for men's chorus and left a number of larger choral works unfinished; Ivar Hallström (1826–1901) and Andreas Hallen (1846–1925), opera composers who also wrote some cantatas; and Johan August Söderman (1832–1876) and Emil Sjögren (1853–1918), each of whom composed a variety of choral pieces.

The Baltics

Choral music in the Baltics during the nineteenth century is bound together with the great awakening of nationalism that occurred in this region somewhat later than in other parts of Europe. In Lithuania, Latvia, and Estonia it began only after 1850 and was then inextricably associated with migration from rural areas to the cities (prior to this, group singing of folk songs was very popular, the old runic songs being in a traditional meter called *regivärss*, common to all Baltic peoples).

Composers who emerged at this time in Latvia were Kārlis Baumanis (1835–1905), Ādams Ore (1855–1927), Andrejs Jurjāns (1856–1922), Jānis Straume (1861–1929), and Jāzeps Vītols (1863–1948).

Kārlis Baumanis composed a simple, homophonic piece to his own words, *Dievs, svētī Latviju* (God Bless Latvia), for the opening of the first national song festival in 1873. It immediately became the unofficial Latvian national anthem, even though it was illegal to say the word "Latvia" during the Czarist Russian regime (later it became the official Latvian national anthem). This was the beginning of a steady stream of part-songs, including the darkly powerful *How the Daugava Moans* (1874, on text by Auseklis), for

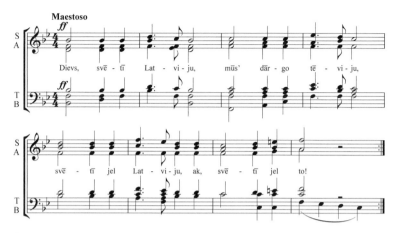

Opening measures of Kārlis Baumanis's *Dievs, svētī Latviju*.

unaccompanied men's choir. This piece, whose text celebrates Baltic mythology, became so popular that a variety of other texts were sung to its music during the 1905 Revolution.

Ādams Ore was influenced by Mendelssohn and other Germans. Primarily known as a brilliant organist, he composed many small choral pieces inspired by folk music, as well as choral arrangements of folk songs.

Andrejs Jurjāns is known as the father of Latvian orchestral music. His *Latvian Folk Music Material* (six volumes, 1894–1926) was the first attempt at a scholarly collection of Latvian folk song. In addition to his folk-song arrangements, he composed over thirty part-songs.

Jānis Straume was the first great Latvian choral conductor. Along with his conducting work, he also wrote many articles on musical subjects and composed a few significant small choral pieces, a good example being *Pie Baltijas jūras* (By the Baltic Sea, on text by the composer), for unaccompanied mixed chorus.

The outstanding choral composers in Lithuania at this time were Juozas Naujalis (1869–1934) and Mikolajus Čiurlionis (1875–1911). The leading figure in Estonia was Rudolf Tobias (1873–1918). Like their Latvian counterparts, all of these men would greatly influence choral music in the next century. Naujalis was somewhat unusual among this generation of Baltic composers because of his interest in church music. Not only did he contribute to the part-song repertoire, but he also composed a number of Masses and other liturgical works. Čiurlionis was an exceptional abstract expressionist painter as well as a composer. Like everyone else in the region, he wrote part-songs and folk-song arrangements. But, taking a page from Naujalis's book, he also composed one of the largest choral works produced in the Baltics up to that time: *De profundis* (1899–1900), for chorus and orchestra. Rudolf Tobias, a student of Rimsky-Korsakov, became an important choral conductor in St. Petersburg and Tartu. As a composer he was quite comfortable in large forms and wrote the first Estonian cantata, *Johannes Damascenus* (1897), for soloists, mixed chorus, and orchestra (see Strimple 2002, 163–71, for more discussion of Baltic composers at century's end).

As in Poland, Eastern Germany, and Russia, Jewish communities in the Baltic countries were very strong, especially in Latvia and Lithuania. Virtually all the ghettos and shtetls had social and educational organizations with group singing activities. Although much of the singing was in Yiddish, there were also organizations (known as Rak Ivrat) at the very end of the century that promoted Hebrew; and new Hebrew songs, created accordingly were sung by coed children's and youth choirs. Unlike Germany, Austria, the Ukraine, and France, where Lewandowski, Sulzer, David Nowakowsky, and Samuel Naumberg were composing new liturgical music, no one stepped to the fore in the Baltic countries until the twentieth century.

7

The Iberian Peninsula and Italy

The Roman Catholic church had traditionally controlled choral music in Portugal and Spain. Secular organizations did not develop in Spain until very late in the century and would not begin in Portugal until 1910. In this environment a lot of sacred choral music was composed, either by church musicians or by famous composers active in the Iberian Peninsula's flourishing opera scene.

The situation was similar in Italy, where many artisan composers labored for the church, and opera composers—who occasionally wrote liturgical works for special occasions—often included prominent choral scenes in their theatrical works; but otherwise secular choral activity was virtually nonexistent. Further, oratorio steadily decreased in popularity throughout the century, virtually disappearing by century's end.

Portugal

João Domingos Bomtempo (1755–1842) spent much of his early professional career outside Portugal, primarily in London and Paris. In 1822 he founded the Philharmonic Society in Lisbon, and he was named principal of the National Conservatory shortly after its founding in 1835. In this position, which he kept until his death, he played a primary role in the reform of Portuguese music. Primarily a pianist, he nevertheless composed a sizable amount of choral music. His choral works are mostly on sacred texts, with the exception of two works inspired by the Napoleonic Wars: *Hymno lusitano* (1811), for soloists, mixed chorus, and orchestra (also known as *La virtù trionfante*, and also arranged for piano four-hands as *March of Lord Wellington*); and the cantata *A paz da Europa* (1814), for four soloists, mixed chorus, and orchestra (also known as *O annuncio da paz*). Other works include a Requiem (1819), for four soloists, mixed chorus, and orchestra; a *Miserere* (n.d.), for four soloists, mixed chorus, and strings; *Libera me* (1835), for mixed chorus and orchestra; and other settings of Latin liturgical texts.

Inácio António de Almeida (1760–1825) served as choirmaster at the collegiate church in Guimaraes and may also have worked at Braga Cathedral. His extant works, of which there is some question of authenticity (Robert Stevenson, "Inácio António de Almeida," in Sadie 1980, 1:286), include pieces for Christmas matins (SSB and piano) and two settings of the Miserere, which together provide excellent examples of the low standard of Portuguese church music in the early decades of the nineteenth century.

João José Baldi (1770–1816) was one of the finest Portuguese composers at the beginning of the nineteenth century. Devoting himself almost exclusively to church music, he composed in the Italian style that dominated Portuguese music at that time. His most celebrated Mass was written in honor of the Count de Borba in 1803. Other works (all for mixed chorus and orchestra) include two *Magnificat*s, two Te Deums, several vesper psalms, and settings of responsories for four matins services (for the feasts of St. Michael, Sacred Heart, Christmas, and the Immaculate Conception).

Joaquim Casimiro Júnior (1808–1862), like several other Spanish and Portuguese composers of this period, managed to work well in both the theatrical and the ecclesiastical worlds. He was, however, set apart from his Portuguese contemporaries by his mastery of contrapuntal technique, which he was particularly fond of displaying in his sacred compositions. The earliest public mention of him (1829) occurs in reference to several large sacred choral works composed in honor of the king. He composed over two hundred theatrical works, culminating in incidental music (for mixed chorus and orchestra) for a biblical drama by José Romano called *Sansão, ou A destrucião dos Philisteus* (Samson, or the Destruction of the Philistines, 1855). He composed ninety-seven liturgical works, of which ten are Masses: eight for mixed chorus and orchestra, and two for unaccompanied mixed chorus.

Others include António Leal Moreira (1750–1819), who composed church music in Italian sacred style and an Italian oratorio after joining the Brotherhood of Saint Caecilia in 1777; and Marcos António Portugal (1762–1830), an internationally known opera composer who, along with his brother, Simão da Ascenção, composed a large number of liturgical works.

Spain

Carlos Baguer (1768–1808) spent most of his brief career as organist at the cathedral in Barcelona, where he was greatly admired. His choral compositions include Masses, motets, and other liturgical works, as well as a cycle of seven oratorios (*dramos sacros*) for soloists, chorus, and orchestra: *La adoration del niño Dios por los ángeles y pastores* (1805), *La resurrección de Lázaro* (1806), *El regreso á Barcelona su patria de Dr. Josef Oriol* (1807), *La partida del hijo pródigo* (1807), *El regreso del hijo pródigo* (1807), *Job* (1808), and *La muerte de Abel* (n.d.). His style was greatly influenced by Italian opera: the choral writing is almost always homophonic, and the solo arias are melodious and frequently florid.

Jaime Balius y Vila (d. 1822) served as *maestro di capilla* in Córdoba for a good part of his career. One of the leading Spanish composers of his era, he focused on church music, writing Masses, motets, and other liturgical works. Like Carlos Baguer, he eschewed the use of contrapuntal techniques in favor of a homophonic style dominated by melody.

Francisco Andrevi y Castellar (1786–1853) began his career as a choirmaster in 1808, gradually moving to more and more important positions, including successive appointments at the cathedrals

of Valencia and Seville, and in 1831 was named choirmaster of the
royal chapel in Madrid. In 1836 he moved to France, becoming
choirmaster at the cathedral at Bordeaux. After his retirement in
1845, he remained in France for a while but eventually returned to
Barcelona, where he worked at the parish church of La Merced
until his death. Unlike many church choirmaster-composers, a
sizable number of Andrevi's sacred choral works were published
(all in Paris), including a Mass, three settings of the *Stabat mater*,
and several motets. Unpublished works include a couple of oratorios, at least eleven Masses, a Requiem, a Te Deum, several psalm
settings, additional motets, and other works for various Roman
Catholic services.

Ramón Carnicer (1789–1855) was a prominent composer known
primarily for his theatrical works. Nevertheless, his sacred choral
music was so highly regarded that the Spanish King Ferdinand
VII commissioned a Requiem (1829) for his third wife. Other important works include a second Requiem (1842), a *Tantum ergo*
(n.d.), a *Tota pulchra* (1814), and a *Missa solemnis* (1828). All of these
are for mixed chorus and orchestra.

Mateo Pérez de Albéniz (1755–1831) was born in the Basque region and worked all of his life in northern Spain, mostly as choirmaster at St. Maria la Redondo in San Sebastián. He composed
many Masses, vespers, motets, and other sacred works that were
very popular during his lifetime and was largely responsible for
introducing Spanish music students to the works of Haydn and
Mozart.

Joaquin Cassadó (1867–1926) was born and died in Barcelona.
Maestro de cappilla at Nuestra Señora de la Merced and organist at
San José (both in Barcelona), he composed a considerable amount
of sacred choral music. Perhaps his greatest achievement, though,
was the establishment in 1890 of the Capilla Catalàna. In 1891 the
opera composer Amadeo Vives (1871–1932) and the choral conductor Luis Millet (1867–1941) followed Cassadó's lead and founded
a choral society in Barcelona called Orfeó Català. At the same
time the music critic, painter, and folklorist Francisco Alió y Brea
(1862–1908) initiated the revival of Catalan folk music. These devel-

opments helped establish vocal repertoire in the Catalan language, furthered the cause of Catalan choral music, and provided, for the first time, opportunities for choral singing outside the church.

Other Spanish composers include Juan Bros y Bertomeu (1776–1852), one of the forgotten masters of Spanish church music, who composed a considerable amount of liturgical music for churches in León and Oviedo; Cosme Damián José de Benito (1829–1888), who composed over two hundred liturgical choral works of all kinds as *maestro de capilla* at El Escorial, and whose choir there was dissolved in 1870 because of financial constraints; Manuel Fernández Caballero (1835–1906), an important composer of zarzuelas, who also contributed several Masses and other church works; Rafael Aceves y Lozano (1837–1876), also a composer of zarzuelas, who contributed to the choral repertoire of the Roman Catholic church, including a *Stabat mater* that was considered important in its day; Enrique Barrera Gómez (1844–1922), one of the finest Spanish composers of the late nineteenth century, who composed many liturgical works for Burgos Cathedral; Tomás Bretón (1850–1923), who contributed the oratorio *El apocalipsis* (1882), for soloists, chorus, and orchestra; and Antonio Nicolau (1858–1933), a Catalan composer and music educator whose choral pieces exhibit a particularly fine understanding of the voice.

Italy

Niccolò Antonio Zingarelli (1752–1837) held important positions in Milan, Rome, and Naples and was internationally famous as a teacher and composer. He composed seven oratorios, some of the later of which were staged, and a large setting of the twelfth chapter of Isaiah, *Canticao d'Isaiah profeta* (1829, for the Birmingham Festival), for soloists, mixed chorus, and orchestra. Among his other works are a large number of Masses and two Requiems, one of which was composed for his own funeral.

Luigi Cherubini (1760–1842) was an important contemporary of Beethoven and Schubert. His opera *Les deux journées* (1800) directly influenced Beethoven's *Fidelio*, and in fact Beethoven considered Cherubini his most important contemporary. Like the Bohemian Antonín Rejcha, Cherubini spent most of his career in Paris, was subject to the whims of French politics during the Revolution and Napoleonic age, and, as professor at the conservatory, had a profound impact on the next generation of French composers. His creative activity falls neatly into three periods, the first devoted to sacred choral music and Italian opera, the second almost exclusively to French opera, and the third to sacred music. During his lifetime the operas were exceedingly important, but after his death they quickly fell out of vogue in France. His mature works cannot be pigeonholed into any national style, but they do exhibit a dramatic expressiveness, seriousness, and classical reserve reminiscent of Gluck; and it was in Germany, thanks initially to the efforts of Mendelssohn, that Cherubini's reputation continued. During the twentieth century his fame rested primarily on two choral works, the Requiem in C Minor and the Requiem in D Minor.

Cherubini began composing as a youngster and had completed an oratorio, three Masses, a *Magnificat*, a Te Deum, and other liturgical works by the time he was sixteen. These works are in the old church style and Italian in character. He devoted 1778–79 to the composition of antiphons in the style of Palestrina. All but one of these *cantus firmus* motets are lost. Even though it may have been written as an exercise, the survivor, *Petrus apostolus* (1778), for six-part mixed chorus, is not without interest. Like the earliest motets of Mozart, it is worthy of close examination by choral conductors looking for new material.

Cherubini's first mature choral work was the Mass in F major (1809), for STB soloists, three-part mixed chorus, and orchestra; it was composed during Cherubini's period of operatic activity. It is important as a marker in his development and introduces the concept of three-part voicing as a symbol of the Trinity; but the writing is academic, especially in fugal movements, and the work as a whole does not compare well with his later Masses. Another important choral work from this time is the *Missa solemnis* in D

Minor (1811), for soloists, mixed chorus, and orchestra. It was composed, like the Mass of Frank Martin in the twentieth century, without external impetus of any kind. Also as in the case of Martin's Mass, Cherubini's would wait several years for performance (it was premiered in the Chapelle Royale in 1821 or 1822, with publication following in 1825). Both the F Major and D Minor Masses are considerably longer than Beethoven's *Missa solemnis*. Also, they are notable for obvious restraint in the vocal solos. It should be noted here that Cherubini held Haydn and Mozart in very high esteem. He also possessed a commanding knowledge of Mozart's Requiem, having conducted the first performance of it in France in 1805. Further, he was a gifted composer of opera in his own right. Even so, Cherubini eschews all operatic influences in his Masses.

Cherubini's last creative period began with his appointment to the Chapelle Royale in 1816. The first piece written in the new job was a *Missa solemnis* in C (1816), for mixed chorus and orchestra. After hearing it in 1837, Robert Schumann offered an assessment:

Call it unsuitable for church performance, strangely wonderful or whatever you like, there is no way of describing the impression which the work makes totally and even more in its separate parts. Sometimes the music, while it seems to resound from the clouds, makes us tremble and shiver. Even what might be called mundane, bizarre and almost theatrical belongs like incense to the Catholic ceremonial and catches the fancy so that we have before us all the grandeur of the rite. As for artistry in harmony, the Mass maybe surpasses even the Requiem in C minor. (Degrada 1985)

Cherubini followed the C Major Mass with his masterpiece, the Requiem in C Minor (1816), for mixed chorus and orchestra. Composed for the anniversary of the death of Louis XVI, Cherubini's setting is universal in its emotional appeal, in reality commemorating not only the death of a royal personage but also those thousands of ordinary people who died in the Revolution and succeeding Napoleonic Wars. Among its remarkable features

are unwavering focus and concentration of thought—aspects pro-
pelled into relief by the omission of soloists—and the use of chromaticism and modulation strictly as aids to the comprehension of
the text's meaning. It studiously avoids the grandiosity of Gossec's
Requiem and other more recent works inspired by the Revolution. That Beethoven, Schumann, Berlioz, and Brahms lavished
praise upon it should be enough to at least pique the curiosity of
thoughtful choral conductors.

Cherubini's profound faith and absolute devotion to the sacred
texts are nowhere more apparent than in the C Minor Requiem.
Still, the Archbishop of Paris objected to its use at the funeral
of Boieldieu in 1834, because there were women's voices in the
choir. While this must have been frustrating for Cherubini, to say
the least, he resolved to compose a piece for his own funeral that
would neatly circumvent the pious peevishness of any archbishop.
The resulting Requiem in D Minor (1834–36), for men's chorus
and orchestra, was duly performed when the composer died. It
is a masterpiece of a different kind from the C Minor Requiem.
Whereas the earlier Requiem is universal and conciliatory, the D
Minor is highly personal and somewhat anguished in its view of
death and paradise. It reinstates the Trinitarian three-part choral
writing of the early F Major Mass, though the first tenor's consistently high tessitura is more in line with a countertenor part.
Further, division of the predominant TTB texture often occurs
in homophonic passages. Lowell Mason, the American music
educator and hymn-tune composer, heard a performance of two
excerpts of the D Minor Requiem in Leipzig on 9 March 1852 and
wrote home about it:

> The music throughout is of a very high character, though it would
> not much interest those who desire musical gratification only from
> pretty tunes or pleasant voices. The first movement, "Requiem
> aeternam," with its accompaniment of violoncellos and double
> basses, is plaintive and sad, and tells only of sorrow, penitence and
> grief. In the "Dies irae," the full powers of the orchestra are brought
> into requisition: and uniting, as was the case on the present oc-

casion, with sixty well-trained and fearless men's voices, the effect was awfully grand and commanding. The majestic movements, the severely dissonant harmonies, the wailings of the strings, the frightful appeals of the instruments of blast and percussion, and the cryings out of the voices, all combined to produce an effect which was, at times, truly terrific and overwhelming. The nineteen stanzas, however, have furnished an opportunity for musical contrasts which have been well introduced, affording variety and relief. (Mason 1854, 59)

Incidentally, Cherubini included settings of the gradual and communion in both Requiems.

Other interesting works include the *Petite messe de la Sainte Trinité*, in D minor (c. 1817), appropriately scored for three-part chorus (organ accompaniment added in 1835 by L. Séjan); the "Coronation" Mass in A major (1825), for three-part mixed chorus (STB, with ad libitum solos) and orchestra; and the multimovement Credo (1806), for eight-part mixed chorus and organ, a contrapuntal tour de force virtually unequaled in the nineteenth century.

Giuseppe Baini (1775–1844) was an official in the papal chapel, where he served as the general administrator of the choirs. As a scholar he began the study and publication of Palestrina's work. His own sacred choral compositions represent an early attempt to reestablish the primacy of sixteenth-century polyphony as the norm for Roman Catholic music. Although his music is now largely forgotten, his ideas were soon embraced by Pietro Alfieri, with much greater success (see below), and were later championed by the Caecilian movement.

Pietro Raimondi (1786–1853), another prolific composer of opera, is interesting also because of his musical experiments. The oratorio trilogy *Giuseppe—Putifar—Giacobbe* (1848), for soloists, mixed chorus, and orchestra, is designed to be performed individually in sequence, and then simultaneously on the same evening. Smither (2000, 619–20) quotes an entertaining contemporary account of the premiere in 1852 detailing the movement on the stage of the 360 performers (120 for each oratorio), the enthusiastic response of the audience, and the aged composer's dramatic fainting spell during the curtain calls. Raimondi composed an extraordinary amount of music; his choral works alone included seven other oratorios, four Masses for mixed chorus and orchestra, two Masses for unaccompanied double chorus, two Requiems for mixed chorus and orchestra, many settings of the Te Deum and *Stabat mater*, and the entire book of Psalms for mixed chorus of four to eight parts.

Michele Carafa (1787–1872) was an Italian nobleman who became a professional composer after the Napoleonic Wars. His music was often performed and generally liked by audiences and critics, but it fell quickly into disuse, possibly because, in the words of Rossini, "he made the mistake of having been born my contemporary" (Julien Budden, "Michele Carafa," in Sadie 1980, 3:768). In addition to his many works for the stage, he also composed a handful of sacred works, including an *Ave verum* (n.d.) for tenor soloist, mixed chorus, and orchestra.

Gioachino Rossini (1792–1868) was one of history's greatest composers of opera, especially excelling in the comic variety. He also composed a number of choral works, some of which are student exercises. In 1820 he collaborated with Pietro Raimondi on a Mass for soloists, mixed chorus, and orchestra, and in 1832 he collaborated with Giovanni Tadolini on a *Stabat mater*. Ten years later he incorporated his movements of this work into his own *Stabat mater* (1842) for soloists, mixed chorus, and orchestra. Rossini's best-known choral work, the *Stabat mater* injects operatic life into the thirteenth-century text. Especially famous is the passionate "Et inflammatus est" for soprano and chorus. Rossini returned to choral music in a big way some twenty years later with his *Petite messe sollennelle* (1863), for SATB soloists, mixed chorus, two pianos, and harmonium. The title itself is a joke: the work is over an hour and a half in length. The first performance was given in a private residence to an invited audience, the Gloria and Credo being separated by a buffet lunch. Only ten singers were used, and the soloists joined with the others to form the chamber chorus. Although Rossini eventually orchestrated this Mass (in his own words: "so that others wouldn't do it"; Phillip Gossett, "Gioachino

Rossini," in Sadie 1980, 16:243), he clearly intended it for intimate performance. He certainly did not expect either his Mass or his *Stabat mater* to find their way into any liturgical setting. Each is an operatic concert work, written at the height of Rossini's powers, containing exceptionally entertaining arias and powerful choruses. Still, he nodded in the direction of Viennese classical church tradition in the *Petite messe* by concluding the Gloria and Credo with large and academic—though immensely entertaining—fugues. Other choral works include several cantatas for soloists, chorus, and orchestra, as well as smaller works, such as the charming *Trois choeurs religieux* (1844) for three-part treble choir and piano (published separately in 1989 by Ricordi with Italian and French texts as "La fede," "La speranza," and "La carità").

Saverio Mercadente (1795–1870), a student of Zingarelli, was celebrated for his numerous operas. He composed a couple of oratorios, of which the first, *Le sette parole di nostre Signore* (1838), for soloists, chorus, and orchestra, became popular enough to be published, an unusual occurrence in Italy at that time (Smither 2000, 617).

Giovanni Pacini (1796–1867) wrote almost ninety operas and was a celebrated composer of cabalettas. His style was an imitation of Rossini's. Pacini also composed Masses, cantatas, and a significant number of oratorios, which was unusual for a time when interest in oratorio was waning in Italy.

Gaetano Donizetti (1797–1848) studied with Mayr and had success in Italy as a composer and teacher. Following political intrigues that prevented him from succeeding Zingarelli as director of the conservatory in Naples and the death of his beloved wife— events that occurred within a couple of months of each other in 1837—he moved to Paris, where, like Cherubini and Rossini, he found success. Donizetti's fame is based, of course, on the enduring popularity of his operas. However, he originally intended to devote his career to church music and composed at least a hundred small sacred works between the years 1818 and 1822. Outstanding among these is the exquisite *Ave Maria* (1842), for soprano solo, mixed chorus, and strings. This five-minute devotional master-

piece showcases Donizetti's understanding of the voice even as he
eschewed theatrical display.

Donizetti also composed two oratorios, *Oratorio sacra* and *Le
siete chiesa*, both for soloists, mixed chorus, and orchestra; as well as
several cantatas, Masses, and Requiem settings. The Requiem (1835,
in memory of Vincenzo Bellini) and *Messa di Gloria e Credo* (1837),
also for soloists, mixed chorus, and orchestra, are good examples of

Initial choral entrance in Gaetano Donizetti's *Ave Maria.*

Donizetti's mature craft. The Requiem is notable for the excellence of the music as well as the unusual soloist configuration (alto, tenor, baritone, and bass). Especially interesting is the "Et incarnatus est," where Donizetti used the dark timbre of the three male soloists to represent the humanity of Christ. The *Messa di Gloria* was commissioned to provide a festive setting for the Feast of San Gennaro, the patron saint of Naples. For this Donizetti incorporated a Kyrie, "Laudamus te," "Qui tollis," "Cum sancto," and parts of the Credo that had been composed earlier during his period of prolific church composition. In keeping with Neapolitan tradition, Donizetti did not set the Sanctus or Agnus Dei. Also, he did not set the first line of Credo text, leaving the priest to open it with a Gregorian intonation. Further, in addition to the normal quartet of vocal soloists (SATB), Donizetti included important solo work for flute and violin. This Mass was performed as intended in 1837 and not heard again until the choir of Berlin's St. Hedwig's Cathedral recorded it in 1976. Because the "Cum sancto" manuscript was illegible, Johannes Wojciechowski made a new edition in which a different "Cum sancto" (also dating from 1818–22) was inserted. In spite of the separate origins of its various sections, the *Messa di Gloria e Credo* is remarkably consistent stylistically, enthusiastically festive, and—like the Requiem—deserving of occasional performance.

Pietro Alfieri (1801–1863) worked somewhat in advance of the Caecilian movement, devoting his life, in the words of Dennis Libby, to "the deliverance of liturgical music from what he saw as the debased theatrical style of contemporary composers and the neglect and incompetence of singers and organists in regard to Gregorian chant and Renaissance music" (Dennis Libby, "Pietro Alfieri," in Sadie 1980, 1:252). This was a very large task, of course, and his success was limited. Palestrina was Alfieri's ideal, and his *Raccolta di Musica sacra*, published in seven volumes from 1841 to 1846, was the first modern edition of Palestrina's music. Alfieri further strove in his compositions and writings to exhibit those qualities in Palestrina's music that, in his mind, raised that master's work above that of others: succinct musical ideas that presented the text clearly, with appropriate and understated expression. Many of

Alfieri's liturgical choral works were published in Rome and were well-known in Italy, as were his manuals for the performance of Gregorian chant. His edition of the Roman Gradual, Antiphonal, and Hymnal did not, however, receive the imprimatur of the church, and was never published.

Antonio d'Antoni (1801–1859) was an Italian conductor who first gained attention by conducting his own Mass for St. Cecilia's Day (1813), for mixed chorus, at the age of twelve. He became well-known as a conductor and opera composer and composed at least one other choral work, the cantata *Il genio di Trieste* (1829).

Michael Costa (1810–1884) was born in Naples and studied with Zingarelli. During his student years he composed a Mass for mixed chorus and a *Dixit Dominus* and oratorio, *La Passione*, for soloists, mixed chorus, and orchestra. In 1829 he journeyed to England to conduct at the Birmingham Festival and thereafter made England his home. He served for many years as music director of Her Majesty's Theatre, music director at Covent Garden, and music director of the Sacred Harmonic Society, and he conducted regularly at the Handel festivals and the Birmingham Festival. His compositions, which stylistically remained true to his Italian heritage, were very popular in England, especially his oratorios *Eli* (1855, text adapted from I Samuel by William Bartholomew), and *Naaman* (1864), both for soloists, mixed chorus, and orchestra (and both written for the Birmingham Festival). *Eli* also received attention across the Atlantic, where it was performed by the Boston Handel and Haydn Society in 1857. George Upton has provided us with comments from a critic who attended that concert neatly summarizing Costa's abilities:

> As a whole, *Eli* is a noble and impressive oratorio. The composition is learned and musician-like, and generally appropriate, tasteful, dignified, often beautiful, and occasionally grand. It is by no means a work of genius, but it is a work of high musical culture, and indicates a mind imbued with the best traditions and familiar with the best masters of the art, and a masterly command of all the modern musical resources, except the "faculty divine." (Upton 1886, 89)

Upton hastened to add that the "faculty divine" was "not included in 'modern musical resources.'"

Gaetano Capocci (1811–1898) was music director at St. John
Lateran in Rome from 1855 until his death. In that position he
composed many liturgical works, including his famous Responses
for Holy Week (n.d.), for mixed chorus. He was also an active par-
ticipant in the Oratorio Filippino, for which he composed *Battista*
(1833) and *Assalone* (1848), for soloists, mixed chorus, and orchestra.

Giuseppe Verdi (1813–1901) was the greatest Italian composer of
the century. He was the antithesis of Richard Wagner: musically
conservative, pragmatic, and uninspired by thoughts of ancient
national epics. There is no mysticism in Verdi whatsoever. He was,
after all, a successful farmer, and his music seems to spring from
the Italian soil like a well-cultivated crop. Many of his operas contain excellent choral music. In particular, his early opera *Nabucco*
(first produced in 1842)—which is often successfully performed
as a concert work—is famous for the vitality of its choral writing,
especially the chorus of Hebrew slaves.

Verdi composed music for the Roman Catholic liturgy in his
youth, a common rite of passage for Italian composers of his generation. But he was not a man of faith and not inclined at all toward sacred music, so these early works hold little interest today,
other than as youthful exercises produced by a budding genius.

He did, however, appreciate certain religious texts for reasons
of his own. When Rossini died on 13 November 1868, Verdi took
it as a national loss. He proposed to his publisher, Tito Ricordi,
that the most distinguished Italian composers each write a movement of the Requiem Mass, the final product to be performed as
a whole on the first anniversary of Rossini's death. Verdi's letter
to Ricordi was published in the press, and the idea immediately
gained enthusiastic public support. A committee was formed, and
Verdi composed the concluding Libera me; then, as squabbles and
rivalries among the various other composers arose, everything fell
apart. Verdi put his Libera me aside, writing to a friend that "men
of talent are almost always overgrown boys."

But a few years later, in 1873, Alessandro Manzoni died. Manzoni had been not only Verdi's friend and Italy's greatest living literary figure, but also a leader in the movement to unify it into a single country. Within a couple of weeks Verdi wrote his publisher that he would compose a complete Requiem to honor Manzoni.

Verdi's Requiem (1874), for SATB soloists, mixed chorus, and orchestra, received its premiere at the church of San Marco in Milan on 22 May 1874, the first anniversary of Manzoni's death. It was an overwhelming success. The only dissenting remark came from Hans von Bülow, who referred to it as Verdi's "latest opera in ecclesiastical garb" (Jaffee 1964, 7). Although Bülow would later apologize for this remark, the sentiment has remained the rallying cry for all whose views are colored by a desire to reclaim for religious music some elusive lost purity.

It is true that the Requiem is awash in primary colors. Its sense of drama is total. And one must search many years in each direction—back to Handel's *Saul* (1739) and forward to Walton's *Belshazzar's Feast* (1931)—in order to find another choral work that presents its case in terms so purely visceral. According to one critic: "To expect Verdi to produce anything like an ecclesiastical music would be humanly absurd. It ill becomes us to dogmatize as to the limits of divine patience; but we may be very sure that Verdi's Requiem stands before the throne at no disadvantage from its theatrical style" (Tovey 1937, 198). Verdi, without false piety, still imbues the work with a kind of realistic reverence.

The day after he conducted the Requiem in Liverpool in 1881, Max Bruch wrote the following to his wife's aunt:

> It had the same powerful and magical effect upon me when I first heard it in 1877. The Requiem contains not places, but whole movements of the highest beauty. True music gushes and sparkles from it, a truly overpowering, melodious abundance enchants and makes me so happy. Even the most peevish German philistines cannot fail to recognize that parts of it . . . are seriously, deeply and truly products of genius, and effected with consummate mastery. Hiller

thinks as I do, and it also made a deep impression upon Brahms. (Fifield 1988, 184–85)

In 1880 Verdi composed a *Padre nostro* for unaccompanied SSATB chorus and an *Ave Maria* for soprano and string orchestra (on paraphrases by Dante of the liturgical text), but these works were not designed for the church and were instead performed at La Scala.

Verdi's last compositions are also settings of religious text. The *Quatro pezzi sacri* were composed over a period of a few years as individual pieces not intended to be performed together. In fact, Verdi implied in letters to Boito in 1896 that he didn't want the last three performed at all. The *Ave Maria*, for unaccompanied four-part mixed chorus, was composed sometime after 3 August 1888 in response to a letter printed in the *Gazzetta musicale* challenging composers to harmonize a curious enigmatic scale: C–D-flat–E–F-sharp–G-sharp–A-sharp–B–C. Verdi sets the scale as a cantus firmus surrounded by a tightly spun web of chromatic counterpoint: one statement of the scale for each voice and the last two transposed up a fourth, followed by a brief coda that returns to the original tonality. The *Ave Maria* was first performed in 1895. The third of the set, *Laudi alla Vergine Maria*, for unaccompanied women's voices, was intended not for chorus, but for four soloists. For text Verdi turned to Dante, as he had for his earlier *Padre nostro* and *Ave Maria*. The second and fourth pieces of the set, the *Stabat mater* (1896–97) and Te Deum (1895–96), are large-scale—though succinct—settings for mixed chorus and large orchestra. The Te Deum is especially grand, with its Gregorian incipit, scoring for double mixed chorus, and brief but vital soprano solo in the concluding sixteen measures. The opening of the *Stabat mater* is particularly dramatic, depicting Mary's view of the cross in four jarring measures. Its terseness stands in bold relief compared to Dvořák's text-painting, for instance. But Dvořák's *Stabat mater* is a devotional work, while the humanistic Verdi, interested in the shock value of a mother watching her son's execution, goes for the jugular. Verdi was eventually persuaded to allow the pieces to

Opening measures of Giuseppe Verdi's *Stabat mater*.

be heard in public, and, during Holy Week, 1898, the last three were performed in Paris, followed by performances in Turin and England. In November 1898 all four pieces were performed by the Gesellschaft der Musikfreunde in Vienna, an event that seems to have begun the tradition of performing *Lauda alla Vergine Maria* with a chorus.

A last choral work of Verdi that deserves mention is the festive *Inno delle nazioni* (1862, on text by Boito), for soloists, mixed chorus, and orchestra, which was later arranged by Arturo Toscanini to include "The Star-spangled Banner."

Teodulo Mabellini (1817–1897) composed a large quantity of liturgical choral music, as well as two oratorios, *Eudosia e Paolo* (1845) and *Ultimo giorno di Gerusalemme* (1848), both for soloists, mixed chorus, and orchestra. They were very popular in Florence, receiving numerous performances there from the time of their premieres until the end of the century, and are unusual among Italian oratorios because of their extensive use of chorus.

Ferruccio Busoni (1866–1924) was an important pianist, composer, and teacher who was mostly influenced by Germans. He was also genuinely inspired by Franz Liszt, although he did not know him and never heard him play. Besides a unique piano concerto that incorporates men's chorus in the finale (see Strimple 2002, 184–85), Busoni composed only two choral works, the cantatas *Primavera, estate, autumno, inverno*, Op. 40 (1882, on text by Pietro Bini), for men's choir and orchestra; and *Il sabato del villagio* (1882), for soloists, mixed choir, and orchestra.

Lorenzo Perosi (1872–1956) became *maestro di cappella* at St. Mark's in Venice in 1894 after completing studies in church music with the great Palestrina scholar Franz Xaver Haberl in Regensburg. He became a priest in 1895 and succeeded to the position of *maestro di cappella* of the Sistine Chapel in 1898. He composed many liturgical works and—beginning with *La Passione di Cristo secondo San Marco: trilogia sacra* (1897), for soloists, mixed chorus, and orchestra—almost singlehandedly rejuvenated the oratorio tradition in Italy. Perosi's innate modesty is apparent in a letter he sent to Giuseppe Martucci on 15 May 1898 in which he included a copy of *La Passione*. The letter does not reflect the extent of *La Passione*'s initial success:

Illustrious Maestro:
I do not have the privilege of knowing you, but knowing of your goodness, I permit myself to write to you, praying that you would

gladly accept a copy of the score to my Passione which I wrote last autumn. As you will see it is no big deal, but I hope that you will accept it as an homage of my esteem and—if I may—my affection for you! . . .

    Believe me [that I am your] devoted servant, D. L. Perosi

Perosi's style is eclectic, combining elements of Wagner, Brahms, and other late nineteenth-century composers with the high-minded objectivity of Palestrina; his best passages are naturally lyrical. Although the choral writing is predominantly homophonic in his oratorios, there is moderate use of counterpoint in his liturgical works. His oratorios, of which he composed fourteen, are quite different from most Italian oratorios. In the words of Howard E. Smither:

> A majority of his oratorios have Latin texts (from the Vulgate and liturgy), and in this respect he follows Liszt's example in *Christus*. Most of Perosi's oratorios include a narrator (called *Storico*) or narrative text for chorus. Thus the oratorios were neither intended to be performed as operas nor are suitable for staging. Relatively brief, deeply spiritual, and thoroughly Roman Catholic works, these oratorios seem to be modeled more on Carissimi's oratorios than on either Italian opera or the oratorios of Handel, Bach, or Mendelssohn. (Smither 2000, 623)

Perosi would become a force in Roman Catholic music in the next century, but his effectiveness was cut short by mental illness in 1915. In conjunction with his position at the Sistine Chapel, Perosi assisted in the writing of the 1903 *motu proprio* of Pope Pius X, which, among other things, decreed an end to operatic influences in Roman Catholic music (Pope Pius X also ended the church's acceptance of castration and the use of castrati in church choirs.)

    Other Italian composers include Paolo Altieri (1745–1820), who composed approximately 400 sacred vocal works as choirmaster for the churches in Noto, Sicily; Luigi Caruso (1754–1822), an opera composer who became *maestro di cappella* at Perugio in

Letter from Lorenzo Perosi to Giuseppe Martucci. Collection of Leonardo Ciampa.

1798, gradually gave up composition for the theater, and produced thereafter a large number of Masses and other works, including a Mass in C (n.d.) and a Requiem (n.d.), both for mixed chorus and orchestra; Bernardo Bittoni (1756–1829), who composed oratorios and many liturgical pieces for the cathedral in his hometown of Fabriani after being named *maestro di cappella* there in 1798; Antonio Calegari (1757–1828), who was already known for his liturgical music during the last decade of the eighteenth century and who also contributed a valuable treatise on vocal ornamentation, *Modi generali del canto*, published posthumously in 1836; Giuseppe Bertini (1759–1852), who composed many liturgical pieces, none of which have survived; Antonio Brunetti (c. 1767–c. 1846), who composed over eighty sacred choral works for the cathedrals in Macarata, Chieta, Bologna, and Urbino; Francesco Basili (1767–1850), who composed a very large number of sacred works for chorus and organ while *maestro di cappella* at St. Peter's in Rome, struggled unsuccessfully to raise musical standards there, and is now remembered primarily as the director who refused Verdi entrance into the Milan Conservatory in 1832; Pietro Casella (1769–1843), who served as *maestro di cappella* in numerous churches and composed a correspondingly large amount of church music; Nicola Benvenuti (1810–1867), who composed a large amount of liturgical music for the cathedral in Pisa as well as cantatas and other choral works for the Grand Duke of Tuscany; Giovanni Tadolini (1785–1872), an eminent choral conductor who collaborated on the first version of Rossini's *Stabat mater*; Raimondo Boucheron (1800–1876), one of the composers invited by Verdi to contribute to the proposed Requiem in memory of Rossini, who wrote many liturgical choral works for the cathedral in Milan, where he was *maestro di cappella*; Vincenzo Bellini (1801–1835), the gifted but ill-fated composer of the popular operas *Norma* and *I Puritani*, who contributed several Masses and other liturgical pieces; Antonio Buzzolla (1815–1871), an opera conductor and composer who also composed a number of excellent church works and was invited by Verdi to contribute to the proposed Requiem in honor of Rossini; Salvatore Agnelli (1817–1874), a student of Zingarelli and Donizetti, who contributed liturgical works and a cantata honoring Napoleon I that required three orchestras; Antonio Bazzini (1818–1897), the teacher of Mascagni and Puccini and one of the few Italian composers of the century to favor instrumental composition over opera, who contributed the symphonic cantata *Sennacheribbo* (c. 1875, on text by V. Meini), for soprano and baritone soloists, mixed chorus, and orchestra; Girolamo Alessandro Biaggi (1819–1897), a composer and prominent music critic who not only composed several liturgical pieces, but also, in his writings, defended the autonomy of the composer in Roman Catholic church music; Giovanni Bottesini (1821–1889), a remarkably gifted double-bass virtuoso, who composed a Requiem (1880) for soloists, mixed chorus, and orchestra, as well as the oratorio *The Garden of Olivet* (1887), for soloists, mixed chorus, and orchestra, commissioned by the Norwich Festival; Gaetano Braga (1829–1907), a virtuoso cellist who also composed several liturgical works for chorus and orchestra; Giovanni Bolzoni (1841–1919), Edgard Varèse's teacher, who contributed a cantata and numerous small choruses; Arrigo Boito (1842–1918), an outstanding poet and composer whose opera *Mefistofele* (1868) contains an extended final scene with chorus that is often given separately as a concert work; Alfredo Catalani (1854–1893), an important, occasionally controversial opera composer and friend of Toscanini, whose sole contribution to the choral repertoire was an early Mass (1872) for mixed chorus and orchestra; Giacomo Puccini (1858–1924), the leading exponent of *verismo* opera, who as a young man produced an attractive *Messa di Gloria* (c. 1880), for tenor and baritone soloists, mixed chorus, and orchestra, which looks back to Verdi's *Nabucco* and ahead to Puccini's own *Manon* and *Edgar*; and Ermanno Wolf-Ferrari (1876–1948), who ended the century with the oratorio *Talitha Kumi (La figlia di Giaro)* (1900), for soloists, mixed chorus, and orchestra, in a mixed style reminiscent of Verdi and Bach.

8

The Americas

The United States

The sturdy American tradition of the itinerant singing master—who taught music to entire communities by renting a public building, selling his own books (which contained both rubrics and choral music for all occasions) and giving group singing lessons—had been under attack since about 1791. A basic musical component in the singing masters' books were fuguing tunes, a bipartite form that had originated in England in the middle of the eighteenth century. These tunes first appeared in American songbooks in 1761 (such as James Lyon's *Urania*) and became popular almost immediately. Thereafter colonial composers embraced the form as their own: fuguing tunes by William Billings, Daniel Read, and others became standard repertoire in churches throughout the land. The B section of the tunes, which were repeated, consisted of contrapuntal vocal entries, and this was initially the focus of criticism. In an essay written in 1808, John Hubbard maintained not only that the contrapuntal sections obscured the text, but that the composers themselves were ignorant of the finer points of composition.

At the time, though, hymnal compilers were not interested in the finer points of composition; rather, they were committed to producing music that could be easily learned and sung by folks with limited musical education. As pressure mounted in urban New England to embrace an educated Eurocentric music, the classics of colonial New England psalmody came to be preserved in books aimed at the rural populations of the South and West. These books, notated in a system of note shapes designed to simplify the process of reading music, not only included works by Billings and Read, but also introduced a new repertoire of folk hymns. These were written primarily, but not exclusively, in three parts (STB), with the tune in the tenor. In practice, some sopranos and tenors would switch parts, creating a five- or six-part texture. The most important of the early shape-note hymnals were John Wyeth's *Repository of Sacred Music, Part Second* (1813); Ananais Davisson's *Kentucky Harmony* (1816); *The Virginia Harmony* (1831), compiled by James P. Carrell and David L. Clayton (containing the first appearance of "Amazing Grace"); William Walker's *The Southern Harmony and Musical Companion* (1835); William Caldwell's *Union Harmony* (1837); and, finally, *The Sacred Harp* (1844), compiled by Benjamin Franklin White and E. J. King. *The Sacred Harp* is still popular, especially in the southern United States.

Lowell Mason (1792–1872) was already conducting his church choir in Medfield, Massachusetts by the time he was sixteen years old. In 1812 he moved to Savannah, Georgia, and gained further

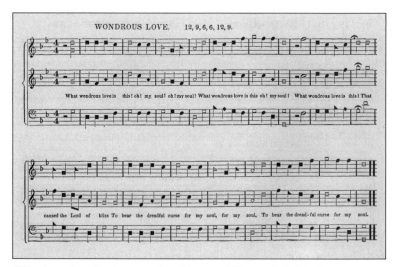

"Wondrous Love" as it appeared in *The Sacred Harp*, 3rd ed. (1859).

experience by teaching singing in schools. Eventually he became organist at the Independent Presbyterian Church. In 1827 he moved to Boston. A leader in the movement to replace the itinerant uneducated singing master with formal music education based on European models, he founded the Boston Academy of Music in 1833 and began teaching music in the public schools in 1837. Considered the father of American music education, his presentation to the Boston School Board proposing the establishment of music programs in public schools relied heavily on the argument that in addition to promoting good health, teaching children to sing would improve music in the churches (such an argument would probably not be successful in the twenty-first century). Mason included his own anthems in the several collections of choral music he edited, including *Handel and Haydn Society's Collection of Church Music* (seventeen editions, beginning in 1822), *Juvenile Lyre* (1829), *Sabbath School Songs* (1836), and *The Psaltery* (1845). The success of these publications made him wealthy enough to be able to travel freely in Europe with essentially no constraints on his time. The diary he kept during his travels (published as *Letters from Abroad*) is an invaluable repository of information concerning choral singing and other musical activities in Europe during the middle of the century. His efforts on behalf of Eurocentric American music were not universally appreciated, however. Early in the twentieth century the pioneering ethnomusicologist George Pullen Jackson referred derisively to the efforts of Mason and his circle to promote "Better Music" (Jackson 1933, 17–21), and an early twenty-first-century Web site, www.amaranthpublishing.com, quotes an anonymous diatribe written as liner notes for the Recorded Anthology of American Music (New World Records):

> Lowell Mason was the latter-day chief of the "scientific" Better Music movement that drove the popular shape-note tune books of the old Yankee singing masters out of New England, leaving what used to be called the Old Southwest (then not including Texas) with the only spirited congregational singing in the country to this day, and bequeathing the Protestant Church in the At-

lantic states its long, sad heritage of hired soloists, paid choirs, and shamefaced congregational mumbling. Not in the more than twelve hundred hymns with which Mason denatured our acts of communal praise nor in the pious secular inanities he pumped into our public-school music books is there a trace of our antecedent musical history or our native musical vitality. His hymns are so dully correct in harmony, so feeble in melody, and so uniform in their watery characterlessness that they constitute a monument to Christian antimusicality.

Of his hundreds of hymn tunes, those that are sung to "Nearer, My God, to Thee," "My Faith Looks Up to Thee," and "Jesus, Thou Joy of Loving Hearts" are still in common use.

Jesse B. Aikin (1808–1900) was a composer and compiler of hymnals. In 1846 he published *Christian Minstrel*, in which he introduced a new system of notes in seven shapes that became extremely popular throughout the United States. Among his other collections are *The Juvenile Minstrel* (1847), *Harmonia ecclesiae* (1853), and *The True Principles of the Science of Music with a Rare Collection of a few of the Best Tunes* (1891). Several of his tunes were included in Lowell Mason's collections.

William Batchelder Bradbury (1816–1868) studied at the Boston Academy of Music and as a teenager sang in the choir under Lowell Mason's direction at the Boudoin Street Church. Although he composed tunes for several of the best-known American Protestant hymns (including "He Leadeth Me," "Jesus Loves Me," "Just as I Am," and "Sweet Hour of Prayer"), his greatest contributions were in children's music education. After moving to New York City in 1840 he established singing classes based on Mason's model and organized highly successful children's-choir festivals that were held annually. With Thomas Hastings he compiled four volumes of music for children's choir, and he was influential in the establishment of music in the New York schools. Bradbury composed a couple of cantatas, several patriotic choruses, numerous anthems and other choral service music for the Baptist church, and over 800 hymn tunes.

Choral Music during the Civil War

In the third week of May, 1861, the Seventy-first New York Regiment gave an afternoon concert for President and Mrs. Abraham Lincoln and about three hundred invited guests.

One private in the regiment was the composer Harrison Millard, who must have had a lot to do with organizing the event. Performers included a choir, a vocal quartet, Harvey Dodworth's band, and at least three soloists. Music by Millard, Stephen Foster, Francis Scott Key, Verdi, Mendelssohn, and now-forgotten composers listed only by their last names (Wallace, Moore) was played. Of the twelve pieces on the program, three required chorus: Millard's *New National Ode: The Flag of the Free*, "Miserere" from Verdi's *Il trovatore*, and, as a finale, "The Star-spangled Banner." The quartet sang Foster's "Come Where My Love Lies Dreaming" and joined in on the finale. The afternoon finished with the Seventy-first marching in review and the president and his party observing the firing of a new naval cannon (Bernard 1966, 22–25). It is typical that the concert was made up of diverse performing forces, including choir, band, and soloists. And while band concerts were preeminently popular, choirs still found a lot to do: many songs published as sheet music were designed to accommodate not only a soloist, but other voices as well.

In concerts organized by religious organizations, choral music was likely to occupy an important position in the proceedings. For example, a Washington, D. C., organization known as the Christian Commission sponsored large meetings every year on the anniversary of its founding. For this event on 29 January 1865, the Washington Handel and Haydn Society performed, opening the program with Bellini's "Mighty Jehovah." After singing a couple of patriotic songs—with audience participation in at least one—they performed Handel's "Hallelujah," from *Messiah*, and concluded with the Doxology (Bernard 1966, 221).

Most sizable church choirs mastered Handel's "Hallelujah." In addition, a new piece, the *President's Hymn* ("Give Thanks All Ye

People"), by J. W. Turner (on text by William A. Muhlenburg), became virtual coin of the realm for all church choirs after it was issued on 2 November 1863. Muhlenburg, an Episcopal minister, had penned the text after reading President Lincoln's proclamation establishing Thanksgiving Day.

Other musically slight but historically significant pieces include Wilson G. Horner's *National Consecration Chant* (1863, on text by Major B. B. French), for mixed chorus; and Alfred Delaney's *Dirge* (1863), also for mixed chorus. Both were sung by the National Union Musical Association of Baltimore immediately before and after Lincoln's address at the Gettysburg battlefield.

During the war, no matter what their circumstances were, people just couldn't help singing. A Northern chaplain, Charles C. McCabe, even organized a choir of captured Union soldiers in the infamous Libby Prison, where they sang French, Irish, Hungarian, Scottish, and German songs, as well as "Home Sweet Home," "We Are Coming, Father Abraham," and other songs, including "Yankee Doodle," which their Southern captors did not particularly like (Bernard 1966, 219).

Composers Active after the Civil War

George Frederick Bristow (1825–1898) was a choral conductor and public-school music teacher in New York City. As music director of the New York Harmonic Society (1851–63), the Mendelssohn Society (1867–71), and several New York churches, he established a reputation as a competent conductor of large choral and orchestral works, a genre in which he also excelled as a composer. Among his works are *Niagara Symphony*, Op. 63 (1893), for SATB soloists, mixed chorus, and orchestra; the oratorio *Daniel*, Op. 42 (1867, on text by W. A. Hardenbrook), for soloists, mixed chorus, and orchestra; and the cantatas *Praise to God*, Op. 33 (1860), and *The Pioneer*, Op. 49 (1872), both for solo voices, mixed chorus, and orchestra. Bristow's compositional style was heavily influenced by Mendelssohn and other nineteenth century Germans.

He also published several pedagogical books and collections of vocal exercises.

Hans Balatka (1826–1899) was a Moravian composer and conductor whose musical and organizational talents were indispensable in the development of large-scale choral singing in the midwestern United States. He immigrated to America after the European revolutions in 1848, settled in Milwaukee in 1849, and established a male chorus almost immediately. Soon he became music director of the Milwaukee Musical Society and was asked to conduct in Chicago, Cincinnati, Cleveland, and Detroit. In 1860 he moved to Chicago, where he served as music director of the Chicago Philharmonic Society and also conducted the Oratorio Society and other choirs. Of his several compositions for chorus, *The Power of Song* (1856), for eight-part male chorus, may be considered representative.

John Knowles Paine (1839–1906) studied in Berlin from 1858 to 1861. Shortly after returning to the United States he joined the faculty at Harvard, becoming the first professor of music at an American university. He was exceptionally important as a pedagogue and established himself as an articulate spokesman on behalf of music as part of the liberal arts. His students included many of the next generation's finest musicians. He composed in all genres, and several of his orchestral and keyboard works (especially those for organ) have remained on the fringes of the repertoire.

Paine's oratorio *St. Peter*, Op. 20 (1872), for SATTB soloists, mixed chorus, and orchestra, is an important contribution to the repertoire. It was a resounding success at its premiere in Portland, Maine, in 1873. Thurston Dox quotes a review from the *Portland Press*:

> The oratorio performance of last evening was a brilliant, important and entire success, which will greatly increase the musical reputation of our city.... It is only within a few years that music and the immortal works of the great masters have been listened to with ever-increasing enjoyment and satisfaction. Nothing could more distinctly indicate the great progress made, than the successful at-

tempt by a native composer in the high and austere department of the oratorio; and its intelligent and adequate performances and cordial reception in his native city. (Pahlen 1990, 256)

By 1886 *St. Peter* had acquired such renown that George Upton included a synopsis of it in his book *The Standard Oratorios*. Written in the classical academic style Paine had learned in Germany, this oratorio has much to recommend it: gratefully written solos, dramatic choruses, effective use of chorales (including "How Brightly Shines the Morning Star"), and clever use of twelve male voices from within the chorus to represent the disciples. As in Bach's *St. John Passion*, Paine places the scene of Peter's denial of Jesus at the end of Part I, followed by a chorus–alto solo–chorus construction that provides hopeful commentary on Peter's resultant anguish. In a departure from Bach's model, Paine's Jesus is a tenor (as is the narrator), while Peter is the bass.

Despite the oratorio's acclaim, Paine's earlier Mass in D, Op. 10 (1864), for SATB soloists, mixed chorus, and orchestra, may be the more significant work. The first composition by an American to be performed in Europe (Berlin, 1867), it is a grandly solemn essay on the liturgical text, obviously designed for the concert hall. In the words of Kenneth G. Roberts, Jr., it goes "beyond mere competence to genuine inspiration and grandeur" (Roberts, "John Knowles Paine," in Hitchcock and Sadie 1986, 3:461). A good example of this inspiration is the intensely intimate "Et incarnatus est," in which accompaniment for the contralto solo is reduced to a string chamber ensemble.

Paine's style underwent a change in the mid-1870s: he began to incorporate more chromatic elements, thereby diluting the strength of his naturally diatonic musical language. His later compositions, therefore, do not generally match the quality of those written before *St. Peter*. Included among his other works are the Christmas cantata *The Nativity*, Op. 38 (1882, revised 1883 as Op. 39, on text by Milton), for soloists, mixed chorus, and orchestra; the brief cantatas *The Realm of Fancy* (1882, on text by Keats), for soprano and baritone soloists, mixed chorus, and orchestra, and *Phoebus,*

Arise (1882, on text by William Drummond), for tenor soloist, male chorus, and orchestra; six male voice choruses on texts related to soldiers and war (1863–65); and incidental music to *Oedipus tyrannus*, Op. 35 (1881, revised 1895, on text by Sophocles), for tenor, male chorus, and orchestra (reorchestrated for larger orchestra in 1908), written for a Harvard University production given entirely in Greek in which the composer conducted the chorus.

Born in Hartford, Connecticut, Dudley Buck (1839–1909) was appointed organist in that city's St. John's Church when he was sixteen years old. He entered the Leipzig Conservatory in 1858, where he studied piano with Moscheles and composition with Hauptman and Richter. In 1860 he moved to Dresden, where as a student of Johann Schneider he focusing his studies on J. S. Bach's music. In 1861 he went to Paris and familiarized himself with the music there. These experiences, especially his study in Germany, profoundly influenced his musical outlook. After returning to America in 1862 he was named organist at the Park Church in Hartford and eventually became organist at St. James's Episcopal Church in Chicago, where his possessions (including many of his compositions) were lost in the great fire of 1871. After this he moved to Boston, where he composed *The Forty-sixth Psalm* (1872) for the Haydn and Handel Society and the cantata *The Legend of Don Munio* (1874, on text by Washington Irving), both for mixed chorus and orchestra. These works caught the attention of the American musical establishment (which at that time was also under the influence of German musical thinking), and in 1875 Buck moved to New York City. Eventually he became organist and choirmaster at Holy Trinity Church, a position he retained until his retirement in 1903.

Buck wrote several other cantatas for soloists, mixed chorus, and orchestra that were successfully performed by prominent organizations in the United States and England, including *The Centennial Meditation of Columbia* (1876), *The Nun of Nidaros* (1878), and *The Golden Legend* (1880), which took the prize at the Cincinnati Festival that year. He also made conspicuous contributions to the genre of secular cantatas for men's chorus and orchestra. Still, his

most significant achievements were in the realm of liturgical music. He composed over a hundred anthems, canticles, and hymns
for the Episcopal Church that were very popular during the last
quarter of the century. The *Festival Te Deum No. 7*, in E-flat, for

Above and opposite: The opening measures of Dudley Buck's *Festival Te Deum.*

soloists, mixed chorus, and organ, may be singled out as typical.
It is straightforward in its rhythmic pulse, with occasional shifts
from duple to triple time; the basic diatonic tonality is generously
flavored with diminished seventh and augmented sixth chords;
the four soloists are prominent; the tonality passes from E-flat
to B-flat back to E-flat and then to A-flat (with change to slower
tempo and 9/8 meter) before returning to the home key in 3/4 for
about thirty measures and 4/4 for the final twenty-five measures.
The opening thematic material returns after the B-flat section and
again for the last ten measures. Most of the effects are obvious,
and the text setting is sometimes awkward (in one instance the
word "Lord," in the phrase "Lord God," is set as a sixteenth-note
pick-up; in another, at "Majesty of thy Glory," the word "of" is set
to a melisma). Buck's international fame was such that two later
cantatas, *Voyage of Columbus* (1885) and *Light of Asia* (1886), were
published in Europe (one in Germany and one in England), an
unusual honor for an American composer at that time.

Arthur Foote (1853–1937) studied with John Knowles Paine
at Harvard. Although his distinguished career stretched far into
the twentieth century, many of his choral works were composed

during the last quarter of the nineteenth. The best-known choral work of his early years is the brief cantata *The Farewell of Hiawatha* (1885), for baritone solo, male chorus, and orchestra, written for the Apollo Club of Boston. Other works include *The Wreck of the Hesperus* (1887–88) and *The Skeleton in Armor*, both for mixed chorus and orchestra, and *Lygeia* (1906), for women's chorus and orchestra. He also composed thirty-five anthems.

Edward MacDowell (1860–1908) is remembered today for his Second Piano Concerto and a small collection of piano pieces entitled *Woodland Sketches*. During his life, however, he was quite important:

> MacDowell occupies a historically important place as the 1st American whose works were accepted as comparable in quality and technique with those of the average German composer of his time . . . since he lived in Germany during his formative years, German culture was decisive in shaping his musical development; even the American rhythms and melodies in his music seem to be European reflections of an exotic art. . . . Lack of musical strength and originality accounts for MacDowell's gradual decline in the estimation of succeeding generations; his romanticism was apt to lapse into salon sentimentality. (Slonimsky 1992, 1105)

Well, sometimes a little sentimentality can be a good thing; and to that end MacDowell was wise enough to limit his choral output to part-songs, mostly for men's chorus. Included among them are *Drei Lieder für vierstimmen Männerchor*, Op. 27 (1887, published in Boston and Leipzig, 1890); *The Witch*, Op. 5, and *War Song*, Op. 6 (both 1898); *Two Songs*, Op. 41 (1890); *Three Choruses*, Op. 52 (1897); and *Two Songs from the Thirteenth Century* (1897). His compositions for other vocal configurations include *Two Northern Songs*, Op. 43 (1891), for mixed chorus, and *Summer Wind* (1902), for women's chorus.

Horatio Parker (1863–1919) is known primarily as the teacher of Charles Ives, but his career included major church positions in Boston and New York before he went to Yale, first as a professor and then as the dean of the School of Music, which he built into one of the nation's finest. In addition to Ives, his students included Quincy Porter and Roger Sessions. His reputation as a composer was established by frequent performances of works he wrote under the tutelage of Josef Rheinberger in Munich. Most of these works were choral and included part-songs, psalm settings, and cantatas. By the time he composed his signature piece, the oratorio *Hora novissima*, Op. 30 (1893, on Latin text by B. de Morlaix), for soloists, mixed chorus, and orchestra, he had established a Eurocentric style that relied heavily on his mastery of polyphonic effects and the moderate use of chromaticism to balance a basically diatonic musical language. After *Hora novissima*, Parker's style became more chromatic and wandered into formulaic sentimentalism, reverting, in his last works, to an exceptionally conservative diatonicism. The lack of a clearly defined personal style no doubt contributed to the quick decline in the number of performances of Parker's music after his death. Still, *Hora novissima* is an impressive work, and other of his choral compositions may be deserving of occasional performances. Among these are his numerous anthems and other service music for the Episcopal church; *Blow, Blow, Thou Winter Wind*, Op. 14 (1888, on text by Shakespeare), for male chorus and piano; and *Two Part-songs*, Op. 27 (1892, on texts by Goethe and Heine), for treble chorus and piano.

Howard Brockway (1870–1951) enjoyed a lengthy career as an educator at institutions such as the Peabody Institute, the Mannes College of Music, and the Juilliard School. He was also a gifted composer who, for some reason, simply stopped composing around 1911. With the exception of his arrangements of Kentucky folk songs, his primary choral works date from the last decade of the nineteenth century. Barton Cantrell offered the opinion that "Brockway was one of the most gifted and consistently inspired American composers. Almost every piece shows a rare sensibility and unique warmth of melody and harmony, surpassing many of his more famous contemporaries . . . he was a Romantic master" (Cantrell, "Howard Brockway," in Sadie 1980, 3:327). His choral works include a *Cantate Domino*, Op. 6 (1893), and *Two Choruses*, Op. 24 (1899), both for mixed chorus.

George Whitefield Chadwick (1854–1931) was one of the first to attempt the creation of a purely American style, free from the grip of a pervading German outlook, by utilizing African American melodies (some years before Dvořák), Caribbean dance rhythms, and other non-European elements. His substantial body of work began around 1878 and did not culminate until well into the twentieth century. Among his choral compositions are over thirty anthems, twenty part-songs for female chorus, nineteen part-songs for male chorus; the cantata *Ecce iam noctis* (1897), for male chorus, organ, and orchestra; and a significant number of cantatas for mixed chorus and orchestra, including *Dedication Ode* (1886), *Lovely Rosabelle* (1888), *Phoenix expirans* (1892), and the pastoral *Noël* (1909), for soloists, mixed chorus, and orchestra.

Other American composers include James C. D. Parker (1828–1916), who wrote a cantata and an Easter oratorio and edited a large anthology of sacred choruses by European composers; George Elbridge Whiting (1842–1923), who composed a significant number of part-songs and anthems; William W. Gilchrist (1846–1916), who edited hymnals for both Presbyterian and Congregational denominations and wrote several large works for chorus and orchestra; Frederick Gleason (1848–1903), a student of Dudley Buck, whose heavily orchestrated cantatas were influenced by Wagner and championed by the conductor Theodore Thomas; and Amy Beach (1867–1944), whose Grand Mass in E-flat, Op. 5 (1895), for soloists, mixed chorus, and orchestra, served notice of her future importance in the twentieth century.

American choral music, which had begun the century in the humble attire of an itinerant singing master, had gained considerable renown by century's end. Through the efforts of Lowell Mason and others, vocal and other music was firmly established in public schools along the eastern seaboard, and most churches, even in rural western communities, had choirs or solo quartets. Accomplished community organizations such as the Handel and Haydn Society in Boston (founded 1815) and its younger cousin, the Oratorio Society of New York (founded in 1873), were producing outstanding choral concerts. The Oratorio Society of New York was particularly active. In the 1880–81 season alone it produced Mendelssohn's *Elijah* (two performances), Berlioz's *Damnation of Faust* (three performances), Handel's *Messiah* and *L'Allegro* (two performances each), and a seven-concert Festival (3–7 May) at the Seventh Regiment Armory that included performances of Handel's "Dettingen" Te Deum and *Messiah*, Anton Rubinstein's *The Tower of Babel*, the Ameri-

Top: An Indian choir in Alaska, c. 1890. Courtesy of the National Archives and Records Administration—Pacific Alaska Region, Anchorage.
Bottom: A Methodist Church choir in Greeley, Colorado, c. 1890. Courtesy of the Denver Public Library, Western History Collection, X-9127.

A performance at the Oratorio Society of New York's Festival of Music, Seventh Regimental Armory, New York City, 3–7 May 1881. Courtesy of the Oratorio Society of New York Archives.

can premiere of Berlioz's Requiem, Beethoven's Ninth Symphony, and selections from Schumann's *Paradise and the Peri* and Verdi's Requiem. In 1891 the society produced an even more extravagant festival for the opening of their new concert hall, built by their board president, Andrew Carnegie. For this event Tchaikovsky was brought to New York as guest conductor. The final concert consisted of Beethoven's Fifth Symphony, Tchaikovsky's first Piano Concerto, the Prelude and Flower Maiden Scene from Wagner's *Parsifal*, songs by Tchaikovsky and Walter Damrosch (the society's music director), and Handel's *Israel in Egypt*.

By the early 1880s even the nation's merchandisers had gotten into the act, first by using professional musicians to sell products and then by establishing performing organizations for their employees, a trend that would last well into the twentieth century:

Most of the large and medium-sized stores sponsored employee choruses, bands, orchestras, and sometimes harmonica bands, mandolin and ukulele clubs, minstrel troupes, and operatic societies. Some of the store groups undertook ambitious programs and achieved considerable renown. The Marshall Field Choral Society, for example, consisting of 150 to 200 employees, performed, among others, Coleridge-Taylor's *Hiawatha's Wedding Feast*, Mendelssohn's *Hymn of Praise*, Rossini's *Stabat mater*, Haydn's *Creation*, and Elgar's *King Olaf* and *The Light of Life*, assisted at different concerts by members of the Theodore Thomas Orchestra and the Chicago Symphony Orchestra. The Strawbridge & Clothier Chorus, tracing its origins back to 1882, performed large-scale works by Frederick Cowan [*sic*], Dudley Buck, Victor Herbert, Mendelssohn, and Elgar at established music halls in Philadelphia and at the outdoor park Willow Grove, accompanied variously by the Philadelphia Orchestra, the Victor Herbert Orchestra, and the Damrosch Orchestra. (Tyler 1992, 89)

African American Choral Music and the Spiritual

Coincidentally with the American Revolution, African American congregations in the North began to break away from the white Protestant churches with which they had traditionally worshiped and began establishing their own churches. In Philadelphia, two such congregations were formed in 1794: the St. Thomas African Episcopal Church, which chose to remain within the American Episcopal communion, and Bethel African Methodist Episcopal Church, which forged ahead under the leadership of the Right Reverend Richard Allen to form the first independent black denomination (the AME church) and publish, in 1801, the first African American hymnal, *A Collection of Spiritual Songs and Hymns Selected from Various Authors by Richard Allen, African Minister*. Independent churches were organized in New York City about the same time, and by 1840 Philadelphia and New York could boast of African American Baptist, Episcopal, Lutheran, Methodist, and Presbyterian congregations, as well as numerous AME and African Methodist Episcopal Zion churches.

Concerns over proper church music were just as strong among
the founders of these churches as among their white brethren, and
before long controversy emerged:

> The AME "doctrines and discipline" firmly established the rules by
> which the church should operate, with regard to music as well as
> other matters. . . . Although these rules were identical to those for
> white Methodists, it was more difficult for the black Methodists to
> observe them strictly. Particularly troublesome were the directives
> about choosing "such hymns as are proper for the congregation" and
> avoiding "the singing of fuge [*sic*] tunes" and "hymns of your own
> composing." It is obvious that the church fathers . . . found it no
> easy job to make their congregations conform to these rules. Indeed,
> there was a controversy early in the nineteenth century between
> those who insisted upon bringing the African heritage to bear on
> the music, primarily by composing their own "spiritual songs." At
> the annual conference of the AME church in 1841, only three reso-
> lutions were passed; significantly one dealt with music: "Resolved,
> that our preachers shall strenuously oppose the singing of fuge [*sic*]
> tunes and hymns of our own composing in our public meetings and
> congregations." It is improbable that the black congregations were
> actually singing the kind of "fugue tunes" popular among whites
> during the period. More likely, rather, their singing in the poly-
> phonic African tradition produced the same effect upon listeners
> as did fugal singing—that is, the exotic polyphonic interweaving of
> melodies obscured the texts of hymns. (Southern 1977, 302–3).

These churches also fell into the same disputes that had em-
broiled white congregations in the previous century concerning
the use of instruments in worship, the singing of anthems by
trained choirs, and singing hymns by "lining out," a process by
which a deacon or other church leader would sing a phrase that
was then repeated by the congregation. In one instance where a
choir was formed for the purpose of singing at the dedication of
a new building, "the older members withdrew from the church,
accusing the advocates of the new practice of having brought the

devil into the church" (Southern 1977, 305).

The controversy over choral singing and the establishment of Eurocentric culture ended in some places earlier than others. For example, a concert at St. Philip's Church in New York City on 23 September 1827 featured a white conductor, a Mr. Rabbeson, who directed the choir, and the eminent black musician Francis Johnson (1792–1844), who directed the orchestra in anthems by Lowell Mason, Samuel Chappell, Handel, and Raynor Taylor. Some years later, in 1841, the choir of the First African Presbyterian Church in Philadelphia presented Haydn's *Creation*, first for its own congregation and then for a white church (Southern 1977, 306–7).

After the Civil War, however, a new attitude developed concerning African American "hymns of our own composing." In a lengthy article on the spiritual, James Weldon Johnson quotes a Mr. Allen (possibly Richard Allen), one of the editors of a collection called *Slave Songs of the United States* (1867):

> There is no singing in parts, as we understand it, and yet no two seem to be singing the same thing; the leading singer starts the words of each verse, often improvising, and others, who "base" him, as it is called, strike in with the refrain or even join in the solo when the words are familiar. When the "base" begins the leader often stops, leaving the rest of the words to be guessed at, or it may be they are taken up by one of the other singers. And the "basers" themselves seem to follow their own whims, beginning where they please, striking or hitting some other note that chords, so as to produce the effect of a marvelous complication and variety and yet with the most perfect time and rarely with any discord. And what makes it all the harder to unravel a thread of melody out of this strange network is that, like birds, they seem not infrequently to strike sounds that cannot be precisely represented by the gamut and abound in "slides" from one note to another and turns and cadences not in articulated notes. (Johnson 1925, 37)

In 1871 George L. White (1883–1895), the music teacher at the newly organized Fisk University in Nashville, Tennessee, heard

The Fisk Jubilee Singers with their accompanist, Ella Sheppard (seated, third
from left); from *The Story of the Fisk Jubilee Singers, with Their Songs* (1877).
Courtesy of the Fisk University Franklin Library's Special Collection.

some of the members of his choir singing together informally.
These students were all former slaves and were singing music
unknown to White, quite unlike anything he had ever heard.
Whether or not they were singing in the fashion described above
is unknown. What is known is that White, completely taken
with the music, formed the Fisk Jubilee Singers with ten of his
best students (a pianist and nine singers) and never looked back.
They toured throughout the eastern United States, Europe, and
Great Britain, presenting a variety of music in addition to the
spirituals that had so impressed White. But it was the spirituals that people came to hear. From President Ulysses S. Grant
to Queen Victoria, the Fisk Jubilee Singers made believers of
everyone who heard them. And the African American spiritual
was on its way.

The songs of the Fisk Jubilee Singers were published in two
collections in the 1880s and as an appendix to the several editions
of the book *The Story of the Fisk Jubilee Singers; and Their Songs*,
wherein they are called "Jubilee Songs," not "spirituals." It had sold
54,000 copies by the time the seventh edition was published in 1877.

"Swing Low, Sweet Chariot," in *The Story of the Fisk Jubilee Singers, with Their Songs,* 7th ed. (1877).

The simplicity of the original Fisk arrangements may surprise contemporary musicians accustomed to the more recent, often complicated, and usually superlative arrangements of Harry Burleigh,
John Work, William Dawson, Jester Hairston, Moses Hogan, and
others. The songs are prefaced by performing instructions:

> It will be observed that in most of these songs the first strain is
> of the nature of a chorus or refrain, which is to be sung after each
> verse. The return to this chorus is to be made without breaking the
> time.
>
> In some of the verses the syllables do not correspond exactly to
> the notes in the music. The adaptation is so easy that it was thought
> best to leave it to the skill of the singer rather than to confuse the
> eye by too many notes. The music is in each case carefully adapted
> to the first verse. Whatever changes may be necessary to singing
> the remaining verses will be found to involve no difficulty. (Marsh
> 1877, 125)

The first song, "Nobody Knows the Trouble I See, Lord!" is for
unaccompanied unison chorus; the others are notated as simple
four-part SATB hymns.

Canada

In Canada, church choirs and bands—many of which had been
organized late in the previous century—remained the primary
performing organizations for much of the nineteenth century.
Virtually none of the great Canadian secular musical organizations existed until the last third of the century; The Toronto Mendelssohn Choir was not founded until 1894, and even then it lasted
for only three years (it was reestablished for good in 1900). Repertoire for the church choirs came primarily from England and
France. There simply were no Canadian composers of professional
quality until the appearance of Charles Sabatier (1802–1862), who
emigrated from Germany in 1848 via a stint in the French navy,

and Calixa Lavallée (1842–1891). Neither of these men composed choral music. Sabatier wrote patriotic songs, Lavalee, piano pieces, and "O Canada," the Canadian national anthem. So Canada had to wait for Healey Willan to arrive from England in 1913 in order to establish any viable choral tradition.

Mexico

Mexican audiences and authorities had become enamored of Italian opera during the last decades of the eighteenth century. This trend continued for much of the nineteenth century, even as native-born composers struggled to incorporate folk materials into the Viennese-classical and Italian-opera models of colonial music. The most prominent composers were Aniceto Ortega (1823–1875) and Melesio Morales (1838–1909). Ortega ignored indigenous material altogether in his Italianate operas. Morales gave lip service to the increasingly popular notion that folk materials were not only important, but necessary; still, he could not free himself from a strictly Eurocentric romantic style influenced by Italian opera. His choral works include a *Misa de gloria* and several cantatas for mixed chorus.

Two other important figures of Mexican choral music were Felipe Villanueva (1862–1893) and José Guadalupe Velázquez (n.d.). Villanueva was a native Indian composer who helped establish the Instituto Musical in 1887. One of the first Mexican composers to utilize folk elements, his style combines these materials easily with more Eurocentric romantic elements. His compositions include *Cantata patriotica (El retrato de benemérito cura Hidalgo)*, for mixed chorus and orchestra; and several motets for mixed chorus and organ (or piano).

Velázquez had come under the influence of the Caecilian movement while studying in Ratisbon, Germany. In 1892 he became director of the new Querétaro School of Sacred Music just as Mexican sacred music was reaching the bottom of an almost century-long downward spiral:

Religious music had become syncretized with secular music during
the turbulent years just before the mid-century. . . . In the popular
albados, villancicos, and motets, published by Ruben M. Campos
as representative music of their epoch, lush thirds and sixths hang
with cloying monotony over their tunes; the harmonies are crush-
ingly banal; and their most exalted moments sound like "lifts" from
tenth-rate Italian operas. At mid-century when a new high altar in
utterly execrable taste was installed in the metropolitan cathedral,
music had catapulted to a disastrous low in the cathedral's history.
(Stevenson 1952, 215)

By the time Velázquez took over the School of Sacred Music,
there was not much he could do to improve the situation, although he tried. As a composer he was Caecilian to the core. His
motet *Ave maris stella*, for mixed chorus, has been described as
"not contrapuntal, not Italian operatic" (Tiemstra 1992, 158). Stevenson's view was more acerbic: "His own compositions, though
not operatic, reach an opposite extreme of complete colorless-
ness. They also notably lack any contrapuntal vitality" (Stevenson
1952, 215).

Other Mexican composers include José Mariano Elízaga
(1786–1842), an especially active musician who composed at least
two Masses and several other liturgical works in the Viennese
classical style; Manuel de Arenzana (flourished 1791–1821), who
composed, in addition to his popular operas and zarzuelas, many
sacred choral works in a rather forward-looking Eurocentric style;
Joaquín Beristáin (1817–1839), a prodigy who left a Mass for mixed
choir but did not live to fulfill his potential; Antonio Juanas (d.
1819), who composed over two hundred liturgical works in the
Viennese classical style; Cenobio Paniagua y Vásques (1821–1882),
who composed numerous sacred works, a significant number of
which are for three-part choir; Luis Baca (1826–1855), who contributed an *Ave María* for mixed choir and organ; Rafael Palacios
(flourished c. 1842), whose extant works consist of a Mass and a
Stabat mater, both for mixed chorus; and Fernando Villalpando
(1844–?), who contributed a Mass for mixed chorus.

The Caribbean

In Cuba, Guillermo M. Tomás (1868–1933), founder of the Havana Symphony Orchestra, composed in a style containing doses of Cuban nationalism flavored with Wagnerian romanticism. His choral compositions include the cantata *La oración del creyente* (n.d.), for tenor solo, mixed chorus, and winds. Other Cuban composers include Antonio Raffelin (1796–1882), whose Mass for mixed chorus demonstrates a thorough knowledge of classical European style; Laureano Fuentes Matons (1825–1898), music director at Havana's cathedral, who composed many sacred choral works in the typical Eurocentric romantic style; the Spanish-born Carlos Anckermann (1829–1909), who composed, among other choral works, the *Gran Misa (Misa de los Asturianos)*, for mixed chorus; Gratilio Guerra (1834–1896), who composed a couple of Masses (in C major and D major) for three-part (SAB) choir and chamber orchestra of flute, clarinet, and strings without viola; and the Spanish-born Oriol Costa Sureda (1836–1892), who contributed sacred choral works.

In the Dominican Republic, the remarkably prolific José María Arredondo (1840–1924) composed well over a hundred Masses, fifty-eight litanies, and many, many additional liturgical pieces in a late nineteenth-century romantic style.

In Puerto Rico, Juan Morel Campos (1857–1896) also contributed to the sacred choral repertoire.

Central America

In Costa Rica, Alejandro Monestel Zamora (1865–?) was the first composer to incorporate folk elements into his music. He founded the Escuela Música de Santa Cecilia in 1894 and served as chapel master at San José Cathedral from 1884 to 1902, before he moved to the United States. Works composed in Costa Rica include a Mass and a Requiem, both for mixed chorus, and five cantatas on the life of Jesus, for mixed chorus and orchestra.

In Guatemala, Vicente Sáenz (1756–1841) and Benedicto Sáenz (1815–1857) were active as composers of liturgical music in the Eurocentric classical style.

South America

Amancio Alcorta (1805–1862) was one of the founders of Argentine music. Although not particularly interested in choral music and famous mostly for salon piano music, he nevertheless contributed a few choral works, including *La Agonía (Canto de Viernes Santo)*, for two-part male chorus and organ; and *Lamentaciones*, for mixed chorus (without sopranos) and keyboard. Juan Pedro Esnaola (1808–1878) also enriched the Argentine repertoire with various choral works in the Eurocentric romantic style.

Unlike most other Latin American countries, whose musical fortunes were in decline, Brazil's colonial music climaxed during the first two decades of the new century, owing primarily to the presence of the Portuguese royal family, who began living in exile in Rio de Janiero in 1808. José Maurício Nunes Garcia (1767–1830), an Afro-Brazilian whose grandparents had been slaves, was the most important composer in Brazil during this period. He provided various musical services to the imperial court, and from 1808 to 1811 he served as chapel master at the cathedral in Rio de Janeiro. His works demonstrate an undiluted mastery of classical European style. He was particularly active as a composer of liturgical works, and many of these were written for mixed chorus (with or without solos) and orchestra. The Requiem Mass (1816), for alto, tenor, and bass soloists, mixed chorus, and winds (flute, two clarinets, two bassoons, two trumpets, and timpani), is perhaps his most important work. Other works include the large *Missa de Santa Cecilia* for SATB soloists, mixed chorus, and orchestra; the large psalm settings *Laudate Dominum omnes gentes* (Psalm 117), for SATB soloists, mixed chorus, and chamber orchestra (two oboes, two horns, and strings without violas); and *Laudate pueri Dominum* (Psalm

113), for SATB soloists, mixed chorus, and chamber orchestra (two flutes, two horns, and strings without violas); as well as a significant number of concerted motets for the Christmas season.

Nunes Garcia's student Francisco Manuel da Silva (1795–1865) also served at the imperial court and royal chapel. In addition to holding other important administrative positions, he founded the National Conservatory in Rio de Janeiro in 1841 (now the Escola Nacional de Música, Universidad de Brazil) and served as its first director. He has been called the "best native composer of his era" as well as the "most active composer from 1800 to 1850" (Tiemstra 1992, 145). In addition to composing the Brazilian national anthem, he produced a significant amount of sacred music, including at least four Masses, two litanies, a Requiem, and numerous motets.

Antônio Carlos Gomes (1836–1896) was the first South American composer to win fame abroad. After study at the National Conservatory, he received a government grant to study in Italy, where his operas (influenced by Verdi) first gained attention in 1871. Among his choral works are a Mass for mixed chorus and the cantata *Colombo*, for mixed chorus and orchestra.

When slavery was abolished and the country became a republic in 1889, Brazil became a leader in the continental struggle to create national American musics free of Eurocentric hegemony. The great pioneer in this effort was Alberto Nepomuceno (1864–1920), who composed in all genres and became known as the father of Brazilian musical nationalism. Nepomuceno studied in Berlin, Paris, and Rome—themselves hotbeds of musical nationalism—and became particularly enamored of the music of Edvard Grieg and Alexandre Guilmant. The first composer to introduce Afro-Brazilian elements into orchestral music (Tiemstra 1992, 113), Nepomuceno developed a style founded on European principles but laced with ethnic Brazilian elements. His works include two settings of an Amazon legend, *As Uyaras* (on text by Mello Morais Filho), the first for women's chorus, soprano soloist, and orchestra, and the second for mixed chorus with *colla parte* instruments; *O salutaris hostia*, for mixed chorus and organ; *Maria mater gratiae*, for mixed chorus, two horns, and strings; and at least one Mass for mixed chorus and orchestra.

Other Brazilians include Marcos Coelho Netto (1745–1823), whose compositions for chorus and orchestra were firmly rooted in Viennese classical style; Damião Barbosa de Araújo (1778–1856), who contributed the little cantata *Memento baiano para côro e urquestra*, for mixed chorus and chamber orchestra of flute, oboe, bassoon, and strings; Elias Álvares Lobo (1834–1901), composer of the first Brazilian opera in Portuguese, who also composed *Missa de São Paulo de Alcántara*, for mixed chorus, in a style containing both romantic and nationalistic elements; José Maria Xavier (1819–1887), a Catholic priest whose works include music for Holy Week as well as the *Matinas de Natal*, for mixed chorus and orchestra; João Gomez de Araújo (1849–1942), who contributed six Masses, two cantatas, and other works for mixed chorus; Prescilliano Silva (1854–1910), who composed *Crux fedeles*, for double mixed chorus, and several other motets for Holy Week; and the Italian-born Glauco Velásquez (1884–1912), who contributed a *Pater noster* for mixed chorus.

In Colombia Julio Quevedo Arvelo (1829–1896), known as the "American Berlioz" (Tiemstra 1992, 131), composed in a style that freely mixed eighteenth-century English oratorio and nineteenth-century Italian opera with more nationalistic elements. He wrote in all genres, including secular and sacred choral music, of which the sacred choral works are more important. These include several Masses for mixed chorus and the impressive *Salve pastoral*, for mixed chorus and orchestra.

The only other significant Colombian composer to contribute to the choral repertoire was José María Ponce de León (1846–1882), a student of Charles Gounod who composed a Requiem Mass for mixed chorus.

In Chile, the popular composer José Zapiola (1802–1885) taught at the National Conservatory and founded the first Chilean music journal. Included among his works are a Mass for unaccompanied mixed chorus, an oratorio, and other sacred and patriotic works.

The Peruvian composer José Bernardo Alcedo (or Alzedo, 1798–1878) spent much of his career in Chile, where he served for many years as chapel master at the cathedral in Santiago. On returning to Peru, he supported the independence movement, composed the Peruvian national anthem, eagerly praised his musical contemporaries, promoted Peruvian folk music, wrote the first music-theory book published in Peru, and composed a large number of sacred works—many in Spanish rather than Latin—including *Hymno Ave maris stella*, *Tantum ergo*, three *Missa solemnes* (in D major, E-flat minor, and F major), and several motets, all for mixed chorus.

Other Peruvian composers of this time include Bonifacio Llaque (1799–1845), who contributed a *Cantada a la Virgen (Pastorala)*, for SSAB choir, soprano solo and chamber orchestra of two oboes, two horns, and strings without viola; and José María Valle Riestra (1859–1925), the first Peruvian to compose an opera, who also contributed a number of motets, including two for four-part treble choirs: *Ave Maria* and *O salutaris*.

Unfortunately, very little music from this period has survived in Uruguay. Two composers who may be considered representative were both born in Spain: Fray Manuel Úbeda (1760–1823) and Antonio Sáenz (1829–?). Úbeda came to Uraguay in 1801. His *Misa para Día de difuntos* (1802), for mixed chorus, is the earliest extant sacred composition in Montevideo (Tiemstra 1992, 154). Sáenz was active in Brazil as well as Uruguay. He contributed a *Misa solemne* and a Te Deum, both for mixed chorus and orchestra.

In Venezuela the revolution of 1811 influenced music in several ways. First, many musicians lost their lives in the conflict, resulting in a dearth of competent composers until the twentieth century. Also, the reluctance of Spain to recognize Venezuela as an independent country created a patriotic music industry that stunted the growth of other secular musical endeavors, and, in a backlash, there was an increase in the performances of music by non-Spanish Europeans. An older composer whose work had a profound effect on the revolution itself was José Angel Lamas (1775–1814).

His *Populus meus* (1811), for mixed chorus and orchestra, became an unofficial national anthem after it was performed on the eve of the war of independence (Tiemstra 1992, 11).

José Francisco Velásquez (n.d.) and Atanasio Bello Montera (d. 1847) are representative composers. Velásquez was the son of another composer of the same name. His *Misa en mi bemol*, for unaccompanied mixed chorus, was highly regarded even though his works in general were not considered "as lofty or inspired" as those of other composers (Tiemstra 1992, 157). He composed a significant number of motets and at least four Masses for unaccompanied mixed chorus, as well as the intriguing *Es María norte y guia*, for mixed chorus and chamber orchestra of flute, oboe, horn, and strings. Bello Montera is best known for his Vigil and Mass for the Dead (1842), which was performed at Simón Bolívar's funeral. Other works include *Pange lingua* (1825), several patriotic songs, and many other liturgical works.

Other Venezuelan composers include Juan Francisco Meserón (flourished early in the century), who composed a Miserere and several Masses for mixed chorus in a classical European style; José Cayetano Carreño (1744–1836), who wrote many liturgical works as chapel master at Caracas Cathedral; the highly regarded José Antonio Caro de Boesi (1750–1814), who also promulgated the Viennese style in his several Masses, motets, and other liturgical pieces; José Antonio Páez (1790–1873), a president of Venezuela, who also composed some part-songs; and José Angel Montero (1839–1881), chapel master at Caracas Cathedral, who composed an *Oficios de difuntos* for mixed chorus.

9

Epilogue

While choral music was flourishing in most of Europe and the Americas, the Balkan countries were left floundering under Turkish occupation. The Serbs revolted early in the century, the spirit of nationalism being carried forward by the creation of various singing societies. In neighboring Croatia the Illyrian Movement attempted to establish a national opera, with singing societies being formed late in the century (perhaps the most famous of these is Kolo, which was not founded until 1899). Greece was liberated from Turkey in 1830. Thereafter it sought identification with Europe through production of Italian opera, while choral music remained largely the domain of the Orthodox church. Orthodox chant had changed little since the fourteenth century and during the nineteenth century still consisted of a melody line over a choral drone. Around 1870 four-part harmonization of Byzantine chant appeared, almost coincidentally with a new type of romantic serenade called *kantades*. Written for four-part male chorus, these were Italianate in style.

Romania and Bulgaria were not liberated from Turkey until 1878. Led by the composers Alexandru Flechtenmacher (1823–1898) and Isidor Vorobchievici (1836–1903), the process of cultural realignment with Europe had already begun in Romania with the foundation of a conservatory in 1860 and the establishment of the National Opera in 1877. In Bulgaria, unison singing groups and school choirs were first formed in 1840 and developed rapidly after 1870. Georgi Baidanov (1853–1927), a choral conductor and educator, wrote articles on music education and published collections of Bulgarian folk songs and church music, paving the way for composers and conductors such as Emanuil Manolov (1860–1902), Georgi Athanassov (1882–1931), and, most important, Angel Bukureshtliev (1870–1951), whose early work would make an impact in the next century.

Albania remained isolated, continuing the traditions of community group singing that had been in place for centuries. Singing groups were normally divided by gender and age, as were singing styles ("women's style," "old men's style," etc.). Many of the songs were monophonic, but polyphonic songs in three and four parts were also common (two solo parts—a melody and countermelody—accompanied by a choral drone of one or two parts).

Along the Pacific Rim, the zeal of Christian missionaries had yet to capture the imagination of composer-converts in most Asian countries. Eurocentric choral music had developed in Japan, where school choirs were formed as early as 1872, and in the Philippines by way of church music introduced into the islands by the Spanish or composed late in the century by Marcelo Adonay (1848–1928). It would not be until the second half of the next century that Filipino composers would begin adding to the choral repertoire (Strimple 2002, 288).

In Australia music was initially provided by military bands in the penal settlements (including music for church services). But once the immigration of free settlers began to increase after 1830, music of all forms, including choral music, thrived. Choral societies sprang up in all the major cities on the east coast, performing standard European repertoire and commissioning new works as well.

Among Australia's new musicians was the talented English choirmaster and conductor Isaac Nathan (1790-1864), who arrived in Melbourne in 1841. He soon moved to Sydney, where he immediately became active in musical life. Nathan composed choral pieces and conducted performances of famous oratorios and other large choral works (Beethoven's C Major Mass, for example) in St. Mary's Cathedral in Sydney.

Leslie Francis Victor (Leon) Caron (1850–1905) immigrated to Australia from France in 1876. Upon arriving in Melbourne, he secured employment as an opera conductor, a career he would successfully pursue throughout Australia and New Zealand for the rest of his life. Among his works are two excellent cantatas, *Victoria* (1880) and *Australian National Cantata* (1888, composed for the Melbourne Centennial Exposition). Both are for soloists, mixed chorus, and orchestra. *Victoria* opened the Melbourne International Exhibition and was performed with a chorus of 1,000 and an orchestra of a 125.

The city of Adelaide was forced to produce its own music because it was relatively isolated and was therefore not visited by traveling artists, as were Sydney, Melbourne, and Brisbane. Founded in 1836, it was not a convict settlement, but relied heavily on German Lutheran immigrants. Choral music became dominant, and choral organizations based on both German and English models flourished, the most notable among them being the Adelaide Choral

The Adelaider Liedertafel at their men's choir Festival in Adelaide, Australia, 1863. Courtesy of the Adelaider Liedertafel 1858.

Society, founded in 1844, and the Adelaider Liedertafel, organized in 1850.

New Zealand was colonized in 1839, and informal choral singing began very soon thereafter. In 1860 the Canterbury Vocal Union was established by nine men. This fledgling group grew into the Royal Christchurch Musical Society. The interest in the English choral tradition continued with the founding of similar groups in other cities and culminated in 1879 with the creation of the Choir School of Christchurch. Although there were numerous fine choral conductors, composers were slow in developing, and, as in Australia, repertoire consisted primarily of European imports.

Throughout the century choral music thrived in areas where Eurocentric choral singing had been introduced. Conductors and composers were quick to take advantage of opportunities afforded by nationalism and secularism, creating the choral societies that would not only provide vital artistic outlets for the masses but also assist in social change. Conservative critics railed against operatic elements in sacred music without realizing that the introduction of symphonic form and the focus on mediant tonal progression in Haydn's late Masses had forever changed the landscape of sacred music, style notwithstanding. In spite of Beethoven's call for universal brotherhood, there was an intensification of national styles, aided by political movements that sought an end to various kinds of oppression.

The issue of propriety in church music was reflected in hundreds if not thousands of choral works. Liberal Judaism created a totally new genre of liturgical pieces that are still sung in synagogues in the twenty-first century. Male choruses took on an unforeseen importance outside of the university. Nationalism forced a new examination of folk sources. Oratorio increased in popularity in many countries but diminished in importance in Italy, the country of its birth. In many places choral music became a basic element in education, and, as seen above, choirs were also formed wherever people sought to establish identity and/or culture.

Revolutionary and nationalistic movements had largely completed their tasks by the last two decades of the century. Some still voiced concern about the future direction of music, but there was little agreement as to what that direction might be: most composers simply attempted to find a comfortable middle ground in their efforts to blend classical and romantic impulses. And yet the agents of incomprehensible change—Claude Debussy, Charles Ives, Arnold Schoenberg, and Igor Stravinsky—were poised to create their own revolutions: revolutions that would reinvigorate the fundamental core of music in the coming century and in which choral music would play a vital role.

Works Lists

The following lists include choral music by nineteenth-century composers mentioned in the text. Lists are organized alphabetically by composer according to type of choral ensemble (mixed, boys' or children's, female or treble, male) and accompaniment (unaccompanied, piano, organ, other instruments, wind orchestra or band, chamber orchestra, full orchestra).

Compositions for Mixed Chorus

UNACCOMPANIED

Adam, Adolphe
  Messe solennelle
Alkan, Charles-Valentin
  Etz chajjim hi
Alcedo, José Bernardo
  Hymno Ave maris stella
  Missa solemnis in D Major
  Missa solemnis in E-flat Minor
  Missa solemnis in F Major
  Tantum ergo
Almqvist, Carl Jonas Love
  Songes
Anckermann, Carlos
  Gran Misa (Misa de los Asturianos)
Arensky, Anton Stepanovich
  Anchar, Op. 14

Four Sacred Choruses from the
    Liturgy of St. John Chrysostom,
    Op. 40
Bachmann, Jacob
  Shirat Jacob
Balakirev, Mily Alekseyivich
  Let All Mortal Flesh Keep Silence
Baumanis, Kärlis
  Dievs, sveti Latviju
Bello Montero, Atanasio
  Pange lingua
  Vigil and Mass for the Dead
Berwald, Franz
  Larghetto, Allegro con Spirito
Bishop, Henry R.
  "Home, Sweet Home"
Borkowski, Bohdan

Natarcie jazdy

Bortniansky, Dmitri Stepanovich

   Glory to God in the Highest

   Let God Arise

   Lord, Make Me to Know My End

   Te Deum

Brahms, Johannes

   Twenty-six German Folk Songs

     "Der englische Jäger"

     "Morgengesang"

     "Täublein weiss"

     "Vom heiligen Märtyrer

       Emmerano, Bischoffen zu

       Regenssburg"

     "Von edler Art"

     "Wach auf!"

   Es ist das Heil uns kommen her, Op.

     29, No. 1

   Drei Gesänge, Op. 42

   Fest- und Gedenksprüche, Op. 109

   Fünf Gesänge, Op. 104

   Lieder und Romanzen, Op. 93a

   Marienlieder, Op. 22

   Missa canonica

   O Heiland Reiss die Himmel auf,

     Op. 74, No. 2

   Schaffe in mir, Op. 29, No. 2

   Sieben Lieder, Op. 62

   Three Motets, Op. 110

   Warum ist das Licht gegeben, Op.

     74, No. 1

Brendler, Eduard

   I de höjda toner skaller

   Spastara död

Brockway, Howard

   Cantate Domino, Op. 6

Two Choruses, Op. 24

Bruch, Max

   Nine Lieder, Op. 60

Bruckner, Anton

   Ave Maria

   Locus iste

   Os justi

   Pange lingua et Tantum ergo

   Virga Jesse floruit

Cherubini, Luigi

   Petrus apostolus

Costa, Michael

   Mass

Crusell, Bernhard Henrik

   Den lilla slavinnan

Cui, César

   Five Choruses, Op. 46

d'Antoni, Antonio

   Mass for St. Cecilia's Day

Delaney, Alfred

   Dirge

Dvořák, Antonín

   Amid Nature, Op. 63

   Four Part-songs, Op. 29

Dvoretsy, I. S.

   Svéte tíniy

Elgar, Edward William

   Four Part-songs, Op. 53

Fauré, Gabriel

   Tantum ergo, Op. 55

Foster, Stephen

   "Come Where My Love Lies

     Dreaming"

Glinka, Mikhail Ivanovich

   Cherubic Hymn

   Let My Prayer Arise

Grell, Eduard
  Mass
Grieg, Edvard
  Ave maris stella
  Four Psalms, Op. 74
  Scenes from "Olav Trygvason," Op.
    50
Herzogenberg, Heinrich von
  Vier Notturnos, Op. 22
Horner, Wilson G.
  National Consecration Chant
Hummel, Johann Nepomuk
  "Herauf Gesang"
  "Kehrt der frohe Tag"
  "Wir steigen frölich"
  "Think On Your Friend"
  Twelve Part-songs to Italian Texts
Liszt, Ferenc (Franz)
  Ungarisches Königslied: "Magyar
    Kiraly-dal"
Lobo, Elias Álvares
  Missa de São Paulo de Alcántara
Lomakin, Gavriil Yakimovich
  All-night Vigil
  The Cherubic Hymn
Lvov, Aleksei Fyodorovich
  It Is Truly Fitting, No. 3
  Of the Mystical Supper
  Standing Before the Cross
MacDowell, Edward
  Two Northern Songs, Op. 43
MacFarren, George Alexander
  *Introits for the Holy Days and
    Seasons of the English Church*
  *Shakespeare Songs for Four
    Voices*

MacKenzie, Alexander Campbell
  Seven Part-songs, Op. 8
Makarov, P.
  Angel vopiyáshe
Meserón, Juan Francisco
  Miserere
Mendelssohn, Fanny Hensel
  Gartenlieder, Op. 3
Mendelssohn, Felix
  "Die Nachtigall," Op. 59, No. 4
  "Ehre sei Gott"
  "Heilig"
  "Psalm 100"
  Six Anthems, Op. 79
  Six Part-songs, Op. 41
Meyerbeer, Giacomo
  Geistliche Oden von Klopstock
  Twelve Psalms
  Stabat mater
  Te Deum
Millard, Harrison
  *New National Ode: The Flag of the
    Free*
Montero, José Angel
  Oficios de difuntos (Requiem)
Morales, Melesio
  Misa de gloria
Naumbourg, Samuel
  Zemriot Israel
Palacios, Rafael
  Stabat mater
Parry, Charles Hubert Hastings
  Songs of Farewell
Ponce de León, José María
  Requiem Mass
Raimondi, Pietro

Mass

Rheinberger, Josef Gabriel

Drei geistliche Gesänge, Op. 69

"Morgenlied"

"Dein sind die Himmel"

"Abendlied"

Missa Sanctissimae Trinitatis, Op. 117

Rimsky-Korsakov, Nikolai

The Lord's Prayer

We Praise Thee, O God

Rubinstein, Anton

Six Part-songs, Op. 62

Sáenz, Antonio

Misa para Día de difuntos

Sáenz, Vicente

Villancicos de Pascua

Schubert, Franz

Christ ist erstanden

Psalm 92: *Tov l'Hodos*

Smetana, Bedřich

Heilig, heilig, ist der Herr Zabaoth

Ich hoffe auf den Herrn

Jesu, meine Freude

Lobet den Herrn

Modlitba

Naše píseň

Píseň na moři

Rolnická

Slavnostni sbor

Tře jezdci

Veňo

Spohr, Louis

Mass, Op. 54

Six Part-songs, Op. 151

Stainer, John

"God So Loved the World"

Stanford, Charles Villiers

Three Motets, Op. 51

Starorrussky

Ot yúnosti moyeyá

Stenhammar, Wilhelm

Three Choral Ballads

Tchaikovsky, Peter

All-night Vigil, Op. 52

Liturgy of St. John Chrysostom, Op. 41

Nine Sacred Choruses

"A Legend"

"Our Father"

The Angel Cried

Turner, J. W.

"The President's Hymn"

Velásquez, Glauco

Pater noster

Velásquez, José Francisco

Misa en mi bemol

Velázquez, José Guadalupe

Ave maris stella

Verdi, Giuseppe

Padre nostro

Quattro pezzi sacri

Ave Maria

Wesley, Samuel

In exitu Israel

Missa solemnis

Zapiola, José

Misa

With Piano

Abeille, Ludwig

Aschermittwoch Lied

Alcorta, Amancio
Lamentaciones
Alkan, Charles-Valentin
Halelouyoh
Balfe, Michael William
Nelly Gray
Berlioz, Hector
Le ballet des ombres, Op. 2
Brahms, Johannes
Five Songs, Op. 104
"Verlorene Jugend," No. 4
"Im Herbst," No. 5
Four Quartets, Op. 92
Kleine Hochzeitskantate
Liebeslieder Walzer, Op. 52
Neueliebeslieder, Op. 65
Seven Songs, Op. 62
"Rosmarin," No. 1
"Vergangen ist mir Glück und
Heil," No. 7
Six Songs, Op. 93a
"Beherzigung," No. 6
Six Quartets, Op. 112
"Nächtens," No. 2
Tafellied, Op. 93b
Three Songs, Op. 42
"Vineta," No. 2
Three Quartets, Op. 64
"Der Abend," No. 2
Zigeunerlieder, Op. 103
Bruckner, Anton
Vergissmeinnicht
de Almeida, Inácio António
Miserere
Glinka, Mikhail
Molitva

Liszt, Ferenc (Franz)
Chorus of Angels from Goethe's Faust
Ungarisches Königslied: "Magyar
Kiraly-dal"
Mendelssohn, Fanny Hensel
Einleitung zu lebenden Bilder
Zum Fest der heiligen Cäcilia
Mussorgsky, Modest
Jesus Nevin
Nietzsche, Friedrich
Christmas Cantata
Hymne an die Freundschaft
Rubinstein, Anton
Songs and Requiem for Mignon,
Op. 91
Schubert, Franz
Lebenslust
Mirjams Siegesgesang
Wolf, Hugo
"Aufblick"
"Im stillen Friedhof"
"Resignation"

With Organ

Adam, Adolphe
Domine salvum
Baca, Luis
Ave Maria
Balfe, Michael William
Save Me, O God
Barnaby, Joseph
"Laudes Domini"
"Merrial"
Brahms, Johannes
Lass dich nur nichts nicht dauren,
Op. 30

Buck, Dudley
  Te Deum
Cherubini, Luigi
  Credo
  Petite messe de la Sainte Trinité, D
    Minor
Dvořák, Antonín
  Mass in D Major, Op. 86
Elgar, Sir Edward William
  Te Deum and Benedictus,
    Op. 34
Fauré, Gabriel
  Tantum ergo
Foerster, Joseph
  Missa Bohemica
Leslie, Henry David
  Jubilate in D
  Let God Arise
  Te Deum
Lewandowski, Lewis
  Deutsche Kedushah
  Haleluyaw (Psalm 150)
Liszt, Ferenc (Franz)
  Missa choralis
  Pater noster
  Via Crucis
Mendelssohn, Felix
  Hear My Prayer
Meyerbeer, Giacomo
  Pater noster
Nepomuceno, Alberto
  O salutaris hostia
Parry, Charles Hubert Hastings
  I Was Glad
Rheinberger, Josef Gabriel
  Mass in F Minor, Op. 159

Schubert, Franz Peter
  Deutsche Trauermesse
Schumann, Robert
  "Gute Nacht," Op. 59, No. 4
Smart, Henry Thomas
  Regent Square
  Lancashire
Stainer, John
  The Crucifixion
Straume, Jānis
  Pie Baltijas jūras
Wesley, Samuel Sebastian
  Let Us Lift Up Our Heart
  The Wilderness and the Solitary
    Place
Witt, Franz Xaver
  Te Deum

With Other Instruments

Apell, David August von
  Missa pontificale
Beethoven, Ludwig van
  Bundeslied, Op. 122
  Elegischer Lied, Op. 118
  Opferlied, Op. 121
Bontempo, João Domingos
  Miserere
Bourgault-Ducoudray, Louis
  Stabat mater
Brahms, Johannes
  Begräbnisgesang, Op. 13
Bruckner, Anton
  Auf, Brüder! Auf zur frohen Feier
  Ecce sacerdos magnus
  Requiem
  Tantum ergo

Chausson, Ernest
  Three Motets, Op. 12
de Bréville, Pierre
  Laudate Dominum
  Mass
Donizetti, Gaetano
  Ave Maria
Fauré, Gabriel
  Cantique de Jean Racine, Op. 11
Glinka, Mikhail
  Pleurons, pleurons sur la Russie
Janáček, Leoš
  Hospodine pomiluj ny
Nepomuceno, Alberto
  As Uyaras
  Maria mater gratiae
Rossini, Gioachino
  Petite messe sollennelle
Saint-Saëns, Camille
  Le déluge, Op. 46
  Les noces de Prométhée, Op. 45
  Oratorio de Noël, Op. 12
Schumann, Robert
  "Das Schifflein," Op. 146, No. 5
  "Zigeunerleben," Op. 29, No. 3

WITH WIND ORCHESTRA OR BAND

Alkan, Charles-Valentin
  Marcia funebre sulla morete d'un papagallo
Berwald, Franz
  Gustaf Adolph the Great's Victory and Death at Lützen
Bruckner, Anton
  Mass in E Minor

Nunes Garcia, José Mauricio
  Requiem Mass
Schubert, Franz Peter
  Deutsche Messe
Schumann, Robert
  Beim Abschied zu singen, Op. 84
Tomás, Guillermo M.
  La oración del creyente

WITH CHAMBER ORCHESTRA

d'Antoni, Antonio
  Il genio di Trieste
de Araújo, Damião Barbosa
  Memento baiano (para coro e orquestra)
Doubravsky, František
  Missa pastoralis
  Missa solemnis in D Major
  Requiem in E-flat Major
  Stabat mater
  Te Deum in C Major
Guerra, Gratilio
  Mass in C
  Mass in D
Llaque, Bonifacio
  Cantada a la Virgen (Pastorala)
Nunes Garcia, José Mauricio
  Laudate Dominum omnes gentes (Psalm 117)
  Laudate pueri Dominum
Schubert, Franz
  Intende voci
  Magnificat
  Mass No. 1 in F Major
  Mass No. 3 in B-flat Major
  Mass No. 4 in C Major

Smetana, Bedřich

Meditabitu in mandatis tuis

Scapulis suis

Winter, P.

Elijah Raising the Widow's Son

WITH FULL ORCHESTRA

Ahlstroem, Olof

Choralbok

Adam, Adolphe

Agnes Sorel

Ariane à Naxos

Cantata

La fête des arts

Les nations

Messe de Ste. Cecile

O salutaris

Victoire

Afanas'yev, Nikolai Yakovlevich

Pir Petra Velikova

Aggházy, Károly

Rákoczí

Akerberg, Erik

Prinsessan och Svennen

Anacker, August Ferdinand

Bergmannsgruss

Andre, Johann Anton

Missa solemnis, Op. 43

Te Deum, Op. 60

Vater unser, Op. 50

Apell, David August von

Magnificat

Mass

Te Deum

Arensky, Anton Stepanovich

The Fountain of Bakhchisaray,

Op. 46

Arvelo, Julio Quevedo

Salve pastoral

Attwood, Thomas

I Was Glad

O Lord, Grant the King a Long Life

Baguer, Carlos

El regreso á Barcelona su patria de

    Dr. Josef Oriol

El regreso del hijo pródigo

Job

La adoration del niño Dios por los

    ángeles y pastores

La muerte de Abel

La partida del hijo pródigo

La resurrección de Lázaro

Baldi, João José

Magnificat

Mass in Honor of Count de Borba

Te Deum

Balfe, Michael William

Mazeppa

Barnett, John

Abraham on the Altar of his Son

Daniel in the Den of Lions

Grand Mass in C Minor

Grand Mass in G Minor

The Omnipotence of the Deity

Barnett, John Francis

The Ancient Mariner

The Raising of Lazarus

Bazzini, Antonio

Sennacheribbo

Beauleiu, Marie Désiré

Requiem

Beer-Walbrunn, Anton

Mahomets Gesang

Beethoven, Ludwig van

  Cantata on the Ascension of
    Emperor Leopold

  Cantata on the Death of Emperor
    Joseph

  Christus am Ölberg, Op. 85

  Der glorreiche Augenblick, Op. 136

  Die Ruinen von Athen, Op. 113

  Die Weihe des Hauses, Op. 124

  Egmont

  Fantasia, Op. 80

  Fidelio

  König Stephan, Op. 17

  Mass in C Major, Op. 86

  Meeresstille und glückliche Fahrt,
    Op. 112 (Calm Sea and
    Prosperous Voyage)

  Missa solemnis, Op. 123

  Preis der Tonkunst

  Symphony No. 9, Op. 125

  Three Hymns, Op. 86a

Bellini, Vincenzo

  Norma

  I Puritani

Bendix, Victor

  Psalm 33, Op. 7

Bendl, Karel

  Smrt Prokopa Velikého

  Štědrý den

  Švanda dudák

  Umírající husita

Bennett, William Sterndale

  The May Queen

Benoit, Camille

  Eleison

Benoit, François

  Mass

Benoit, Peter

  De Rhijn

  Lucifer

  Prometheus

  Quadrilogie religieuse

    Cantate de Noel

    Messe solennelle

    Requiem

    Te Deum

Berlijn, Anton

  Die Matrosen am Ufer

  Mass

  Moses auf Nebo

Berger, Wilhelm

  Meine Göttin, Op. 72

Berlioz, Hector

  Grand messe des morts

  Huit scènes de Faust

  La damnation de Faust, Op. 24

  Lélio ou Le retour à la view, Op. 14

  L'enfance du Christ, Op. 25

  Messe solennelle

  Requiem, Op. 5

  Roméo et Juliette, Op. 17

  Te Deum, Op. 22

Berneker, Constanz

  Judith

Berton, Henri-Montan

  Cantata for the Marriage of
    Napoleon and Marie-Louise

Berwald, Franz

  Chorale

Bexfield, William Richard

  Israel Restored

Bierey, Gottlieb Benedikt
  Wie an dem stillen Abend
Bizet, Georges
  Carmen
  Clovis et Clothilde
  David
  Les pécheurs de perles
  Te Deum
Blockx, Jan
  Antwerpen's schutsgeest
  Een droom van 't paradijs
  Klokke Roeland
Blondeau, Pierre-Augueste-Louis
  Te Deum
Blumner, Martin
  Abraham, Op. 8
  Der Fall Jerusalems, Op. 30
Boito, Arrigo
  Mefistofele
Bomtempo, João Domingos
  A paz da Europa
  Hymno lustiano
  Libera me
  Requiem
Borkowski, Bohdan
  *Hymn for the Feast of the
    Annunciation of the Blessed
    Virgin Mary*
Borodin, Alexander
  "Polovtsian Dances"
  Prince Igor
Bortniansky, Dmitri Stepanovich
  Cherubic Hymn
Bottesini, Giovanni
  Requiem
  The Garden of Olivet

Boutmy, Laurent-François
  Le naufrage
Brahms, Johannes
  Ein deutsches Requiem, Op. 45
  Gesang der Parzen, Op. 89
  Liebeslieder Suite
  Nänie, Op. 82
  Schicksalslied, Op. 54
  Triumphlied, Op. 55
Braun, Wilhelm Theodor Johannes
  Mass
Brendler, Eduard
  Edmund och Clara
Bretón, Tomás
  El apocalipsis
Bristow, George Frederick
  Daniel, Op. 42
  Niagara Symphony, Op. 63
  The Pioneer, Op. 49
  Praise to God, Op. 33
Bruch, Max
  Achilleus, Op. 50
  Das Feuerkreuz, Op. 52
  Das Lied von der Glocke, Op. 45
  Hebräische Gesänge
  Moses: ein biblisches Oratorium,
    Op. 67
  Odysseus, Op. 41
Bruckner, Anton
  Mass in D Minor
  Mass in F Minor
  Psalm 150
  Te Deum
Bruneau, Alfred
  Requiem
Buck, Dudley

The Centennial Meditation of
  Columbia
The Forty-sixth Psalm
The Golden Legend
The Legend of Don Munio, Op. 62
The Light of Asia
Bungert, August
  Warum? Woher? Wohin?, Op. 60
Burghersh, John Fane
  Grand Mass
Busoni, Ferruccio
  Il sabato del villagio
Cahen, Albert
  Jean le Precurseur
Capocci, Gaetano
  Assalone
  Battista
Carafa, Michele
  Ave verum
Carnicer, Ramón
  Missa solemnis
  Requiem (1829)
  Requiem (1842)
  Tantum ergo
  Tota pulchra
Caron, Leslie Francis Victor (Leon)
  Australian National Cantata
  Victoria
Caruso, Luigi
  Mass in C Major
  Requiem
Castillon, Alexis
  Mass
  Paraphrase du psaume 84
Catalani, Alfredo
  Mass

Cellier, Alfred
  Grey's Elegy
Chadwick, George Whitefield
  Dedication Ode
  Lovely Rosabelle
  Noël
  Phoenix expirans
Charpentier, Gustave
  La vie du poète
  Le chant d'apothéose
  Louise
  Sérénade à Watteau
Cherubini, Luigi
  Les deux journées
  Magnificat
  Mass in F Major
  Mass in A Major ("Coronation")
  Missa solemnis in C Major
  Missa solemnis in D Minor
  Requiem in C Minor
  Te Deum
Čiurlionis, Mikolajus
  De profundis
Corder, Frederick
  The Bridal of Triermain
  The Cyclops
Costa, Michael
  Dixit Dominus
  Eli
  La Passione
  Naaman
Cowen, Frederic H.
  Ruth
  The Sleeping Beauty
de Bréville, Pierre
  La tête de Kenwarc'h

de Lange, Samuel
  Mozes
Donizetti, Gaetano
  Le siete chiesa
  Messa di Gloria e Credo
  Oratorio Sacra
  Requiem
Dvořák, Antonín
  Hymnus: Dědicové Bílé Hory, Op. 30
  Requiem, Op. 89
  Stabat mater, Op. 58
  Svatá Ludmila, Op. 71
  Svatební Košile, Op. 69
  Te Deum, Op. 103
  The American Flag, Op. 102
  The Old Folks at Home
Elgar, Sir Edward William
  Caractacus
  Lux Christi
  Scenes from the Saga of King Olaf
  Spirit of England, Op. 80
  The Apostles
  The Black Knight
  The Dream of Gerontius
  The Kingdom
  The Light of Life
  The Music Makers
Eybler, Joseph Leopold, Edler von
  Requiem in C Minor
  Te Deum
Fauré, Gabriel
  Requiem, Op. 48
David, Félicien
  Moïse au Sinai
Fibich, Zdeněk

The Bride of the Wind
Foote, Arthur
  The Skeleton in Armor, Op. 28
  The Wreck of the Hesperus, Op. 17
Franck, César
  Les Béatitudes
  Psalm 150
  Psyché
  Trois Offertoires
Gade, Niels
  Der Strom, Op. 64
  Elverskud, Op. 30
Glinka, Mikhail
  Velik nash Bog
Goldschmidt, Adalbert von
  Die sieben Todsünden
Gomes, Antônio Carlos
  Colombo
Gossec, François Joseph
  Hymn to the Supreme Being
  Requiem
  Te Deum
Gounod, Charles
  La rédemption
  Mors et vita
  St. Caecilia Mass
  Tobias
Grell, Eduard
  Die Israeliten in der Wüste
  Te Deum
Grieg, Edvard
  Peer Gynt
Grimm, Julius Otto
  An die Musik
Hadyn, Franz Joseph
  Missa in angustiis ("Nelsonmesse")

in D Minor
Mass in B-Flat
("Harmoniemesse")
Mass in B-Flat
("Schöpfungsmesse")
Mass in B-Flat
("Theresienmesse")
Missa Sancti Bernardi von Offida
("Heiligmesse") in B-flat Major
Missa in tempore belli
("Paukenmesse") in C Major
Die Schöpfung (The Creation)
Die Jahreszeiten (The Seasons)
Halévy, Jacques-François-Fromental
Ave verum
La juive
Prométhée enchaîné
Hatton, John Liphot
Robin Hood
Hiller, Ferdinand
Saul
Zerstörungs Jerusalems
Hummel, Johann Nepomuk
Mass in E Major
Te Deum
Josephson, Axel
Islossningen
Quando corpus
Júnior, Joaquim Casimiro
Sansão, ou A destrucião dos
Philisteus
Lamas, José Angel
Populus meus
Leslie, Henry David
Holyrood
Immanuel

Judith
The Daughter of the Isles
Liszt, Ferenc (Franz)
Christus
Dante Symphony
Die Legende von der heiligen
Elisabeth
Faust Symphony
Hungarian Coronation Mass
Missa solemnis
("Granerfestmesse")
Mabellini, Teodulo
Eudosia e Paolo
Ultimo giorno di Gerusalemme
MacFarren, George Alexander
Christmas
Joseph
Leonora
May Day
St. John the Baptist
The Lady of the Lake
The Resurrection
MacKenzie, Alexander Campbell
A Jubilee Ode, Op. 36
Rose of Sharon, Op. 30
The Story of Sayid, Op. 34
Veni creator spiritus, Op. 46
Mahler, Gustav
Das klagende Lied
Symphony No. 2 ("Resurrection")
Massenet, Jules
La terre promise
Mayr, Johann Simon
La Passione
Stabat mater
Měchura, Leopold Eugen

Christmas Eve

Mendelssohn, Fanny Hensel

  Hiob

  Lobgesang

  Oratorium nach den Bildern der
    Bibel

Mendelssohn, Felix

  Athalie, Op. 74

  Christus, Op. 97

    "There Shall a Star Come out
      of Jacob"

  Elijah, Op. 70

  Die erste Walpurgisnacht, Op. 60

  Hear My Prayer

  Lauda Sion, Op. 73

  Psalm 42, Op. 42

  Psalm 95, Op. 46

  St. Paul, Op. 36

    "The Conversion of St. Paul"
      (Part I, ed. Charles Hirt)

    "How Lovely Are the
      Messengers"

  Symphony No. 2, Op. 52
  ("Lobgesang")

Meyerbeer, Giacomo

  Gott und die Natur

Mussorgsky, Modest

  Boris Godunov

  Shamil's March

  The Destruction of Sennacherib

Nietzsche, Friedrich

  Hymne an das Leben

Nunes Garcia, José Mauricio

  Missa de Santa Cecilia

Paine, John Knowles

  Mass in D, Op. 10

The Nativity, Op. 38

St. Peter, Op. 20

The Realm of Fancy, Op. 36

Parker, Horatio

  Hora novissima, Op. 30

Parry, Charles Hubert Hastings

  An Ode to the Nativity

  Judith

  Ode to Music

  Ode to Solemn Music: "Blest Pair
    of Sirens"

  *Scenes from Shelley's 'Prometheus
    Unbound'*

Perosi, Lorenzo

  *La Passione de Cristo secondo San
    Marco: trilogia sacra*

Puccini, Giacomo

  Edgar

  Manon

  Messa di Gloria

Raimondi, Pietro

  Giuseppe—Putifar—Giacobbe

  Mass

  Requiem

  Stabat mater

  Te Deum

Rejcha, Antonín

  Der neue Psalm

  Requiem

  Te Deum

Rheinberger, Josef Gabriel

  Mass in E-flat Major, Op. 109

  Mass, Op. 169

  Star of Bethlehem, Op. 164

Rimsky-Korsakov, Nikolai

  "Procession of the Nobles" from

Mlada

Rossini, Gioachino

  Stabat mater

Rubinstein, Anton

  Christus, Op. 117

  Moses, Op. 112

  Paradise Lost, Op. 54

  The Maccabees

  The Tower of Babel, Op. 80

Sáenz, Antonio

  Misa solemne

  Te Deum

Saint-Saëns, Camille

  Mass, Op. 4

  Requiem, Op. 54

  Samson et Dalila, Op. 47

Schubert, Franz

  Lazarus

  Mass No. 2 in G Major

  Mass No. 5 in A-flat Major

  Mass No. 6 in E-flat

  Raising of Lazarus

Schumann, Robert

  Adventlied, Op. 71

  Das Glück von Edenhall, Op. 143

  Das Paradies und die Peri, Op. 50

  Der Königssohn, Op. 116

  Der Rose Pilgerfahrt, Op. 112

  Des Sängers Fluch, Op. 139

  Festival Overture on the

    "Rheinweinlied," Op. 123

  Missa sacra, Op. 147

  Requiem, Op. 148

  Requiem für Mignon, Op. 98b

  Szenen aus Goethe's "Faust"

  Vom Pagen und der Königstochter,

    Op. 140

Silva, Prescilliano

  Crux fideles

Škroup, František

  Dratenik

Smart, Henry Thomas

  Jacob

  King Rene's Daughter

  The Bride of Dunkerron

Smetana, Bedřich

  Česka piseň

Smythe, Dame Ethyl

  Mass in D

Spohr, Louis

  Psalm 84, Op. 134

Stanford, Charles Villiers

  Requiem, Op. 63

  Stabat mater, Op. 96

Stenhammar, Wilhelm

  I rosengård

Sullivan, Arthur Seymour

  The Golden Legend

  The Light of the World

  The Martyr of Antioch

  The Prodigal Son

Taneyev, Sergey Ivanovich

  At the Reading of a Psalm, Op. 36

  John of Damascus, Op. 1

Tchaikovsky, Pyotr Il'yich

  To Joy

Tenel, Edgar

  Franciscus

Thomas, Ambroise

  Messe des mort

  Messe solemnelle

Thomas, Arthur Goring

The Swan and the Skylark

Tobias, Rudolf

  Johannes Damascenus

Veit, Jindřich

  Mass in D Major

  Te Deum

Velázquez, José Guadalupe

  Es Maria norte y guia

Verdi, Giuseppe

  Inno delle nazioni

  Nabucco

  Requiem

  Quattro pezzi sacri

    Stabat mater

    Te Deum

Villanueva, Felipe

  Cantata patriotica (El retrato de benemérito cura Hidalgo)

Voříšek, Jan Hugo

  Mass in B-flat Major

Wade, Joseph

  The Prophecy

Wagner, Richard

  Neujahrs-Kantate

Weber, Carl Maria von

  Der erste Ton, Op. 14

  Jubal-Cantata, Op. 58

  Mass in E-flat Major, Op. 75a

  Mass in G Major, Op. 76

Wolf, Hugo

  Der Feuerreiter

Wolf-Ferrari, Ermanno

  Talitha Kumi

Xavier, José Maria

  Matinas de Natal

Zelter, Carl Friedrich

  Requiem

  Te Deum

Zingarelli, Niccolo Antonio

  Canticao d'Isaiah profeta

Compositions for Boys' or Children's Chorus

UNACCOMPANIED

Cui, César
  Les oiseaux d'Argenteau
Liszt, Ferenc (Franz)
  Ungarisches Königslied: "Magyar Kiraly-dal"

WITH PIANO

Berlioz, Hector
  Prière du matin, Op. 19, No. 4
Rheinberger, Josef Gabriel
  May Day, Op. 64
Schubert, Franz
  Gott in natur
Stanford, Charles Villiers
  Nine Songs for Children, Op. 30

WITH ORGAN

Parry, Charles Hubert Hastings
  "Jerusalem"
Sulzer, Salomon
  Duda'im

WITH FULL ORCHESTRA

Blockx, Jan
  De kleine Bronnen
Mahler, Gustav
  Symphony No. 3 in D Minor
Rheinberger, Josef Gabriel
  Daughter of Jairus, Op. 32

Compositions for Female or Treble Chorus

UNACCOMPANIED

Bendl, Karel

   Four Songs

Bortniansky, Dmitri Stepanovich

   Let My Prayer Arise, No. 2

Brahms, Johannes

   Geistliche Chöre, Op. 37

   Thirteen Canons, Op. 113

   Twelve Songs and Romances, Op. 44

Cui, César Antonovich

   Mystic Chorus, Op. 28

Fauré, Gabriel

   Tantum ergo, Op. 65, No. 2

Hummel, Johann Nepomuk

   "O ihr Geliebten"

MacDowell, Edward

   Summer Wind

Mahler, Gustav

   Symphony No. 3 in D Minor

Mussorgsky, Modest

   Three Vocalises

Rheinberger, Josef Gabriel

   Mass in A, Op. 126

Smetana, Bedřich

   Three Choruses for Women's Voices

Valle Riestra, José María

   Ave Maria

   O salutaris

Verdi, Giuseppe

   Quatro pezzi sacri

   Laudi alla Vergine Maria

WITH PIANO

Alkan, Charles-Valentin

   Stances de Millevoye

Arensky, Anton Stepanovich

   Tsvetnik, Op. 69

Berlioz, Hector

   Tantum ergo

   Veni creator

Bruch, Max

   Six Christkindlieder, Op. 92

Chausson, Ernest

   Jeanne d'Arc

Dvořák, Antonín

   Moravian Duets, Op. 32 & Op. 38

Liadov, Anatal

   Songs, Op. 50

MacDowell, Edward

   Two Part-songs, Op. 27

Rossini, Gioachino

   Trois choeurs religieux

Schubert, Franz Peter

   Ständchen

Schumann, Robert

   Romanzen, Op. 69 & Op. 91

With Organ

Besozzi, Louis-Désiré
La chapelle du convent
Brahms, Johannes
Ave Maria, Op. 12
Psalm 13, Op. 27
Fauré, Gabriel
Messe basse
Mendelssohn, Felix
Three Latin Motets, Op. 39
Rheinberger, Josef Gabriel
Mass, Op. 155

With Other Instruments

Brahms, Johannes
Songs for Female Chorus, Op. 17
de Bréville, Pierre
Hymne à Venus
Elgar, Edward William
Two Part-songs, Op. 26
Liadov, Anatal
Slava, Op. 47

With Full Orchestra

Blockx, Jan
De kleine bronnen

Vredezang
Bruch, Max
Die Flucht nach Ägypten, Op. 31,
No. 1
Morgenstunde, Op. 31, no. 2
de Bréville, Pierre
Chant des divinités de la forêt
Médeia
Diepenbrock, Alphons
Les elfes
Foote, Arthur
Lygeia, Op. 58
Grieg, Edvard
*At a Southern Convent's Gate, Op.
20*
McEwen, John
Scene from "Hellas"
Nepomucena, Alberto
As Uyaras
Rubinstein, Anton
The Water-sprite, Op. 63
Smart, Henry Thomas
The Fishermaidens
Wolf, Hugo
Elfenlied

Compositions for Male Chorus

UNACCOMPANIED

Adam, Adolph
Les enfants de Paris
La garde mobile
La marche républicaine
Les métiers
La muette

Arensky, Anton Stepanovich
Two Choruses, Op. 31

Balatka, Hans
The Power of Song

Baumanis, Kārlis
How the Daugava Moans

Bella, Ján Levoslav
Drei ernste Gesänge
Vier heitere Gesänge
Haec dies
Tu es Petrus

Bendl, Karel
Pochod Táborů

Benoit, Peter
Aan Antwerpen
De Maaiers

Berwald, Franz
Apoteos

Blockx, Jan
De Heide
Licht

Borodin, Alexander
Serenade of Four Cavaliers to One Lady

Bortniansky, Dmitri Stepanovich
Let My Prayer Arise, No. 2
Liturgy

Brahms, Johannes
Five Songs, Op. 41

Bruch, Max
In der Nacht, Op. 72

Bruckner, Anton
Träumen und Wachen

Buya, Ludwig Felix Brandts
Avondrood
Zegepraal

Cui, César Antonovich
Two Choruses, Op. 58

David, Félicien
Le désert

Diepenbrock, Alphons
Stabat mater

Dvořák, Antonín
Four Part-songs

Elgar, Edward William
Five Part-songs, Op. 45

Gade, Niels
Five Songs, Op. 33

Glinka, Mikhail Ivanovich

Great Litany
Janáček, Leoš
  Ave Maria
  Choral Elegy
  Three Male-voice Choruses
Josephson, Axel
  Sjung, sjung, du underbara sang
  Stjänklart
Křížkovský, Pavel
  Dar za Lásku
  Odpadlý od srdca
  Odvedeného prosba
  Requiem
  Te Deum
  Utonulá
  Zaloba
  Zatoč ze
Liszt, Ferenc (Franz)
  Pater noster
  Ungarisches Königslied: "Magyar
    Kiraly-dal"
MacDowell, Edward
  Drei Lieder für vierstimmen
    Männerchor, Op. 27
MacKenzie, Alexander Campbell
  Two Toasts for Male Voices
Mussorgsky, Modest
  Five Russian Folk Songs
Nordraak, Rikard
  "Ja, vi elsker dette landet"
Rubinstein, Anton
  Three Part-songs, Op. 61
Schubert, Franz
  "An die Frühling"
  "Die Nacht"
  "Ewige Liebe"

Sibelius, Jean
  Rakastava, Op. 14
Smetana, Bedřich
  Odrodilec
Spohr, Louis
  Six Part-songs, Op. 44
  Six Part-songs, Op. 90
Stanford, Charles Villiers
  Three Cavalier Songs, Op. 17
Sulzer, Salomon
  Schir Zion
Svendsen, Johan
  Two Part-songs for Men's Voices,
    Op. 2
Wagner, Richard
  An Webers Grabe
Weber, Carl Maria von
  Leyer und Schwert, Op. 42
Wolf, Hugo
  "Mailied"

WITH PIANO

Andre, Johann Anton
  Liederkranz, Op. 57
  Liederkranz, Op. 61
  Twenty-four Maurergesänge
Baumgartner, Wilhelm
  O mein Heimatland, Op. 11, No. 1
Berlioz, Hector
  Chant guerrier
  Chanson à boire
Borodin, Alexander
  Requiem
  Song of the Dark Forest
Dvořák, Antonín
  From a Bouquet of Slavonic Folk

Songs, Op. 43

Janáček, Leoš

Festival Chorus

Křížkovský, Pavel

Vyprask

Liszt, Ferenc (Franz)

Ungarisches Königslied: "Magyar Kiraly-dal"

MacDowell, Edward

Three Choruses, Op. 52

Two Songs, Op. 41

Two Songs from the Thirteenth Century

War Song, Op. 6

The Witch, Op. 5

Parker, Horatio

Blow, Blow, Thou Winter Wind, Op. 14

Schubert, Franz Peter

Nachtelle

"Trinklied"

Schumann, Robert

"Die Lotusblume," Op. 33, No.1

Wolf, Hugo

"Die Stimme des Kindes"

WITH ORGAN

Alcorta, Amancio

La Agonia (Canto de Viernes Santo)

Benoit, Peter

Mass

Berwald, Franz

Nordiska fatasibilder

Brzowski, Josef

La foi messe

Requiem

Diepenbrock, Alphons

Missa in die festo

Halévy, Jacques-François-Fromental

Agnus Dei and Sanctus (from *Messe de l'Orphéon*)

Křížkovsky, Pavel

Hvězdy dvě se z východu

Rheinberger, Josef Gabriel

Mass, Op. 172

Mass in F Major, Op. 190

WITH OTHER INSTRUMENTS

Bruckner, Anton

Abendzauber

Das deutsche Lied

Elgar, Sir Edward William

Christmas Greeting, Op. 52

Goldmark, Carl

Frülingsnetz, Op. 15

Meeresstille und glückliche Fahrt, Op. 16

Hummel, Johann Nepomuk

"Have"

Křížkovsky, Pavel

Modlitba Sv. Cyrilla na sotnach

Liszt, Ferenc (Franz)

Requiem

Mendelssohn, Felix

An die Künstler: Festgesang, Op. 68

Der Jäger Abschied, Op. 50

Schubert, Franz Peter

Gesang der Geister über den Wassern

Schumann, Robert

Jagdlieder, Op. 137

Taneyev, Sergey Ivanovich

Sixteen Choruses, Op. 35

With Wind Orchestra or Band

Bruckner, Anton

   Auf Brüder, auf, und die Saiten zur Hand

With Full Orchestra

Akerberg, Erik

   Der barde

Berlioz, Hector

   La mort de Sardanapale

Borodin, Alexander

   Requiem

   Song of the Dark Forest

Bovy-Lysberg, Charles Samuel

   Les Alpes

Brahms, Johannes

   Rhapsodie, Op. 53

   Rinaldo, Op. 50

Bruch, Max

   Frithjof: Szenen aus der Frithjof-Sage, Op. 23

Buck, Dudley

   The Nun of Nidaros, Op. 83

   The Voyage of Columbus

Busoni, Ferruccio

   Primavera, estate, autumno, inverno, Op. 40

Chadwick, George Whitefield

   Ecce iam noctis

Cherubini, Luigi

   Requiem in D Minor

David, Samuel

   Le génie de la terre

Dvořák, Antonín

   Psalm 149, Op. 79

Foote, Arthur

   The Farewell of Hiawatha, Op. 11

Gade, Niels

   Choruses, Op. 26

   Den Bergtagne, Op. 52

Gevaert, François-Joseph

   Requiem

Grieg, Edvard

   Album, Op. 30

   Landsighting, Op. 31

   Songs from "Sigurd Jorsalfar," Op. 22

Liszt, Ferenc (Franz)

   Ungarisches Königslied: "Magyar Kiraly-dal"

Mendelssohn, Felix

   Festgesang on the Anniversary of the Gutenberg Bible

Paine, John Knowles

   Oedipus tyrannus, Op. 35

   Phoebus Arise, Op. 37

Schumann, Robert

   Verzweifle nicht im Schmerzenstal, Op. 93

Sibelius, Jean

   Kullervo, Op. 7

   Laulu Lemminkäiselle, Op. 31, No. 1

Wagner, Richard

   Das Liebesmahl der Apostel

Bibliography

Abraham, Gerald, ed. 1982. *The Age of Beethoven, 1790–1830*. Vol. 8 of *New Oxford History of Music*. London: Oxford University Press.

———, ed. 1990. *Romanticism, 1830–1890*. Vol. 9 of *New Oxford History of Music*. London: Oxford University Press.

Albright, Daniel. 2001. *Berlioz's Semi-operas: "Roméo et Juliette" and "La Damnation de Faust."* Rochester, N.Y.: University of Rochester Press.

Balthazar, Scott L. 1988. "Rossini and the Development of the Mid-century Lyric Form." *Journal of the American Musicological Society* 41, no. 1: 102–25.

Beckerman, Michael, ed. 1993. *Dvořák and His World*. Princeton, N.J.: Princeton University Press.

Beckwith, R. Sterling. 1968. "How to Write a Russian Mass." *American Choral Review* 10, no. 4: 178–85.

Beller-McKenna, Daniel. 2004. *Brahms and the German Spirit*. Cambridge, Mass.: Harvard University Press.

Béhague, Gerard. 1979. *Music in Latin America: An Introduction*. Englewood Cliffs, N.J.: Prentice Hall.

Bell, A. Craig. 1996. *Brahms: The Vocal Music*. Madison, N.J.: Fairleigh Dickinson University Press.

Berger, Melvin. 1993. *Guide to Choral Masterpieces: A Listener's Guide*. New York: Doubleday.

Bernard, Kenneth A. 1966. *Lincoln and the Music of the Civil War*. Caldwell, Id.: Caxton Printers.

Bethell, Leslie, ed. 1998. *A Cultural History of Latin America: Literature, Music and the Visual Arts in the 19th and 20th Centuries*. New York: Cambridge University Press.

Black, Leo. 2005. *Franz Schubert: Music and Belief*. Rochester, N.Y.: Boydell & Brewer.

Blocker, Robert, ed. 2004. *The Robert Shaw Reader*. New Haven, Conn.: Yale University Press.

Blom, Eric, ed. 1954. *Grove's Dictionary of Music and Musicians*. 9 vols. 5th ed. London: Macmillan.

Bloom, Peter. 1981. "Berlioz and the 'Prix de Rome' of 1830." *Journal of the American Musicological Society* 34, no. 2: 279–304.

Blume, Friedrich. 1975. *Protestant Church Music: A History*. London: Victor Gollancz.

Blyth, Alan. 1991. *Choral Music on Record*. Cambridge: Cambridge University Press.

Bolton, Jacklin Talmage. 1964. "Religious Influences on American Secular Cantatas, 1850–1930." Ph.D. diss., University of Michigan.

Brahms, Johannes. 1984. *Messe: Für vier- bis sechsstimmigen gemischten Chor und Continuo (Orgel)*. Edited by Otto Biba. Vienna: Doblinger.

Breuning, Gerhard von. 1992. *Memories of Beethoven: From the House of the Black-robed Spaniards*. Edited by Maynard Solomon. Cambridge: Cambridge University Press.

Brockway, Wallace, and Herbert Weinstock. 1950. *Men of Music: Their Lives, Times and Achievements*. Revised ed. New York: Simon & Schuster.

Brodbeck, David. 2007. "Dvořák's Reception in Liberal Vienna: Language Ordinances, National Property, and the Rhetoric of *Deutschtum*." *Journal of the American Musicological Society* 60, no. 1: 71–131.

Brown, A. Peter. 1986. *Performing Haydn's 'The Creation': Reconstructing the Earliest Renditions*. Bloomington: Indiana University Press.

Broyles, Michael. 1985. "Lowell Mason on European Church Music and Transatlantic Cultural Identification: A Reconsideration." *Journal of the American Musicological Society* 38, no. 2: 316–48.

———. 1991. "Music and Class Structure in Antebellum Boston." *Journal of the American Musicological Society* 44, no. 3: 451–93.

Buch, Mary. 2000. "A Guide to a Historically Accurate Performance of Edvard Grieg's *Fire Salmer* [*Four Psalms*], Op. 74." *Choral Journal* 41, no. 5: 9–23.

Budden, Julian. 2008. *Verdi*. 3rd ed. London and New York: Oxford University Press.

Carley, Lionel. 2006. *Edvard Grieg in England*. Rochester, N.Y.: Boydell & Brewer.

Cassaro, James P. 2000. *Gaetano Donizetti: A Guide to Research*. New York: Garland.

Chase, Gilbert. 1959. *The Music of Spain*. New York: Dover.

Chase, Robert. 2003. *Dies Irae: A Guide to Requiem Music*. Lanham, Md.: Scarecrow Press.

Chesnut, John Hind. 1977. "Mozart's Teaching of Intonation." *Journal of the American Musicological Society* 30, no. 2: 254–71.

Chusid, Martin. 1970. "Some Observations on Liturgy, Text, and Structure in Haydn's Late Masses." *Studies in Eighteenth-century Music: A Tribute to Karl Geiringer on His Seventieth Birthday*. Edited by H. C. Robbins Landon. New York: Oxford University Press.

Clapham, John. 1966. *Antonín Dvořák: Musician and Craftsman*. London: Faber.

———. 1972. *Smetana*. London: J. M. Dent & Sons.

———. 1979. *Dvořák*. New York: W. W. Norton.

Clive, Peter. 2006. *Brahms and His World: An Annotated Bibliography of Primary and Secondary Sources*. Lanham, Md.: Scarecrow Press.

Colles, J. A., ed. 1927. *Grove's Dictionary of Music and Musicians*. 5 vols. 3rd ed. London: Macmillan.

———. 1940. *Grove's Dictionary of Music and Musicians*. 5 vols. 4th ed. London: Macmillan.

Commanday, Robert Paul. 1962. "Repertory for Men's Choruses: Romantic Music." *American Choral Review* 4, no. 2: 1–4.

Cook, Grant W., III. 2001. "Bach in Boston: The Emergence of the *St. Matthew Passion*, from 1868 to 1879." *Choral Journal* 41, no. 9: 21–33.

Cook, Grant William, III. 2005. "Beethoven's Choral Director, Ignaz Karl Dirzka (1779–1827)." *Choral Journal* 46, no. 6: 49–53.

Cook, Nicholas. 1993. *Beethoven: Symphony No. 9*. Cambridge: Cambridge University Press.

Cooper, Barry. 2001. *Beethoven*. New York: Oxford University Press.

Cooper, Martin, ed. 1974. *The Modern Age, 1890–1960*. New Oxford History of Music 10. London: Oxford University Press.

Dahlhaus, Carl. 1991. *Nineteenth-century Music*. Translated by J. Bradford Robinson. Berkeley and Los Angeles: University of California Press.

Daverio, John. 1993. "The *Wechsel der Tone* in Brahms's *Schicksalslied*." *Journal of the American Musicological Society* 46, no. 1: 84–113.

Davis, Oma Grier. 1967. "A Selected, Annotated Bibliography of Te Deums in the Library of Congress, and a History of This Hymn in Ceremonial Music since 1600." Ph.D. diss., University of Iowa.

Degrada, Francesco. 1985. "Luigi Cherubini: 'Coronation' Mass in A." Liner notes for *Luigi Cherubini: "Coronation" Mass in A*. Translated by Gwyn Morris. Philharmonia Orchestra and Chorus; Roberto Benaglio, chorus master; conducted by Riccardo Muti. LP. London: EMI Records, DS-38240.

DeVenney, David P. 1987. *Nineteenth-century American Choral Music: An Annotated Guide*. Berkeley: Fallen Leaf Press.

———. 1988. *Early American Choral Music: An Annotated Guide*. Berkeley: Fallen Leaf Press.

———. 1990. *American Masses and Requiems: A Descriptive Guide*. Berkeley: Fallen Leaf Press.

Dibble, Jeremy. 2007. *John Stainer: A Life in Music*. Rochester, N.Y.: Boydell & Brewer.

Di Grazia, Donna M. 2002. "Volcanic Eruptions: Berlioz and His *Grande Messe des morts*." *Choral Journal* 43, no. 4: 27–52.

Downs, Philip G. 1992. *Classical Music: The Era of Haydn, Mozart, and Beethoven*. New York: W. W. Norton.

Dox, Thurston J. 1986. *American Oratorios and Cantatas: A Catalog of Works Written in the United States from Colonial Times to 1985*. 2 vols. Metuchen, N.J.: Scarecrow Press.

Dvořák, Otakar. 1993. *Antonín Dvořák, My Father*. Edited by Paul J. Polansky. Translated by Miroslav Němec. Spillville, Ia.: Czech Historical Research Center.

Eliach, Yaffa. 1998. *There Once Was a World: A Nine-hundred-year Chronicle of the Shtetl of Eishyshok*. Boston: Little, Brown.

Fairtile, Linda B. 1999. *Giacomo Puccini: A Guide to Research*. New York: Garland.

Faucett, Bill F. 1998. *George Whitefield Chadwick: A Bio-bibliography*. Westport, Conn.: Greenwood Press.

Ferguson, J. Scott. 2001. "Slovak Choral Music: Part 1." *Choral Journal* 42, no. 5: 37–44.

———. 2002. "Slovak Choral Music: Part 2." *Choral Journal* 42, no. 7: 27–33.

Ficher, Miguel, Martha Furman Schliefer, and John M. Furman, ed. 2002.

Latin American Classical Composers: A Biographical Dictionary. Lanham, Md.: Scarecrow Press.

Fifield, Christopher. 1988. *Max Bruch: His Life and Works*. New York: George Braziller.

Filler, Susan Melanie. 1989. *Gustav and Alma Mahler: A Guide to Research*. New York: Garland.

Fiske, Roger. 1979. *Beethoven's Missa solemnis*. New York: Charles Scribner's Sons.

Floros, Constantin. 1993. *Gustav Mahler: The Symphonies*. Translated by Vernon Wicker and Jutta Wicker. Portland, Ore.: Amadeus Press.

Forbes, Elliot. 1960. "The Choral Music of Beethoven." *American Choral Review* 2, no. 3: 1–6.

———. 1969. "The Choral Music of Beethoven." Special issue, *American Choral Review* 11, no. 3.

———, ed. 1967. *Thayer's Life of Beethoven*. 2nd ed. Princeton, N.J.: Princeton University Press.

Foster, Myles Birket. 1901. *Anthems and Anthem Composers: An Essay upon the Development of the Anthem from the Time of the Reformation to the End of the Nineteenth Century*. London: Novello.

Friddle, David, ed. 2006. *Liszt: Christus; Oratorium nach texten aus der Heiligen Schrift und der katholischen Liturgie*. Vocal score. Kassel: Bärenreiter.

Fuller-Maitland, ed. 1900. *Grove's Dictionary of Music and Musicians*. 5 vols. 2nd ed. London: Macmillan.

Gabrielová, Jarmila. 2007. "Antonín Dvořák: From the Point of View of Contemporary Musicology and the New Complete Edition of his Work." *Czech Music Quarterly* 2: 32–35.

Gangemi, Marie. 1995. *The Oratorio Society of New York, 1873–1995*. New York: Oratorio Society of New York.

Garretson, Robert L. 1993. *Choral Music: History, Style, and Performance Practice*. Upper Saddle River, N.J.: Prentice-Hall, Inc.

Gaussens, Jean-Gabriel. 1972. "Saint-Saëns: Requiem Mass." Liner notes for *Saint-Saëns: Requiem Mass*. Orchestre Lyrique de l'O.R.T.F.; Ensemble choral "Contrepoint"; Danielle Galland, soprano; Jeannine Collard, alto; Francis Bardot, tenor; Jacques Villisech, bass; Micheline Lagache, organ; conducted by Jean-Gabriel Gaussens. LP. New York: RCA, AGL1-1968.

Geck, Martin. 1971. *Deutsche Oratorien 1800 bis 1840*. Wilhelmshaven: Heinrichshofen.

Geiringer, Karl. 1961. *Brahms: His Life and Work.* 2nd ed. Garden City, NY: Doubleday/Anchor Books.

Gradenwitz, Peter. 1996. *The Music of Israel: From the Biblical Era to Modern Times.* 2nd ed. Portland, Ore.: Amadeus Press.

Grim, William E. 1988. *Max Reger: A Bio-bibliography.* Westport, Conn.: Greenwood Press.

Grimley, Daniel M. 2006. *Grieg: Music, Landscape and Norwegian Cultural Identity.* Rochester, N.Y.: Boydell & Brewer.

Grove, George, ed. 1878. *Grove's Dictionary of Music and Musicians.* 4 vols. 1st ed. London: Macmillan.

———. 1898/1962. *Beethoven and His Nine Symphonies.* 3rd ed. London: Novello. Reprint, New York: Dover.

Hadden, J. Cuthbert. 1934. *Haydn.* Revised ed. London: J. M. Dent & Sons.

Hancock, Virginia. 1983. *Brahms's Choral Compositions and His Library of Early Music.* Ann Arbor: UMI Research Press.

Harrandt, Andrea. 1996. "Bruckner and the Liedertafel Tradition: His Secular Music for Male Voices." *Choral Journal* 37, no. 5: 15–21.

Harwood, Gregory W. 1998. *Giuseppe Verdi: A Guide to Research.* New York: Garland.

Heintze, James R. 1990. *American Music before 1865 in Print and on Records: A Biblio-discography.* Brooklyn: Institute for Studies in American Music, Conservatory of Music, Brooklyn College of the City University of New York.

Henderson, Donald G., and Alice H. Henderson. 1990. *Carl Maria von Weber: A Guide to Research.* New York: Garland.

Hitchcock, H. Wiley. 2000. *Music in the United States: A Historical Introduction.* 4th ed. Upper Saddle River, N.J.: Prentice Hall.

Hitchcock, H. Wiley, and Stanley Sadie, eds. 1986. *The New Grove Dictionary of American Music.* 4 vols. London: Macmillan.

Hoggard, Lara, ed. 1984. *Johannes Brahms: A German Requiem.* Chapel Hill, N.C.: Hinshaw Music.

Houtchens, Alan, and Janis P. Stout. 2004. "'This Dreadful Winnowing-fan': Rhetoric of War in Edward Elgar's *The Spirit of England.*" *Choral Journal* 44, no. 9: 9–19.

Huneker, James. 1911. *Franz Liszt.* New York: Charles Scribner's Sons.

Huntington, Robert R. 1996. "The 'Real' Fauré Requiem? The Search Continues." *Choral Journal* 37, no. 3: 9–15.

Idelsohn, Abraham Z. 1929/1992. *Jewish Music in Its Historical Development.* New York: Henry Holt. Reprint, New York: Dover.

Jackson, George Pullen. 1933. *White Spirituals in the Southern Uplands: The Story of the Fasola Folk, Their Songs, Singings, and "Buckwheat Notes."* Chapel Hill: University of North Carolina Press.

Jacobs, Arthur, ed. 1963. *Choral Music: A Symposium.* Harmondsworth: Penguin Books.

Jacobson, Joshua R. 1997. "Franz Schubert and the Vienna Synagogue." *Choral Journal* 38, no. 1: 9–15.

Jaffee, Kay. 1964. "Messa da Requiem, Composed in Memory of Alessandro Manzoni (1785–1873) by Giuseppe Verdi (1813–1901): A Chronology and Commentary." Booklet notes for *Verdi Requiem.* The Philadelphia Orchestra; the Westminster Choir, George Lynn, director; Lucine Amara, soprano; Maureen Forrester, alto; Richard Tucker, tenor; George London, bass; conducted by Eugene Ormandy. LP boxed set. New York: Columbia Records, M2S 707.

Jensen, Eric Frederick. 2005. *Schumann.* Oxford and New York: Oxford University Press.

John, James. 2003. "Brahms and the 'Clara Emblem': Musical Allusion as a Key to Understanding the Thematic Sources at the Heart of *Ein deutsches Requiem.*" *Choral Journal* 44, no. 5: 15–27.

John, James A. 2005. "Poetry and Text Setting in Brahms's *Nänie*, Op. 82." *American Choral Review* 47, no. 2: 1–6.

Johnson, Eric A. 2002. "Franz Joseph Haydn's Late Masses: An Examination of the Symphonic Mass Form." *Choral Journal* 42, no. 7: 19–24.

Johnson, James Weldon, and J. Rosamond Johnson. 1925. *The Book of American Negro Spirituals.* New York: Viking.

———. 1926. *The Second Book of American Negro Spirituals.* New York: Viking.

Jones, Marice Allen. 1975. "American Theater Cantatas, 1852–1907." D.M.A. diss., University of Illinois.

Kean, Ronald. 2002. "Medievalism in Hector Berlioz's *Grande Messe de [sic] mortes.*" *Choral Journal* 43, no. 5: 7–23.

Kennedy, Michael. 1991. *Mahler.* Revised ed. New York: Schirmer Books.

Kent, Christopher. 1993. *Edward Elgar: A Guide to Research*. New York: Garland.

Kerst, Friedrich, comp. 1964. *Beethoven: The Man and the Artist, as Revealed in His Own Words*. Translated and edited by Henry Edward Krehbiel. New York: Dover.

Krehbiel, Henry Edward. 1898. *Music and Manners in the Classical Period*. New York: Charles Scribner's Sons.

———. 2007/1896. *How to Listen to Music: Hints and Suggestions to Untaught Lovers of the Art*. New York: Bibliobazaar.

Kroeger, Karl. 1993. *American Fuging-tunes, 1770–1820: A Descriptive Catalog*. Westport, Conn.: Greenwood Press.

Kuna, Milan. 1887–2004. *Antonín Dvořák: Korespondence a Dokumenty*. 10 vols. Prague: Editio Bäreneiter Praha.

Kuzma, Marika C. 2001. "Dmitry Bortniansky at 250: His Legacy as a Choral Symphonist." *Choral Journal* 42, no. 1: 9–16.

Lang, Paul Henry. 1976. "The Symphonic Mass." Special issue, *American Choral Review* 17, no. 2: 7–38.

Langford, Jeffrey, and Jane Denker Graves. 1989. *Hector Berlioz: A Guide to Research*. New York: Garland.

Large, Brian. 1970. *Smetana*. 1st American ed. New York: Praeger.

Lester, Joel. 1970. "Revisions in the Autograph of the *Missa Solemnis Kyrie*." *Journal of the American Musicological Society* 23, no. 3: 420–38.

Lindsley, Charles Edward. 1968. "Early Nineteenth-century American Collections of Sacred Choral Music, 1800–1810." Ph.D. diss., University of Iowa.

Littlewood, Julian. 2004. *The Variations of Johannes Brahms*. London: Plumbago.

Locke, Benjamin. 1998. "Christiane: Cryptography in Brahms's *Ein deutsches Requiem*." *Choral Journal* 39, no. 2: 9–14.

Longyear, Rey M. 1988. *Nineteenth-century Romanticism in Music*. 3rd ed. Englewood Cliffs, N.J.: Prentice-Hall.

Lowens, Irving. 1957. "Writings about Music in the Periodicals of American Transcendentalism (1835–50)." *Journal of the American Musicological Society* 10, no. 2: 71–85.

Macdonald, Hugh. 2002. "Berlioz's Napoleonic *Te Deum*." *Choral Journal* 43, no. 4: 9–17.

[Mann, Alfred.] 1965. "Handel and Haydn Society: Legacy of a Pioneer" [editorial]. *American Choral Review* 8, no. 1: 1–2.

Marek, George R. 1985. *Schubert*. New York: Viking.

Marsh, J. B. I., ed. 1877. *The Story of the Jubilee Singers with Their Songs*. 7th ed. London: Hodder & Stoughton.

Mason, Daniel Gregory. 1929. *Contemporary Composers*. New York: Macmillan.

Mason, Lowell. 1854. *Musical Letters from Abroad*. New York: Mason Brothers.

McVeagh, Diana. 2007. *Elgar the Music Maker*. Rochester, N.Y.: Boydell & Brewer.

Meredith, Victoria. 1997. "The Pivotal Role of Brahms and Schubert in the Development of the Women's Choir." *Choral Journal* 37, no. 7: 7–12.

Miller, Ronald A. 1996. "The Motets of Anton Bruckner." *Choral Journal* 37, no. 2: 19–25.

Minear, Paul Sevier. 1987. *Death Set to Music: Masterworks by Bach, Brahms, Penderecki, Bernstein*. Atlanta: John Knox Press.

Mintz, Donald. 1961. "Schumann as an Interpreter of Goethe's *Faust*." *Journal of the American Musicological Society* 14, no. 2: 235–56.

Mitchell, Donald. 2003–5. *Gustav Mahler*. 3 vols. Rochester, N.Y.: Boydell & Brewer.

Morosan, Vladimir. 1986. *Choral Performance in Pre-revolutionary Russia*. Ann Arbor, Mich.: UMI Research Press.

———1991. "One Thousand Years of Russian Church Music: An Introduction." In *Monuments of Russian Sacred Music*, series 2, vol. 1, *One Thousand Years of Russian Church Music*, edited by Vladimir Morosan. Washington, D.C.: Musica Russica.

———1996. "The Sacred Choral Works of Peter Tchaikovsky." In *Monuments of Russian Sacred Music*, series 2, *Peter Tchaikovsky: The Complete Sacred Choral Works*, edited by Vladimir Morosan. Madison, Conn.: Musica Russica.

Music, David W. 1998. "Camille Saint-Saëns's *Christmas Oratorio*: Description, Accessibility, Comparison." *Choral Journal* 39, no. 5: 49–53.

Mussulman, Joseph A. 1979. *Dear People . . . Robert Shaw*. Chapel Hill, N.C.: Hinshaw Music.

Nejedlý, Zdeněk. 1924. *Frederick Smetana*. London: Geoffrey Bless.

Nettl, Paul. 1951. *Forgotten Musicians*. New York: Philosophical Library.

Neufeld, Gerald. 1996. "Structure, Symbolism, and Thematic Transformation in Edward Elgar's *The Dream of Gerontius*." *Choral Journal* 36, no. 8: 9–14.

Newmarch, Rosa. 1942. *The Music of Czechoslovakia*. London and New York: Oxford University Press.

Notley, Margaret. 2006. *Lateness and Brahms: Music and Culture in the Twilight of Viennese Liberalism*. Oxford and New York: Oxford University Press.

Ochs, Siegfried. 1972. "Encounter with Bruckner and Brahms." *American Choral Review* 14, no. 4: 12–15.

Oldman, Cecil B. 1965. "Thomas Attwood: An English Choral Composer." *American Choral Review* 8, no. 2: 1–5.

Olleson, Philip. 2003. *Samuel Wesley: The Man and His Music*. Rochester, N.Y.: Boydell & Brewer.

Osborne, Richard. 2007. *Rossini*. 2nd ed. London and New York: Oxford University Press.

Ossenkop, David. 1988. *Hugo Wolf: A Guide to Research*. New York: Garland.

Pahlen, Kurt. 1990. *The World of the Oratorio: Oratorio, Mass, Requiem, Te Deum, Stabat Mater, and Large Cantatas*. Translated by Judith Schaefer. Portland, Ore.: Amadeus Press.

Pekacz, Jolanta T. 2002. *Music in the Culture of Polish Galicia, 1772–1914*. Rochester, N.Y.: University of Rochester Press.

Pemberton, Carol A. 1988. *Lowell Mason: A Bio-bibliography*. Westport, Conn.: Greenwood Press.

Phillips, Edward R. 2000. *Gabriel Fauré: A Guide to Research*. New York: Garland.

Plantinga, Leon. 1984. *Romantic Music: A History of Musical Style in Nineteenth-century Europe*. New York: W. W. Norton.

Pocock, Peter. 1998. "The Choral Music of Hugo Wolf." *Choral Journal* 39, no. 3: 25–30.

Poos, Heinrich, ed. 1983. *Chormusik und Analyse: Beiträge zur Formanalyse und Interpretation mehrstimmiger Vokalmusik*. Part 1, 2 vols. Mainz: Schott.

———, ed. 1997. *Chormusik und Analyse: Beiträge zur Formanalyse und Interpretation mehrstimmiger Vokalmusik*. Part 2, 2 vols. Mainz: Schott.

Radant, Else, ed. 1968. "The Diaries of Joseph Carl Rosenbaum, 1770–1829." Translated by Eugene Hartzell. *Haydn Yearbook* 5. Vienna: Universal Edition.

Rainbow, Bernarr. 1970. *The Choral Revival in the Anglican Church, 1839–1872*. Rochester, N.Y.: Boydell & Brewer.

Rakhmanova, Marina. 1999. "The Sacred Choral Works of Nikolai Rimsky-Korsakov." In *Monuments of Russian Sacred Music*. Series 3, *Nikolai Rimsky-Korsakov: The Complete Sacred Choral Works*. Edited by Vladimir Morosan. Madison, Conn.: Musica Russica.

Rhodes, Lila. 1997. "Verdi's Opera Choruses: Songs That Rallied a Nation." *Choral Journal* 38, no. 4: 9–16.

Ricks, Robert. 1974. "The Published Masses of Joseph Eybler (1765–1846)." *American Choral Review* 16, no. 3: 3–12.

Robertson, Alec. 1945. *Dvořák*. London: J. M. Dent & Sons.

———. 1968. *Requiem: Music of Mourning and Consolation*. New York: Frederick A. Praeger.

Robertson, Patricia. 2001. "Early American Singing Organizations and Lowell Mason." *Choral Journal* 42, no. 4: 17–24.

Robbins Landon, H. C. 1975. *Beethoven: A Documentary Study*. Translated by Richard Wadleigh and Eugene Hartzell. New York: Macmillan/Collier.

Robinson, Ray, ed. 1978. *Choral Music: A Norton Historical Anthology*. New York: W. W. Norton.

———. 1994. "*Quis desiderio sit*: A Newly Discovered Work by Felix Mendelssohn." *Choral Journal* 35, no. 10: 27–30.

Rosen, Charles. 1972. *The Classical Style: Haydn, Mozart, Beethoven*. New York: W. W. Norton.

Rothmüller, Aron Marko. 1954. *The Music of the Jews: An Historical Appreciation*. New York: Beechhurst Press.

Rubin, Emanuel, and John H. Baron. 2006. *Music in Jewish History and Culture*. Sterling Heights, Mich.: Harmonie Park Press.

Sabaneyeff, Leonid. 1927. *Modern Russian Composers*. Translated by Judah A. Joffe. New York: International.

Sachs, Joel. 1972. "Authentic English and French Editions of J. N. Hummel." *Journal of the American Musicological Society* 25, no. 2: 203–29.

———. 1974. "A Checklist of the Works of Johann Nepomuk Hummel." *Notes*, 2nd ser., 30, no. 4: 732–54.

Sadie, Stanley, ed. 1980. *The New Grove Dictionary of Music*. 20 vols. London: Macmillan.

Sadie, Stanley, and John Tyrell, eds. 2001. *The New Grove Dictionary of Music and Musicians*. 2nd ed. 29 vols. London: Macmillan.

Saffle, Michael Benton. 1991. *Franz Liszt: A Guide to Research*. New York: Garland.

Schenbeck, Lawrence. 1996. *Joseph Haydn and the Classical Tradition*. Chapel Hill, N.C.: Hinshaw Music.

Schmidt-Görg, Joseph. 1967. *Geschichte der Messe*. Cologne: Arno Volk Verlag.

Seaman, Gerald R. 1988. *Nikolai Andreevich Rimsky-Korsakov: A Guide to Research*. New York: Garland.

Sharp, Avery T. 1978. "A Descriptive Catalog of Selected, Published Eighteenth- through Twentieth-century Stabat Mater Settings for Mixed Voices with a Discussion of the History of the Text." Ph.D. diss., University of Iowa.

Shelley, Harry Rowe. 1913. "Dvořák as I Knew Him." *Etude* 31: 541–42.

Silantien, John Joseph. 1980. "The Part-song in England, 1837–1914." D.M.A. diss., University of Illinois.

Slonimsky, Nicolas. 1992. *Baker's Biographical Dictionary of Musicians*. 8th ed. New York: Schirmer Books.

———. 2000. *Lexicon of Musical Invective: Critical Assaults on Composers since Beethoven's Time*. New York: W. W. Norton.

Smith, Richard Langham, and Caroline Potter, eds. 2006. *French Music since Berlioz*. Aldershot: Ashgate.

Smither, Howard E. 2000. *A History of the Oratorio*. Vol. 4, *The Oratorio in the Nineteenth and Twentieth Centuries*. Chapel Hill: University of North Carolina Press.

Solomon, Maynard. 2003. *Late Beethoven: Music, Thought, Imagination*. Berkeley and Los Angeles: University of California Press.

Southern, Eileen J. 1977. "Musical Practices in Black Churches of Philadelphia and New York, ca. 1800–1844." *Journal of the American Musicological Society* 30, no. 2: 296–312.

Sposato, Jeffrey S. 2005. *The Price of Assimilation: Felix Mendelssohn and the Nineteenth-century Anti-Semitic Tradition*. Oxford and New York: Oxford University Press.

Stanford, Charles Villiers, and Cecil Forsyth. 1925. *A History of Music*. 2nd ed. New York: Macmillan.

Steinberg, Michael. 2005. *Choral Masterworks: A Listener's Guide.* Oxford and New York: Oxford University Press.

Štěpánek, Vladimir, and Bohumil Karásek. 1964. *An Outline of Czech and Slovak Music.* Prague: Orbis.

Stevenson, Robert. 1952. *Music in Mexico: A Historical Survey.* New York: Thomas Y. Crowell.

———. 1966. *Protestant Church Music in America: A Short Survey of Men and Movements from 1564 to the Present.* New York: W. W. Norton.

Strimple, Nick. 1993. "Te Deum and the American Flag." In *Dvořák in America, 1892–1895,* edited by John Tibbetts. Portland, Ore.: Amadeus Press.

———. 1995. "Dvořák's Stabat Mater." 1995. Booklet notes for *Antonín Dvořák: Stabat Mater.* Oregon Bach Festival Choir and Orchestra; Marina Shaguch, soprano; Ingeborg Danz, alto; James Taylor, tenor; Thomas Quasthoff, bass; conducted by Helmut Rilling. CD. Stuttgart: Hänssler Verlag, 98.935.

———. 1997. "The Choral Works of Antonín Dvořák: An Annotated Discography." *Choral Journal* 37, no. 9: 45–52.

———. 1998. "The Choral Music of Leoš Janáček: An Annotated Discography." *Choral Journal* 38, no. 9: 47–52.

———. 2002. *Choral Music in the Twentieth Century.* Portland, Ore.: Amadeus Press.

———. 2006. "Dvořák's *Svatá Ludmila*: Genesis, Premiere, and Aftermath." *American Choral Review* 48, no. 1: 1–5.

Studwell, William E. 1987. *Adolphe Adam and Léo Delibes: A Guide to Research.* New York: Garland.

Subotnik, Rose Rosengard. 1971. "Adorno's Diagnosis of Beethoven's Late Style: Early Symptom of a Fatal Condition." *Journal of the American Musicological Society* 29, no. 2: 242–75.

Sullivan, J. W. N. 1960. *Beethoven: His Spiritual Development.* New York: Vintage Books.

Summer, Robert J. 2007. *Choral Masterworks from Bach to Britten: Reflections of a Conductor.* Lanham, Md.: Scarecrow Press.

Temperley, Nicholas, ed. 2006. *William Sterndale Bennett: Lectures on Musical Life.* Woodbridge: Boydell.

Thrall, Josephine. 1908. *Oratorios and Masses.* Introduction by Edward Dickinson. Vol. 7 of *The American History and Encyclopedia of Music,* edited by

W. L. Hubbard. Toledo: Irving Squire.

Tibbetts, John C., ed. 1993. *Dvořák in America, 1892–1895*. Portland, Ore.: Amadeus Press.

Tiemstra, Suzanne Spicer. 1992. *The Choral Music of Latin America: A Guide to Compositions and Research*. New York: Greenwood Press.

Todd, R. Larry. 2003. *Mendelssohn: A Life in Music*. Oxford and New York: Oxford University Press.

Tovey, Donald Francis. 1937. *Essays in Musical Analysis*. Vol. 5, *Vocal Music*. London: Oxford University Press.

———. 1945. *Beethoven*. Edited by Hubert J. Fox. London: Oxford University Press.

Tyler, Linda L. 1992. "'Commerce and Poetry Hand in Hand': Music in American Department Stores, 1880–1930." *Journal of the American Musicological Society* 45, no. 1: 75–120.

Ulrich, Homer. 1973. *A Survey of Choral Music*. Belmont: Schirmer/Thomson Learning.

Upton, George P. 1886. *The Standard Oratorios: Their Stories, Their Music, and Their Composers*. Chicago: A. C. McClurg.

———. 1899. *Woman in Music*. 6th ed. Chicago: A. C. McClurg.

———. 1907. *The Standard Cantatas: Their Stories, Their Music, and Their Composers*. 9th ed. Chicago: A. C. McClurg.

Urban, Ladislav. 1919. *The Music of Bohemia*. New York: Czechoslovak Arts Club.

Valentin, Erich. 1984. *Handbuch der Chormusik*. Revised ed. 2 vols. Regensburg: Gustav Bosse.

Watson, Derek. 1996. *Bruckner*. Revised ed. Oxford and New York: Oxford University Press.

Weinert, William. 1996. "Bruckner's Mass in F Minor: Culmination of the Symphonic Mass." *Choral Journal* 37, no. 2: 9–16.

Wellesz, Egon, and Frederick Sternfeld, eds. 1973. *The Age of Enlightenment, 1745–1790*. Vol. 7 of *New Oxford History of Music*. London: Oxford University Press.

Werner, Jack. 1965. *Mendelssohn's "Elijah": A Historical and Analytical Guide to the Oratorio*. London: Chappell.

Wienandt, Elwyn A. 1965. *Choral Music of the Church*. New York: Free Press.

———, and Robert H. Young. 1970. *The Anthem in England and America*.

New York: Free Press.

White, Chris D. 1998. "Mendelssohn's *Der zweite Psalm, 'Warum toben die Heiden'*: Personal Perspective or Political Enlightenment?" *Choral Journal* 39, no. 2: 17–22.

Williamson, Richard A. 2006. "Reawakening the Romantic Spirit: Nineteenth-century Sources on Expression." *Choral Journal* 46, no. 11: 11–24.

Wolverton, Vance. 2001. "Baltic Portraits: Rudolph Tobias of Estonia." *Choral Journal* 41, no. 7: 17–25.

———. 2003. "Baltic Portraits: Jāzeps Vītols, Patriarch of Latvia's Art Music Tradition." *Choral Journal* 44, no. 1: 9–17.

Worthen, John. 2007. *Robert Schumann: Life and Death of a Musician*. New Haven, Conn.: Yale University Press.

Yoell, John. 1983. "Czechoslovakia and Music." Los Angeles: Unpublished monograph.

Young, Percy M. 1962. *The Choral Tradition: An Historical and Analytical Survey from the Sixteenth Century to the Present Day*. New York: W. W. Norton.

———. 1976. "Samuel Wesley and the Sublime." *American Choral Review* 18, no. 1: 3–16.

———. 1977. "The Madrigal in the Romantic Era." Special issue, *American Choral Review* 19, no. 4.

Index

Abeille, Ludwig, 41

Ábrányi, Kornél, 142–43

Abt, Franz Wilhelm, 76

Aceves y Lozano, Rafael, 175

Adam, Adolphe, 83–84, 121

Adams, Thomas, 118

Addison, John, 118

Adelburg, August, 143

Adonay, Marcelo, 226

Afanas'yev, Nikolai Yakovlevich, 160

Aggházy, Károly, 143

Agnelli, Salvatore, 192–93

Ahlstroem, Olof, 166

Aiblinger, Johann Kaspar, 42

Aikin, Jesse B., 198

Aimon, François, 96

Akerberg, Erik, 166

Aksakov, K. S., 152

Albéniz, Mateo Pérez de, 174

Albrecht, Karl, 151

Albrecht, Konstantin Karl, 151

Albrechtsberger, Johann Georg, 21, 41

Alcedo [Alzedo], José Bernardo, 223

Alcorta, Amancio, 220

Alfieri, Pietro, 179, 183

Alió y Brea, Francisco, 174

Alkan, Charles-Valentin, 88

Allen, Richard, 211, 213

Almeida, Inácio António de, 172

Almqvist, Carl Jonas Love, 165–66

Altieri, Paolo, 190

Alzedo, José Bernardo See Alcedo, José Bernardo

Alyabyev, Alexander Alexandrovich, 160

Ambros, August Wilhelm, 76

Amon, Johannes Andreas, 41

Anacker, August Ferdinand, 43–44

Anckermann, Carlos, 219

Ancot, Jean, 101

André, Charles-Louis-Joseph, 98

Andre, Jean Baptiste, 79

Andre, Johann, 41

Andre, Johann Anton, 41, 79

Andrevi y Castellar, Francisco, 173–74

Apell, David August von, 40

Arensky, Anton Stepanovich, 155

Arnold, Edwin, 111

Arredondo, José María, 219

Asafiev, Boris Vladimirovich, 157

Athanassov, Georgi, 226

Attwood, Thomas, 118

Augustus, Frederick, 43
Auseklis, 167

Baca, Luis, 218
Bach, Johann Sebastian, 3, 4, 7, 27,
　31, 37, 39, 41, 53, 55, 71, 76, 98, 104,
　105, 109, 133, 136, 154, 162, 190, 193,
　202, 203
Bachmann, Jacob, 160
Baguer, Carlos, 173
Baidanov, Georgi, 226
Baini, Giuseppe, 6, 179
Balakirev, Mily Alekseyivich, 6,
　155–56, 157, 159
Balatka, Hans, 201
Baldi, João José, 172
Balfe, Michael William, 106
Balius y Vila, Jaime, 173
Balmont, Konstantin, 154
Bargiel, Woldemar, 79
Barnard, Kenneth, 8
Barnby, Joseph, 110, 133
Barnekow, Christian, 162
Barnett, John, 105–6
Barnett, John Francis, 110
Barrett, William Alexander, 104
Bartalus, István, 142
Bartay, András, 142
Bartholomew, William, 184
Bartók, Béla, 88, 97, 125, 142, 143
Bartoš, František, 132
Basili, Francesco, 192
Bastiaans, Gijsbertus Johannes, 98
Baszny, József, 146
Baumanis, Kārlis, 167–68
Baumgartner, Wilhelm, 97–98

Bazin, François, 97
Bazzini, Antonio, 193
Beach, Amy, 208
Beale, William, 118
Beaulieu, Marie Désiré, 82-83
Beers, J. van, 100
Beer-Walbrunn, Anton, 80
Beethoven, Ludwig van, 2, 3, 5, 20–31,
　32, 39, 41, 42, 53, 58, 67, 68, 93, 97, 152,
　162, 175–76, 177, 178, 210, 227, 228
Behrens, Johan Diderik, 164
Beliczay, Gyula, 143
Bella, Ján Levoslav, 140
Bellerman, Heinrich, 79
Beller-McKenna, Daniel, 61, 62
Bellini, Vincenzo, 182, 192, 199
Bello Montera, Atanasio, 224
Bendix, Victor, 162
Bendl, Karel, 130–31
Benedetti, G., 97
Benedict, Julius, 104, 118
Benito, Cosme Damián José de, 175
Bennett, Joseph, 111
Bennett, William Sterndale, 108–9
Benoit, Camille, 96, 97
Benoit, François, 96
Benoit, Peter, 99–100
Benson, R. H., 61
Benvenuti, Nicola, 192
Berger, Wilhelm, 76
Berggreen, Andreas Peter, 161
Bergt, August, 46–47
Beristáin, Joaquín, 218
Berlijn, Anton, 98–99
Berlioz, Hector, 2, 4, 68, 71, 84–88, 95,
　97, 100, 121, 178, 209, 210, 222

Berneker, Constanz, 79

Bernstein, Leonard, 29

Berton, Henri-Montan, 82

Bertini, Giuseppe, 192

Berwald, Franz, 165

Besozzi, Louis-Désiré, 96–97

Bexfield, William Richard, 118–19

Biaggi, Girolamo Alessandro, 193

Biangini, Felice, 96

Bierey, Gottlieb Benedikt, 47

Billings, William, 195–96

Bini, Pietro, 189

Binyon, Laurence, 116

Bishop, Henry R., 105

Bittoni, Bernardo, 192

Bizet, Georges, 83, 92–93

Bjørnson, Bjørnstjerne, 164, 165

Blake, William, 112

Blockx, Jan, 100–101

Blondeau, Pierre-Auguste-Louis, 96

Blumner, Martin, 74

Boesi, José Antonio Caro **de**, 224

Boieldieu, Adrien, 83, 178

Boito, Arrigo, 189, 193

Bolívar, Simón, 224

Bolzoni, Giovanni, 193

Boman, Peter Conrad, 167

Bomtempo, João Domingos, 171–72

Borba, Count de, 172

Bordes, Charles, 96

Borghese, Pauline, 96

Borkowski, Bohdan, 146

Borodin, Alexander, 6, 155, 156, 159

Bortniansky, Dmitri Stepanovich, 6, 147–49, 150, 152, 159

Bottesini, Giovanni, 193

Boucheron, Raimondo, 192

Bouhélier, Saint-Georges de, 95

Bourgault-Ducoudray, Louis, 97

Boutmy, Laurent-François, 101

Bovy-Lysberg, Charles Samuel, 98

Bradbury, William Batchelder, 198

Braga, Gaetano, 193

Brahms, Johannes, 2, 47, 52–67, 72, 73, 75, 76, 78, 79, 80, 131, 132, 133, 178, 187, 190

Bräuer, Ferenc, 142

Braun, Wilhelm Theodor Johannes, 47

Bree, Johannes Bernardus van, 98

Brendler, Eduard, 166–67

Bretón, Tomás, 175

Bréville, Pierre de, 95–96

Bridge, Frederick, 119

Bristow, George Frederick, 200

Britten, Benjamin, 35

Brockway, Howard, 207–8

Brockway, Wallace, 64, 66

Bros y Bertomeu, Juan, 175

Browning, Robert, 115

Bruch, Margarethe, 75

Bruch, Max, 73, 74, 186

Bruckner, Anton, 3, 47, 48–52, 53, 79

Brüll, Ignaz, 80

Bruneau, Alfred, 97

Brunetti, Antonio, 192

Brzowski, Josef, 146

Buck, Dudley, 8, 203–5, 208, 211

Buck, Zechariah, 118

Bukureshtliev, Angel, 226

Bülow, Hans von, 53, 186

Bulthaupt, H., 75
Bungert, August, 80
Burghersh, John Fane, 118
Burion, Amédée, 92
Burleigh, Harry, 216
Burnett, W. A., 106
Busoni, Ferruccio, 88, 89
Butler, Samuel, 119
Buya, Ludwig Brandts, 49
Buzzolla, Antonio, 192
Byron, George Gordon, 73, 106, 157

Caballero, Manuel Fernández, 175
Cahen, Albert, 97
Caldwell, William, 196
Calegari, Antonio, 192
Calkin, John Baptiste, 119
Call, Leonhard von, 46
Callcott, John Wall, 104
Camidge, Matthew, 116, 118
Campenhout, François van, 101
Campion, Thomas, 113
Campos, Juan Morel, 219
Campos, Ruben M., 218
Cantrell, Barton, 207
Canudo, Ricciotto, 92
Capocci, Gaetano, 185
Carafa, Michele, 180
Cardinal Newman, John Henry, 115
Carissimi, Giacomo, 190
Carnegie, Andrew, 210
Carnicer, Ramón, 174
Caron, Leslie Francis Victor (Leon), 227
Carré, Albert, 83
Carrell, James P., 196

Carreño, José Cayetano, 224
Caruso, Luigi, 190
Casella, Pietro, 192
Casimiro Júnior, Joaquim, 172–73
Cassadó, Joaquin, 174
Castillon, Alexis, 93
Catalani, Alfredo, 193
Catoire, Georgy, 160–61
Čelakovský, František, 128
Cellier, Alfred, 119
Chadwick, George Whitefield, 208
Chappell, Samuel, 213
Chard, George William, 118
Charpentier, Gustave, 95
Chausson, Ernest, 93, 97
Cherubini, Luigi, 26, 53, 82, 96, 124,
    175–79, 181
Chmelensky, Josef Krasoslav, 124
Chopin, Frédéric, 88, 143, 144
Chorley, Henry F., 108–9
Choron, Alexandre-Etienne, 4
Čiurlionis, Mikolajus, 168–69
Clapham, John, 132
Clapisson, Louis, 83
Clayton, David L., 196
Coleridge-Taylor, Samuel, 110, 211
Corder, Frederick, 119, 151
Cornelius, Peter, 79
Costa, Michael, 184
Costa Sureda, Oriol, 219
Cowen, Sir Frederic Hymen, 114,
    119, 211
Crusell, Bernhard Henrik, 162
Cui, César Antonovich, 6, 155,
    156–57
Czerny, Joseph, 142

d'Albano, Gaston, 92
d'Antoni, Antonio, 184
da Ascenção, Simão, 173
da Silva, Francisco Manuel, 221
d'Agoult, Marie, Countess, 141
Damrosch, Walter, 210
Dante Alighieri, 187
Darwin, Charles, 105
Daumer, Georg Friedrich, 58
David, Félicien, 96
David, Samuel, 97
Davies, John, 113
Davisson, Ananais, 196
Dawson, William, 216
de Araújo, Damião Barbosa, 222
de Araújo, João Gomez, 222
de Arenzana, Manuel, 218
Dean, Winton, 92–93
Debussy, Claude, 95, 229
Delaney, Alfred, 200
Deschamps, Emile, 87
Devrient, Eduard, 37
Diabelli, Antonio, 47
Diepenbrock, Alphons, 99
d'Indy, Vincent, 89, 93
Ditson, Oliver, 154
Dodworth, Harvey, 199
Donizetti, Gaetano, 181–83, 192
Donne, John, 113
Doubravsky, František, 123–24
Dox, Thurston, 201
Drake, Henry Rodman, 136
Drechsler, Joseph, 47
Drummond, William, 202
Dryden, John, 111
Dubois, Théodore, 95

Duni, Egidio, 96
Duparc, Henri, 93
Duruflé, Maurice, 93
Dvořák, Antonín, 5, 131–138, 139, 187, 208
Dvořák, Otakar, 132
Dvoretsy, I. S., 160

Eichendorff, Joseph, Freiherr von, 34, 40, 78
Elgar, C. Alice, 116
Elgar, Edward William, 5, 112, 114, 115–16, 117, 211
Elízaga, José Mariano, 218
Elliot, J. H., 81
Elsner, Józef, 144
Emerson, Ralph Waldo, 31
Engel, Joel, 161
Erben, K. J., 130, 139
Erkel, Ferenc, 143
Esnaola, Juan Pedro, 220
Esterházy, Josepha Maria, 11, 13, 21, 140
Esterházy, Prince Nicolaus II, 11, 21, 23
Eybler, Joseph, 41

Fasch, Johann Friedrich, 40, 73
Fauré, Gabriel, 4, 93–94, 95
Favart, Charles-Simon, 96
Fels, E., 52
Feofan, Archimandrite, 160
Ferdinand VII, King, 174
Feuerbach, Anselm, 60
Fibich, Zdeněk, 131, 132
Filho, Mello Morais, 221

Fischer-Dieskau, Dietrich, 38

Flechsig, Emil, 35

Flechtenmacher, Alexandru, 225

Flemming, Paul, 54

Foerster, Josef Bohuslav, 131

Foerster, Joseph, 131, 132

Foote, Arthur, 205–6

Förster, Aloys, 21

Forsyth, Cecil, 114

Foster, Stephen, 138, 199

Franck, César, 92, 95, 97, 121

Frederick Augustus, King, 43

French, Major B. B., 200

Führer, Robert, 47

Fuller-Maitland, John Alexander, 113

Gabrieli, Giovanni, 50, 55

Gade, Niels, 161–62

Gallet, Louis, 92–93

Galuppi, Baldassare, 6, 147

Gassmann, Therese, 12

Gaussen, Jean-Gabriel, 94

Geijer, Eric Gustav, 166

Geiringer, Karl, 61, 62

Gevaert, François-Joseph, 101

Gilbert, William S., 112

Gilchrist, William W., 208

Giulini, Carlo Maria, 23

Glazunov, Aleksandr
    Konstantinovich, 156

Gleason, Frederick, 208

Glinka, Mikhail, 6, 149–50

Gluck, Christoph Willibald, 176

Goethe, Johann Wolfgang von, 32,
    34, 35, 38, 40, 58, 59, 60, 74, 78, 80,
    87, 140, 151, 162, 207

Goldmark, Carl, 79

Goldschmidt, Adalbert von, 80

Gomes, Antônio Carlos, 221

Gómez, Enrique Barrera, 175

Goring Thomas, Arthur, 114, 119

Goss, John, 118

Gossec, François Joseph, 81, 84, 92, 178

Gounod, Charles, 4, 5, 83, 89–91, 95,
    97, 121, 222

Graff, W. P., 75

Grant, Ulysses S., 214

Grell, August Eduard, 73–74, 79

Grétry, André, 82, 92

Grieg, Edvard, 163, 164, 165, 221

Grillparzer, Franz, 32, 52

Grimm, Jacob, 67

Grimm, Julius Otto, 52, 54, 79

Grimm, Wilhelm, 67

Guéranger, Dom Prosper, 4

Guerra, Gratilio, 219

Guilmant, Alexandre, 221

Haberl, Franz Xaver, 189

Hadden, J. Cuthbert, 12

Hairston, Jester, 216

Hálek, Vítězslav, 132

Halévy, Jacques-François-Fromental,
    83

Hallen, Andreas, 167

Hallström, Ivar, 167

Hamerling, Robert, 80

Hamilton, Lady Emma, 18

Handel, George Frideric, 61, 82, 103,
    106, 119, 186, 190, 199, 209, 210, 213

Hanslick, Eduard, 52

Hardenbrook, W. A., 200

Hartmann, August Wilhelm, 161

Hartmann, Johann Peter Emilius, 161

Hastings, Thomas, 198

Hatton, John Liphot, 118

Hauptmann, Moritz, 203

Haydn, Franz Joseph, 1, 2, 3, 11–20, 20–21, 27, 48, 49, 82, 98, 104, 124, 139, 174, 177, 211, 213, 228

Haydn, Michael, 15, 49

Heine, Heinrich, 34, 39, 207

Hensel, Fanny Mendelssohn, 30, 46

Herbert, Victor, 211

Herold, A. F., 96

Herzogenberg, Elisabeth von, 75

Herzogenberg, Heinrich von, 75–76

Hiller, Ferdinand, 79, 186

Hirt, Charles C., 38

Hitler, Adolf, 49

Hoffman, E. T. A., 47

Hogan, Moses, 216

Hölderin, Friedrich, 59

Horn, Moritz, 36

Horner, Wilson G., 200

Horsley, Charles E., 104

Hubbard, John, 195

Hummel, Johann Nepomuk, 139, 140, 142

Hus, Jan, 128

Ibsen, Henrik, 164

Ingelman, G., 165

Irving, Washington, 203

Ives, Charles, 206–7, 209

Jackson, George Pullen, 197

Jacobson, J. P., 166

Jahn, Jiljí, 128

Janáček, Leoš, 5, 125, 126, 127, 130, 138–39

Joachim, Joseph, 52, 54

Johnson, Francis, 213

Johnson, James Weldon, 213

Josephson, Jacob Axel, 166

Josquin des Prez, 31, 76

Juanas, Antonio, 218

Jurjāns, Andrejs, 167, 168

Kabalevsky, Dmitri, 160

Kâlidâsa, 96

Kastalsky, Alexander, 153

Kean, Ronald, 86

Keats, John, 202

Keller, Gottfried, 67, 98

Kelterborn, Louis, 64

Kennedy, Michael, 72

Key, Francis Scott, 199

Khomiakov, Aleksey, 154

Kind, Friedrich, 43

King, E. J., 196

Kinkade, Thomas, 31

Kinkel, Gottfried, 131

Kittl, Jan Bedřich, 139

Kjerulf, Halfdan, 163

Klein, Gideon, 128

Kleist, Ewald von, 32

Klopstock, Friedrich Gottlieb, 34, 68, 69

Kodály, Zoltán, 142, 143

Körner, Theodor, 43

Kotzebue, August von, 25

Krehbiel, Henry E., 30

Krogzemis, Mikus See Auseklis

Křížkovský, Pavel, 5, 125–27, 128, 139
Krumacher, Friedrich, 32

Lamas, José Angel, 223
Lamm, Paul, 157
Lange, Samuel de, 99
Large, Brian, 127, 129
Lavallée, Calixa, 216–17
Lauridsen, Morton, 63
Leconte de l'Isle, 95
Lemaire, Ferdinand, 94
Lenau, Nikolaus, 78
Leo VIII, Pope, 77
Leslie, Henry David, 109–10
Lesueur, Jean François, 82, 84
Lewandowski, Lewis, 4, 88, 144–46,
    169
Liadov, Anatol, 160
Libby, Dennis, 183
Lidley, Thomas, 19
Lincoln, Abraham, 8, 199, 200
Lincoln, Mary Todd, 199
Lindblad, Otto, 167
Liszt, Ferenc (Franz), 3, 6, 52, 68, 88,
    95, 121, 134, 139, 140–42, 143, 151,
    162, 166, 189, 190
Littleton, Alfred, 137
Llaque, Bonifacio, 223
Lobo, Elias Álvares, 222
Lockhart, John Gibson, 113
Lomakin, Gavriil Yakimovich,
    150–51
Longfellow, Henry Wadsworth, 112
Louis XVI, King, 177
Ludwig I, King, 42
Luther, Martin, 55, 56

Lvov, Aleksei Fyodorovich, 149
Lyon, James, 195

Mabellini, Teodulo, 189
MacCunn, Hamish, 119
MacDowell, Edward, 206
MacFarren, George Alexander, 106–7
MacKenzie, Alexander Campbell,
    110–11, 114
Mahler, Gustav, 44, 47, 67–73, 85
Mahlmann, Siegfried Augustus,
    121–22
Maitland, Frederic William, 64
Makarov, P., 160
Mannheimer, Isaac Noah, 45
Manolov, Emanuil, 226
Manzoni, Alessandro, 186
Marek, Jan Jindřich, 129
Maria Theresa, Empress, 17, 18
Marinelli, Karl von, 51
Martin, Frank, 177
Martucci, Giuseppe, 189
Mascagni, Pietro, 193
Mason, Daniel Gregory, 111, 115
Mason, Lowell, 3, 7, 42, 178, 196–98,
    208, 213
Massenet, Jules, 97
Matons, Laureano Fuentes, 219
Mattig, H. von der, 52
Mayr, Johann Simon, 46, 181
McCabe, Charles C., 200
McEwen, John, 119
Měchura, Leopold Eugen, 139
Méhul, Etienne Nicolas, 82, 83
Meini, V., 193
Meisl, Carl, 25

Mendelssohn Hensel, Fanny *See* Hensel, Fanny (Mendelssohn)

Mendelssohn, Abraham, 37

Mendelssohn, Alexander, 144

Mendelssohn, Felix, 4, 5, 30, 32, 35, 36–40, 41, 44, 46, 56, 58, 68, 73, 82, 89, 104, 106, 107, 130, 135, 144, 146, 151, 161–62, 163, 166, 168, 176, 190, 199, 209, 211

Mendelssohn, Moses, 4, 36

Mercadente, Saverio, 181

Méry, Joseph, 83

Meserón, Juan Francisco, 224

Metliński, Ambrož, 128

Meyerbeer, Giacomo, 44, 89, 100

Millard, Harrison, 199

Millet, Luis, 174

Milton, John, 202

Montero, José Angel, 224

Monteverdi, Claudio, 26, 31, 76

Montgomery, R., 106

Moore, Thomas, 35

Morales, Melesio, 217

Moreira, António Leal, 173

Mörike, Eduard, 34, 78

Morlaix, B. de, 207

Morosan, Vladimir, 148, 152

Moscheles, Ignaz, 203

Mosonyi, Mihály, 142

Mozart, Wolfgang Amadeus, 31, 34, 41, 58, 73, 174, 176, 177

Muhlenburg, William A., 200

Mussorgsky, Modest, 6, 155, 157, 159

Napoleon I, 103, 193

Nathan, Isaac, 226–27

Naujalis, Juozas, 168–69

Naumbourg, Samuel, 4, 88–89, 169

Nejedlý, Zdeněk, 132

Nelson, Lord Horatio, 16–17, 18

Nepomuceno, Alberto, 221

Netto, Marcos Coelho, 222

Neumann, Johann Philipp, 33

Newmarch, Rosa, 124, 127

Nicolau, Antonio, 175

Niemeyer, August, 34

Nietzsche, Friedrich, 72, 79

Nordraak, Rikard, 164

Nowakowsky, David, 169

Nunes Garcia, José Maurício, 220, 221

Ockeghem, Johannes, 76

Olleson, Edward, 18

Ore, Ādams, 167, 168

Orlov, Vasily, 153

Ortega, Aniceto, 217

O'Shaughnessy, Arthur, 116

Ostrčil, Otakar, 132

Oxenford, John, 106

Pacini, E., 83

Pacini, Giovanni, 181

Pacius, Frederik, 163

Páez, José Antonio, 224

Paine, John Knowles, 201, 205

Palacios, Rafael, 218

Palestrina, Giovanni Pierluigi da, 6, 7, 51, 76, 79, 150, 176, 179, 183, 189, 190

Paniagua y Vásques, Cenobio, 218

Parker, Horatio, 206–207

Parker, James C. D., 208

Parry, Charles Hubert Hastings, 5, 112–13, 114

Pears, Peter, 35

Penderecki, Krzysztof, 26

Perosi, Lorenzo, 189–91

Pfau, Ludwig, 79

Pius VII, Pope, 40

Pius X, Pope, 7, 190

Plath, Wolfgang, 41

Polonsky, Yakov Petrovich, 154

Ponce de León, José María, 222

Porter, Quincy, 207

Portugal, Marcos António, 173

Proske, Karl, 3

Puccini, Giacomo, 193

Purcell, Henry, 106

Pushkin, Alexander, 155

Quevedo Arvelo, Julio, 222

Racine, Jean, 40

Raffelin, Antonio, 219

Raimondi, Pietro, 179–80

Rankin, Jessica, 106

Read, Daniel, 195–6

Reinecke, Carl, 100

Reinick, R., 75

Rejcha, Antonín, 5, 83, 96, 121–23, 176

Rheinberger, Josef Gabriel, 75, 77–78, 207

Rhumfeld, Anna, 12

Richard, A., 98

Richter, Hans, 203

Ricordi, Tito, 185

Rieger, Gottfried, 125

Riestra, José María Valle, 223

Rimsky-Korsakov, Nikolai, 6, 155, 156, 157–60, 169

Roberts, Kenneth G., Jr., 202

Robertson, Alec, 136

Robespierre, Maximilien, 82

Rochlitz, Friedrich, 25

Röckel, Joseph, 23

Rodenbach, A., 100

Romano, José, 173

Roquette, Otto, 141

Rosenbaum, Joseph Carl, 12

Rossi, Salomone, 89

Rossini, Gioachino, 6, 118, 180–81, 185, 192, 211

Rubinstein, Anton, 151, 154, 209

Rückert, Friedrich, 34

Runeberg, J., 163

Rungenhagen, Carl Friedrich, 73

Rutter, John, 93, 159

Sabatier, Charles, 216–17

Sáenz, Antonio, 223

Sáenz, Benedicto, 220

Sáenz, Vicente, 220

Saint-Saëns, Camille, 4, 83, 94–95

Salieri, Antonio, 21, 41

Sarti, Giuseppe, 147

Schenk, Johann, 21

Schiller, Friedrich, 20, 25, 28, 31, 32, 40, 59, 60, 74, 152

Schneider, Johann, 203

Schoenberg, Arnold, 229

Scholz, Benedikt, 23, 52

Schreiber, Christian, 23

Schubert, Ferdinand, 34

Schubert, Franz Peter, 2, 3, 5, 15, 32–34, 41, 46, 47, 67, 124, 146, 175

Schulze, Ernst, 32

Schumann, Robert, 32, 34–36, 41, 52, 58, 59, 61, 93, 161, 177, 178, 210

Schütz, Heinrich, 55, 61, 133

Schütz, Johann Jakob, 54

Schwarz, Rudolf Israel, 71

Scott, Walter, 75

Seidl, Anton, 32

Séjan, L., 179

Sessions, Roger, 88, 207

Shakespeare, William, 78, 87, 207

Shaw, George Bernard, 64, 66

Shaw, Robert, 27, 58

Shelley, Harry Rowe, 136

Shelley, Percy Bysshe, 119

Sheppard, Ella, 214

Sheremetev, Count, 150

Sibelius, Jean, 163

Silva, Prescilliano, 222

Simrock, Fritz, 133, 137

Sinding, Christian, 165

Sjögren, Emil, 167

Škroup, František, 124–25

Sládek, J. V., 130

Smart, Henry Thomas, 107–8

Smetana, Bedřich, 2, 5, 124, 126, 127–130, 132

Smither, Howard E., 107, 179, 190

Smulders, Charles, 99

Smythe, Dame Ethel, 119

Söderman, Johan August, 167

Sophocles, 203

Spengel, Leonhard von, 63

Spitta, L., 75

Spitta, Philipp, 75, 76

Spohr, Louis, 42–43

Srb-Debrnov, Josef, 128

Stainer, John, 119

Stanford, Charles Villiers, 5, 112, 113, 114–15, 119

Starorussky, Vasily, 160

Steinberg, Michael, 86

Steinberg, William, 116

Stenhammar, Wilhelm, 166

Stern, Daniel See d'Agoult, Marie, Countess

Stern, Julius, 73

Stevens, Halsey, 95

Stevenson, Robert, 218

Stevenson, Robert Louis, 115

Stockhausen, Julius, 73

Stokowski, Leopold, 156

Stratton, S. S., 111

Straume, Jānis, 167, 168

Strauss, Richard, 67, 140

Stravinsky, Igor, 159, 229

Sullivan, Arthur Seymour, 5, 112, 114, 119

Sullivan, J. W. N., 30

Sulzer, Salomon, 4, 44–46, 47, 88, 145, 169

Sušil, František, 125

Sveinbjörnsson, Sveinbjörn, 163

Svendsen, Johan, 164

Swieten, Gottfried van, 19

Tadolini, Giovanni, 180, 192

Taneyev, Sergey Ivanovich, 154–55, 159

Taylor, Raynor, 213

Tchaikovsky, Pyotr Il'yich, 148,
    152–54, 155, 210
Tegnèr, Esaias, 74
Temperley, Nicholas, 108, 118
Tenel, Edgar, 101
Tersteegen, G., 75
Thomas, Ambroise, 83, 88
Thomas, Theodore, 19, 208
Thomson, James, 19
Thrall, Josephine, 35, 89, 115
Thun, Count Leopold, 127
Thurber, Jeanette, 137
Tobias, Rudolf, 168–69
Tolstoy, Aleksey Konstantinovich,
    154
Tomás, Guillermo M., 219
Tomášek, Václav Jan, 139
Toscanini, Arturo, 189, 193
Toulmon, Auguste Bottée de, 96
Tours, Berthold, 137
Tovey, Donald Francis, 30
Traquair, E. M., 61
Traumihler, Ignaz, 51
Trnobranský, Václav, 128
Troutbeck, Rev. Dr. J., 135
Turner, J. W., 200
Tyutchev, Fyodor Ivanovich, 154

Úbeda, Fray Manuel, 223
Udbye, Martin Andreas, 164
Upton, George P., 35, 106, 108–9,
    184, 202

Varèse, Edgard, 193
Vaughan Williams, Ralph, 29, 97, 125
Vaughan, Henry, 113

Veit, Jindřich, 139
Velásquez, Glauco, 222
Velásquez, José Francisco, 224
Velázquez, José Guadalupe, 217–18
Verdi, Giuseppe, 2, 6, 86, 133, 185–89,
    192, 193, 199, 221
Verlaine, Paul, 95
Victoria, Queen, 112, 214
Villalpando, Fernando, 218
Villanueva, Felipe, 217
Vinogradov, Mikhail
    Aleksandrovich, 160
Vitásek, Jan August, 139
Vītols, Jāzeps, 167
Vives, Amadeo, 174
Vogler, Abbé Georg Joseph, 44
Volkmann, Robert, 79
Voříšek, Jan Hugo, 5, 124
Vorobchievici, Isidor, 225
Vrchlický, Jaroslav, 130, 135

Wade, Joseph, 118
Waelput, Hendrik, 101
Wagner, Cosima, 141
Wagner, Richard, 42, 47–48, 50, 52,
    53, 67, 71, 73, 75, 78, 95, 100, 115, 141,
    162, 166, 185, 190, 208, 210
Walker, William, 196
Walton, William, 186
Webber, Robert, 26
Weber, Bernard Anselm, 44
Weber, Carl Maria von, 43, 47, 118
Webern, Anton, 60
Weigl, Joseph, 124
Weinstock, Herbert, 64, 66
Weiss, Johann Baptist, 79

Weisse, Michael, 57

Weissenbach, Aloys, 24

Wennerberg, Gunnar, 167

Wesley, Charles, 104

Wesley, John, 104

Wesley, Samuel, 104–5, 106

Wesley, Samuel Sebastian, 106

White, Benjamin Franklin, 196

White, George L., 213–14

Whiting, George Elbridge, 208

Wilhelm II, King, 98

Willan, Healey, 217

Winter, P., 118

Witt, Franz Xaver, 3, 49, 51, 77, 126

Wojciechowski, Johannes, 183

Wolf, Hugo, 52, 75, 78–79

Wolf-Ferrari, Ermanno, 193

Wolle, J. Fred, 7

Work, John, 216

Wouters, A., 100

Wyeth, John, 196

Xavier, José Maria, 222

Zamora, Alejandro Monestel, 219

Zapiola, José, 222

Żeleński, Władysław, 146

Zelter, Carl Friedrich, 37, 40–41, 44, 73, 74

Zenger, Max, 79

Zingarelli, Niccolò Antonio, 175, 181, 184, 192